IMAGES
of America

EMMETT AND GEM COUNTY

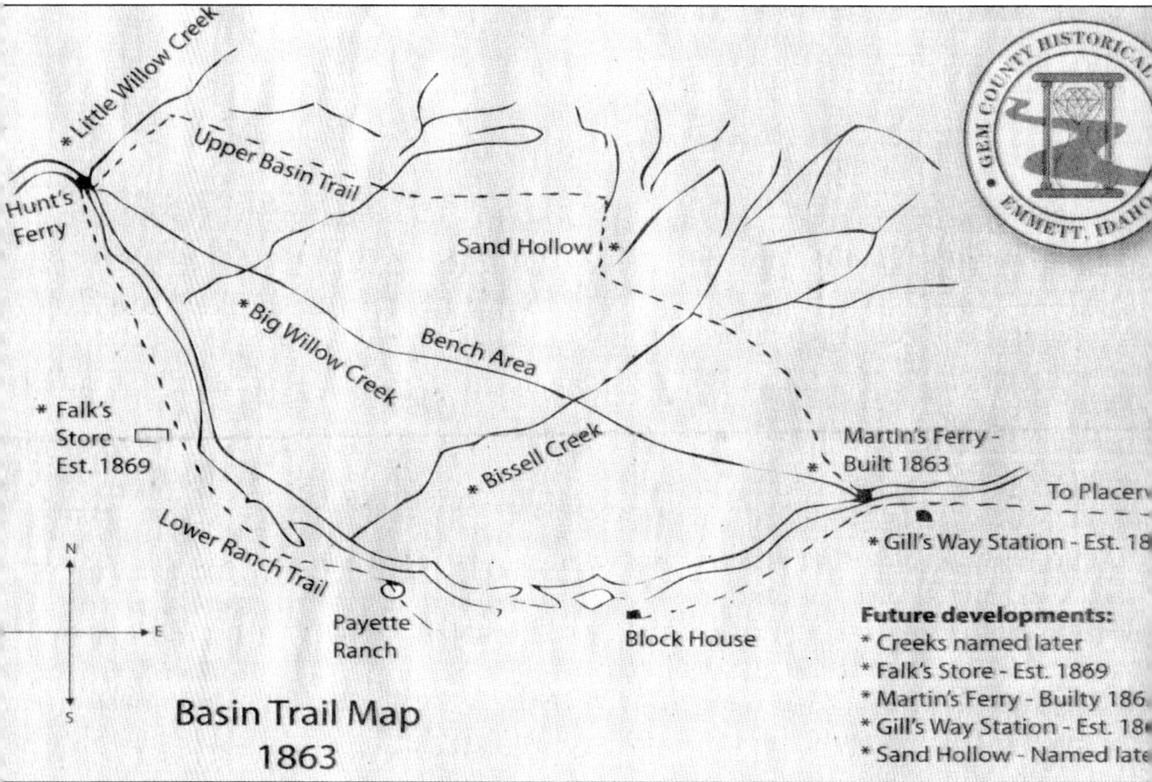

This early-1860s map shows the location of Martinsville, founded in 1863. Displayed are the well-traveled trails to the goldfields found both east and west. People were beginning to fill up the country, taking the opportunity to create new lives for themselves. There was already a way station and a ranch, and a ferry was a much-needed addition. (Courtesy of Gem County Historical Society.)

On the Cover: One means of communication between Emmett and the upper country was the Thunder Mountain Stagecoach. The stage, which was operated by John F. Hall, left Emmett in the morning after the mail arrived from Nampa on the train. By changing to fresh teams of horses, it was able to reach Van Wyck, which is near Cascade, in 18 hours. It delivered supplies to Sweet, Ola, Dry Buck, and Smiths Ferry and provided the mining camps access to much-needed goods. In this image, the stage is being driven by Edward Ingman; J.R. Hughes is beside him, and George Flake on top. (Courtesy of Gem County Historical Society.)

IMAGES
of America

EMMETT AND GEM COUNTY

Julianne Rekow Peterson and
the Gem County Historical Society

ARCADIA
PUBLISHING

ISBN 978-1-4671-3244-2

Published by Arcadia Publishing
Charleston, South Carolina

Printed in the United States of America

Library of Congress Control Number: 2014937595

For all general information, please contact Arcadia Publishing:
Telephone 843-853-2070
Fax 843-853-0044
E-mail sales@arcadiapublishing.com
For customer service and orders:
Toll-Free 1-888-313-2665

Visit us on the Internet at www.arcadiapublishing.com

To all people of Gem County who have provided encouragement, stability, and opportunity for the rising generations

Contents

ACKNOWLEDGMENTS

I would like to thank the Gem County Historical Society and the museum for their dedication to preserving and sharing the contributions of past generations. It is through their encouragement that this book was created.

All photographs without a specific credit are part of the general collection of the Gem County Historical Society. I would like to thank Meg Davis for her help in obtaining photographs and for the writing assistance provided by Karla Standley, Karen Bruner, and Andrea Peterson. I also extend a special thank-you to my husband for his assistance.

A particular debt is owed to Ruth B. Lyon for her book *The Village That Grew,* which served as a reference.

Introduction

With the United States' purchase of nearly 530 million acres of land from France in 1803 and Lewis and Clark's challenging exploration of it, the westward migration was launched. The onset of the Civil War gave many Americans impetus to seek a peaceful and more pleasant residence. It is estimated that 300,000 people came west to Oregon between 1842 and 1862 in pursuit of free land or of gold. In 1862, Tim Goodell led 60 ox-drawn wagons down Freezeout Hill. He blocked the back wheels and, with one steep slide, descended into the valley, and others followed.

The Basin Trail, or the Umatilla-Placerville road, was well established by 1863. With the discovery of gold at Placerville, people came pouring into Idaho. There were individuals from all walks of life seeking their fortunes. *The Village That Grew* documents an Oregonian correspondent who reported on the influx, saying, "On my way (to the Basin), we met on average not less than 10 pack trains per day, many consisting of from 50 to 100 animals and not less than five 5,000-pound freight wagons beside the countless other vehicles and travelers."

Jonathan Smith and Nathaniel Martin were in eastern Oregon, placer mining, when they heard the news of gold in the Boise Basin. They had been at Burnt River, Oregon, since 1861 and were ready for a change, so they started for the basin. While traveling, they camped for the night at the junction of the lower and upper basin trails. It was probably a pleasant evening, with plenty of grass for their animals and water and wood for themselves. They could see the need for a ferry at this spot and, having tired of mining, they settled and cut logs for one. They prospered and expanded their operation by adding a large log roadhouse and a feed barn across the road from it. They provided valuable services at Martinsville to hundreds of miners who were hurrying to the goldfields.

Mail was delivered three days a week from Kelton, Utah, to Umatilla, Oregon. It was a natural extension to establish a post office in Martinsville in 1864. The post office was moved in 1870 to the Payette Ranch, where it was named Emmettsville after postmaster Thomas Cahalan's seven-year-old son. A few years later, the post office was reestablished in Martinsville, but it continued to be called Emmettsville.

The native Weiser Shoshoni camped north of the Payette River near the site of the Gill School House near Lower Bluff Road as they traveled to their wintering grounds in Indian Valley. In 1877, there was talk of the Snakes, Blackfeet, and Nez Perce joining forces to drive the settlers from the Payette Valley. The Emmettsville settlers were alarmed and some of them erected a fort of cottonwood logs north of the present-day Messenger-Index for protection. Some families even moved to Boise where they had the protection of Fort Boise; others left their homes and hid in the trees, grasses, and bushes for several weeks. War threatened; however, no fighting occurred. Eventually, the natives were forced back onto the reservation.

William Burdge brought the first roan Durham cattle and Morgan-strain horses to Idaho in 1864. Nine years had passed since Martin came to the valley, and more permanent settlers interested in free land began filing for homesteads in Emmettsville. Nathaniel Martin filed on October 11, 1872, for 48.38 acres.

Emmett is regarded as the garden spot of Idaho. Because of rich soil, abundant water, and a mild, temperate climate, a wide variety of crops can be grown. Jonathan Smith knew from experience the tasty fruits and vegetables that could be grown. These, as well as fish, turkeys, chickens, and eggs, were sold to the mining camps for a source of cash. Today, Emmett is still the garden spot, producing delectables for cash.

The following is from a Community Economic Profile for Gem County, Idaho, in September 2009:

> Despite being a mature industry, agriculture is big business in Gem County. There were 822 farms in the county in 2007, with total crop and livestock sales of $30.8 million. Most of the farms are small, hobby farms both in size and sales, with 485 farms having less than $10,000 in sales. Beef cattle, sheep and alfalfa hay are the mainstays of Gem County with dairy, small grains, and fruit making contributions. There were 2,831 horses and 1,169 goats in 2007. In 2011 there were 2,831 horses and 1,169 goats in 2007. In 2011 there were 6500 head of sheep and 22,000 head of cattle with beef cattle accounting for 10,000.
>
> Livestock cash receipts increased 29 percent in 2010, totaling $3.23 billion. Livestock receipts were once again higher than crop receipts after dropping below in 2009. Higher marketing combined with record high prices resulted in record cash receipts for the year. Receipts from sheep and lambs totaled $22.7 million in 2010, an increase of 38 percent from 2009.

The demand for lamb in the nation's grocery and restaurant chains is not being met, and the American Sheep Industry is encouraging ranchers and prospective ranchers to ramp up production and take advantage of this trend. This is certainly a bright spot in the economy of Gem County. The timber industry, the fruit industry, the railroad, and mining and have matured and are all now in decline. Many people commute to the larger cities around Emmett in order to support themselves. Tourism, recreation, and retirees provide bright spots in the local economy. The challenge is to innovate, just as residents' predecessors did, and use the community's resources to the best advantage.

One

The Weiser-Shoshoni Indians

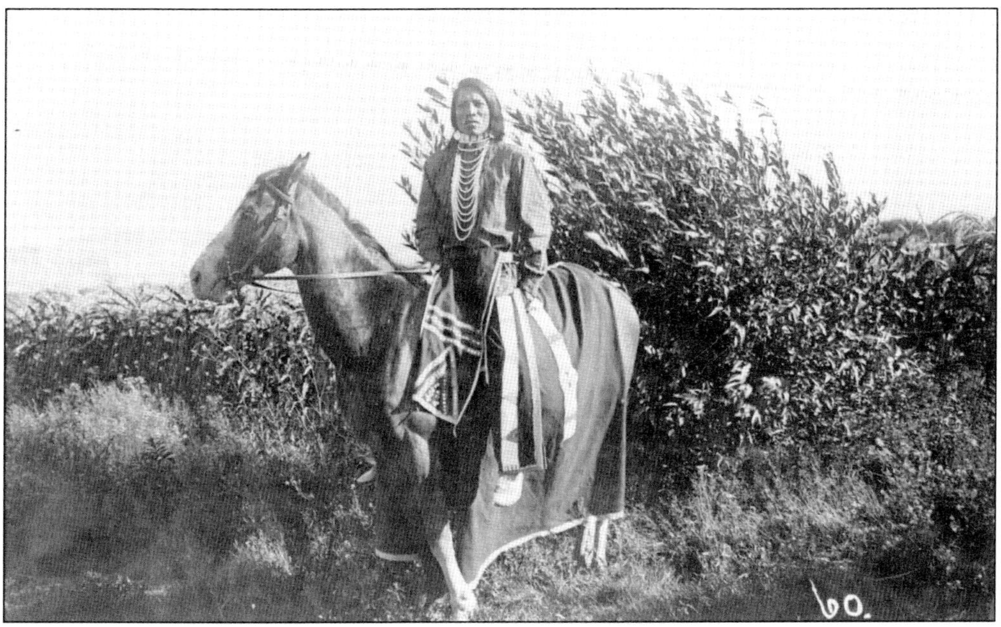

The first known human footprints in Gem County were made by the Weiser band of the Shoshoni, who were native to the area. These peoples were interrelated with the Bannock and the Paiute and extended from Canada to Mexico. They covered hundreds of miles each year as they gathered roots, berries, and seeds; fished for spawning salmon in the rivers and streams; and hunted and trapped animals for their sustenance. The man pictured is Patsevonoquedar. (Courtesy of Idaho State Historical Society, No. 77-69.6.)

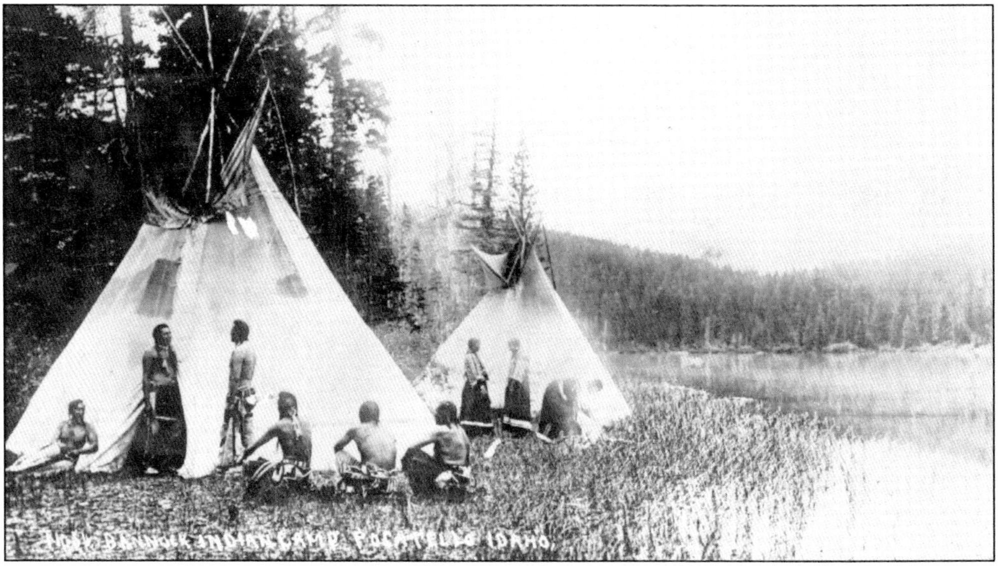

The Weiser band of the Shoshoni and the related Bannock wintered in the sheltered valleys of the Weiser River. In the spring, they began their migration to the cooler, higher elevation around the Payette Lakes. Fall drew them down the Payette River and tributaries to hunt elk and deer. They had seasonal campsites in the Sweet-Ola area, on the butte, at the hot springs, and in the Emmett Valley. (Courtesy of Idaho State Historical Society, No. 79-148.8.)

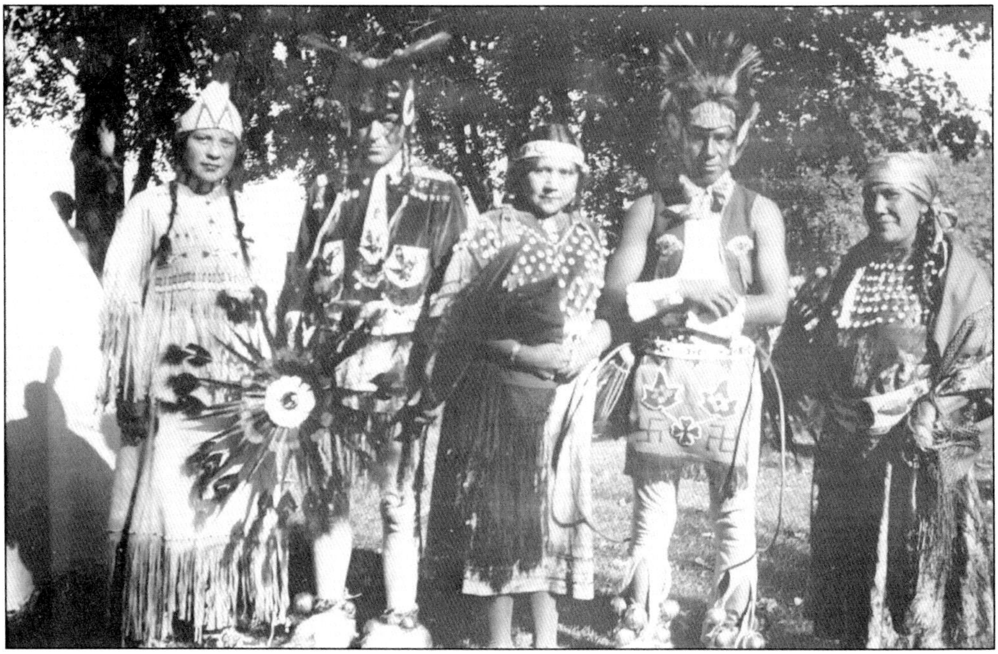

The *Idaho Statesman*, on October 7, 1875, mentions the extensive fisheries that are worked by Indians "who shoot, spear and otherwise catch large quantities of delicious salmon every fall which are dried and cached for winter market. The family groups were often identified by names for the areas they traveled or by the food they hunted or gathered. Shoho agaideka: means cottonwood-salmon eaters, living around Payette and Weisers Rivers." (Courtesy of Idaho State Historical Society, No. 891.)

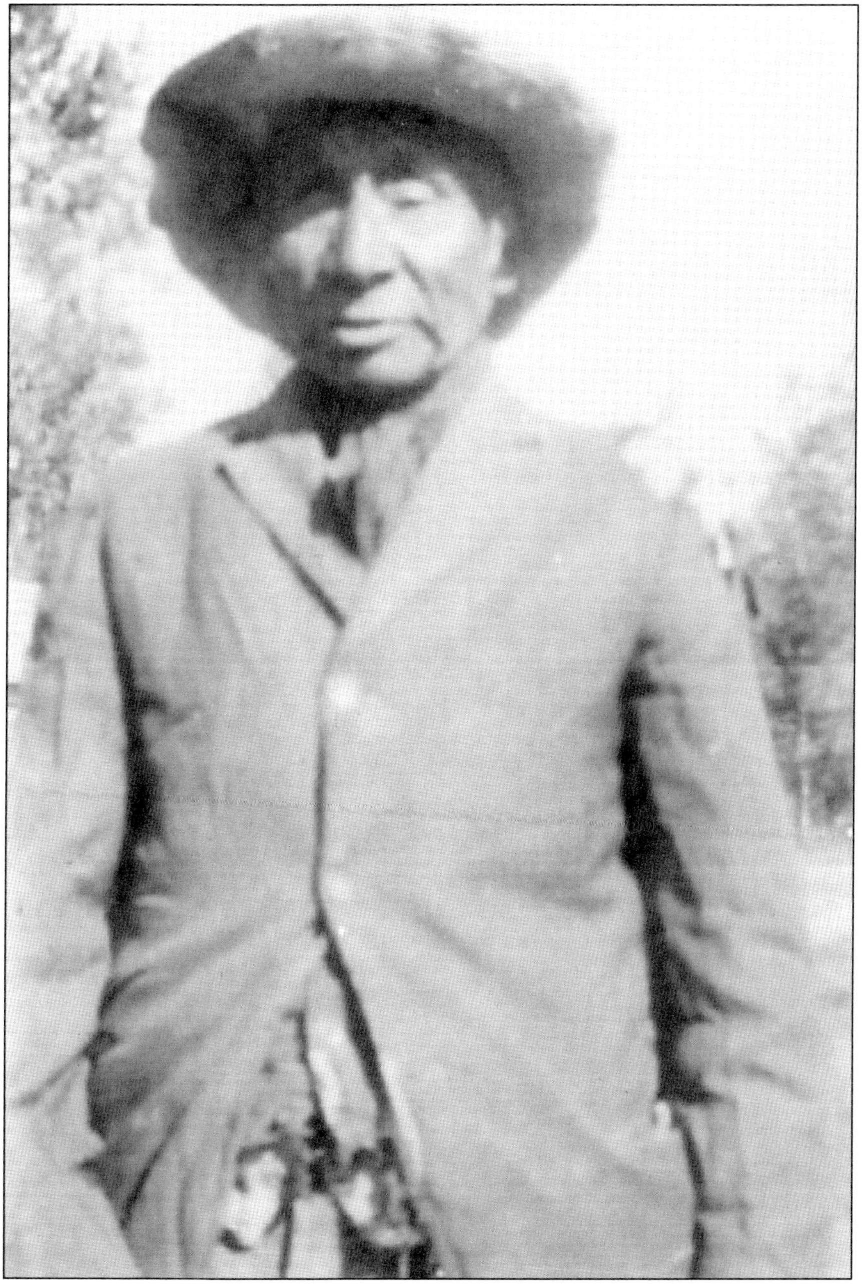

Eagle Eye, the Shoshone peacemaker, led his Weiser band deep into the central mountains to avoid soldiers searching for them. They were successful, assimilating with white settlers north and east of the Sweet area for over 20 years. In 1894, Eagle Eye was buried by his followers on Timber Butte overlooking the rivers, valleys, and mountains of his people. In about 1900, the last of the Weiser Indians quietly gathered their belonging and finally settled on the Fort Hall Reservation, where some of their descendants are tribal leaders to this day. This photograph is purported to show Charles Eagle, son of Bannock chief Indian Charley of the Eagle Eye Weiser and the last Shoshone Bannock group to go into the Fort Hall Reservation. The photograph was taken by Mary Burdell Lopshire at Bear Valley in 1920.

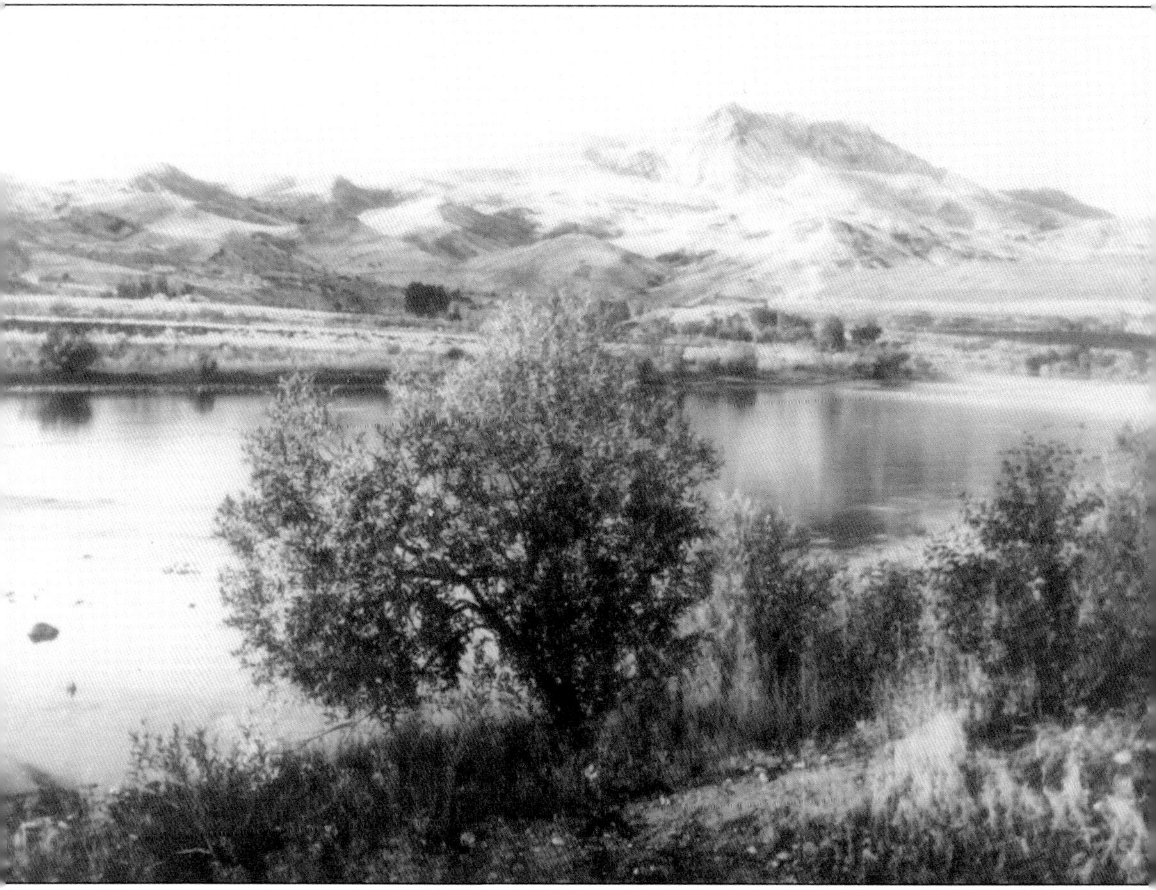

The prominent feature of Gem County is a lone mountain that stands as a sentinel. It is known as the "Sorrowing Mother." According to legend, some Indian women and their babies were left in camp while the men went hunting. While they were gone, some drunken fur trappers massacred the innocent women and children. To mark this tragic event, the Great Spirit gave the order that a monument be raised from Mother Earth; thus, a butte was born, a sorrowing mother, to honor those who were robbed of their lives and land. (Courtesy of Gem County Museum.)

Two

Contributions of Pioneers

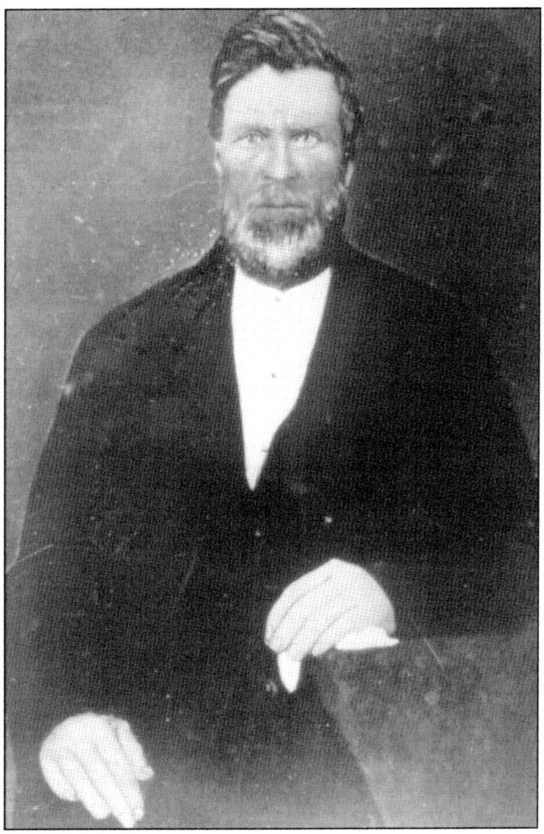

Nathaniel Martin (pictured) owned the ferry, and Jonathan Smith, the hostelry. Martin was affectionately called "the squire," as he performed weddings and acted as justice of the peace. Martin served as postmaster from 1871 to 1875 in a log cabin with a dirt-covered roof and floor, at which time Martinsville became Emmettsville. It remained Emmettsville until 1885, when it became Emmett. Martin homesteaded 48.38 acres.

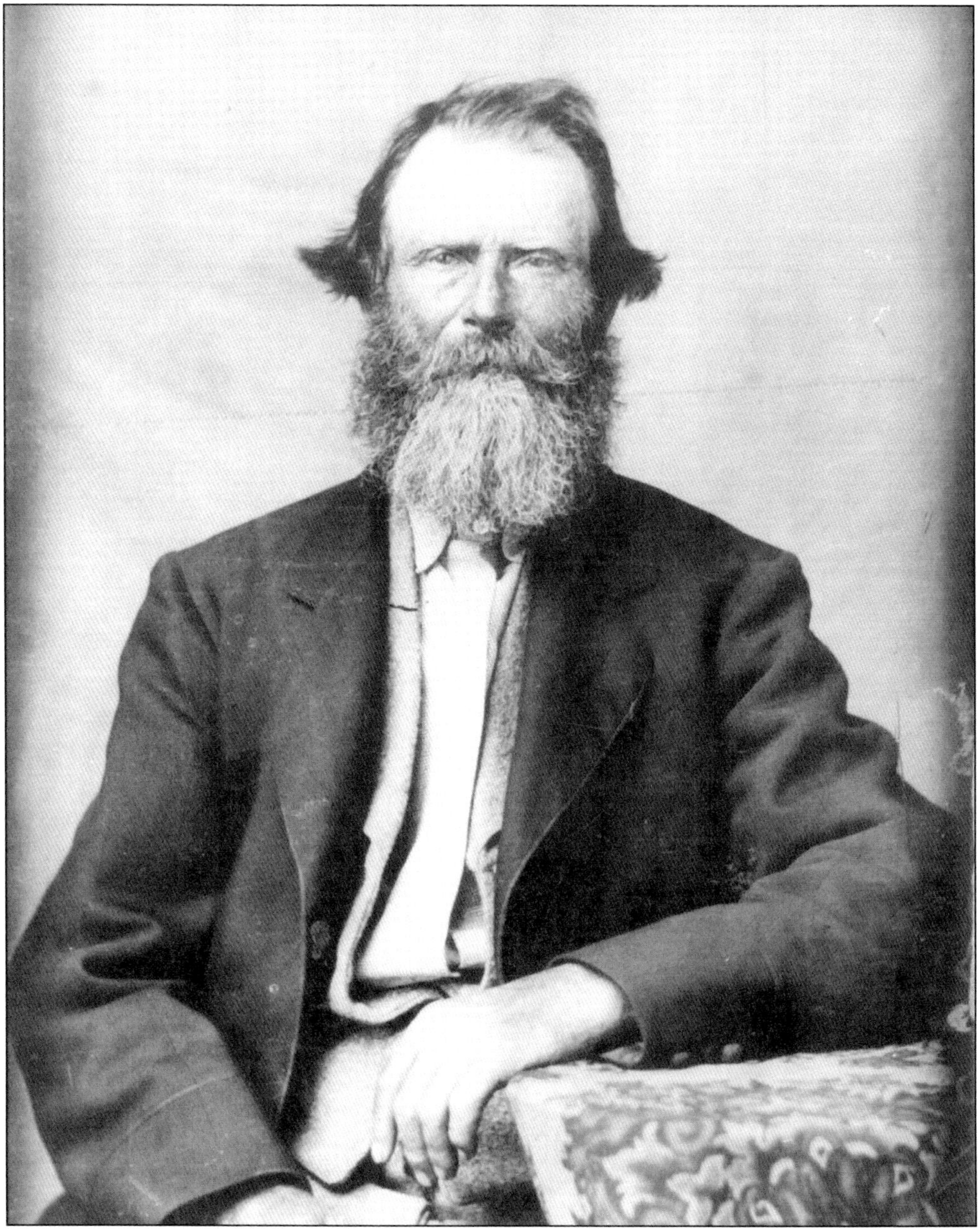

This image of Jonathan Smith has been reproduced from a tintype. Smith served as postmaster from 1867 to 1868. He and some of his neighbors dug the first irrigation ditch in about 1870. Smith wanted to enlarge and extend the ditch, so he obtained water rights (the right to use water from a particular source) on September 12, 1874. He reserved the right to raise the banks two feet higher and to claim 3,000 inches of water from the Payette River. He also claimed the right to extend the ditch from the sawmill to a place now owned by Absalom Wells and to use and sell the water for milling and irrigating purposes. Eventually, Smith formed a ditch company with nontaxable shares that are still in effect today, administered by the Farmers Cooperative Canal. Smith loved to garden, and he created a delightful place with fruit, grapes, berries, and all kinds of vegetables and flowers. His home was located near the river bridge.

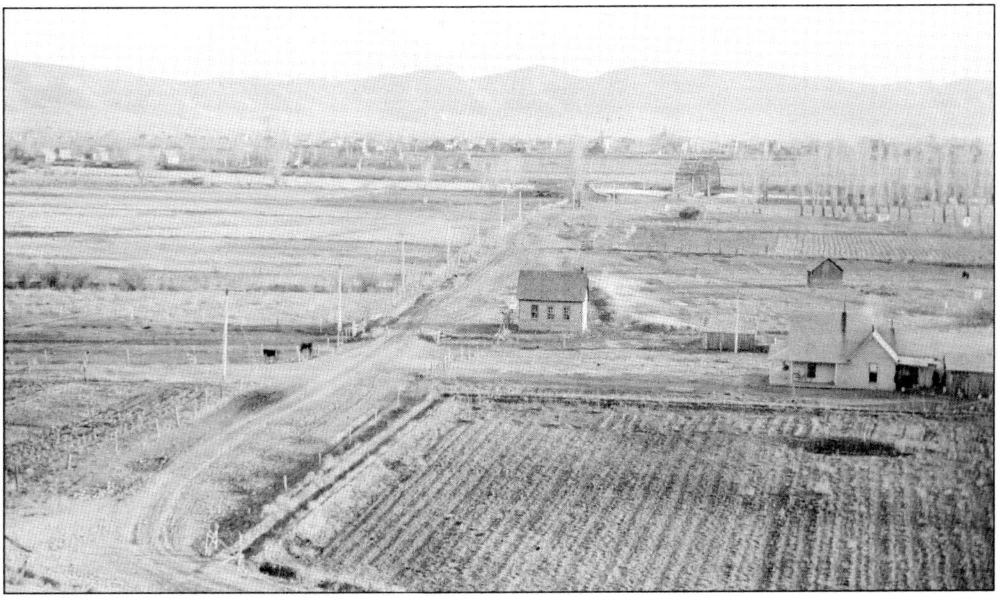

This picture is taken from the Riverside Cemetery, with a view looking south toward the river. In the background is the river bridge. Note the lack of all commercial development. The Gills sold the roadhouse and were the first to move across the river, where they built another comfortable and hospitable hostelry. They also built up an extensive cattle business. This formerly had been the traditional camping grounds of the Native Americans. The Weiser band of the Shoshoni camped here on the way to their winter camp in Indian Valley.

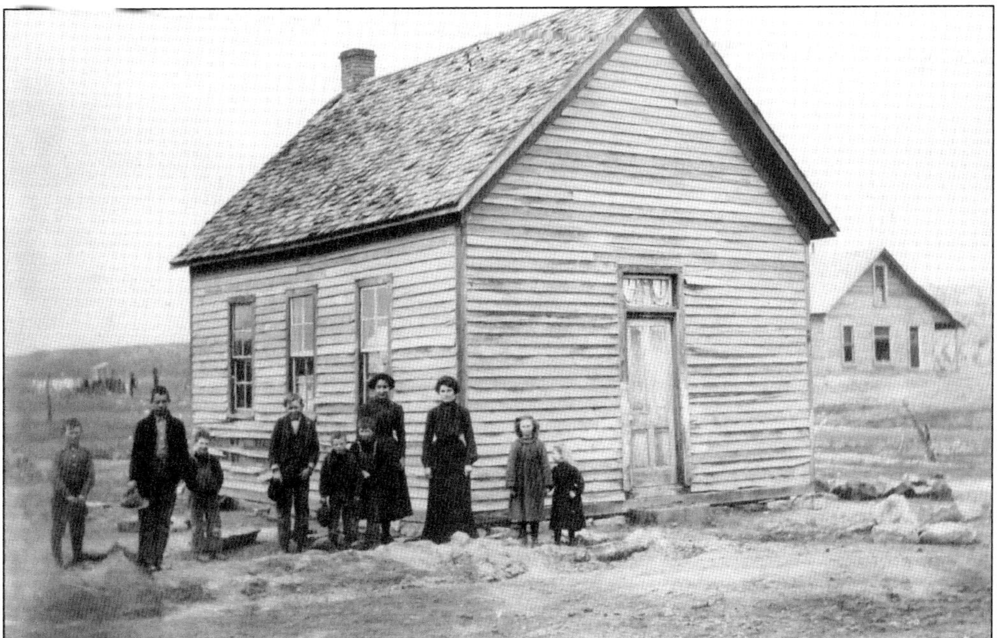

Blanche Bishop (third from right) was the teacher at Gill School in 1903. The settlers wanted their children to be able to read and write, so one-room schools were established throughout the county. There were onetime between 28 and 30 schools operating in the Gem County, and Gill School was a typical school of the period.

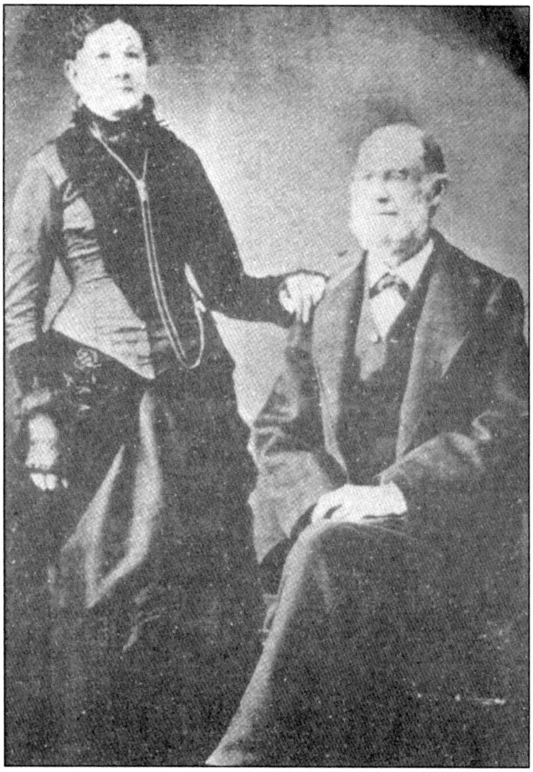

Lorenzo Gill was a Missouri gentleman who wore formal clothing and had been a banker and a dance master before coming west. Louisa Gill wore beautiful clothes and jewelry and loved a good party. After the railroad came, she often returned home to Ohio. They knew how to entertain and provide for the travelers that came for accommodations. Their son managed the cattle business and entertained the guests as well.

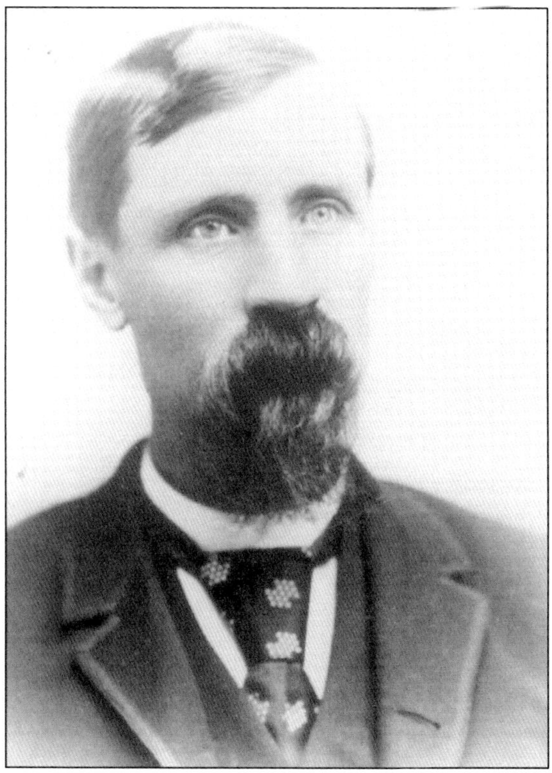

James "Mat" Madison Martin and his father, Nathaniel, built a spacious house in which the family hosted social activities. The house was well built with hand-selected lumber, and it still stands on the corner of North Wardwell and Riverside Streets. Mat served in the territorial and state legislatures and on the school board. He was a farmer and orchardist specializing in fruit, vegetables, and cider, which he sold in the mining camps.

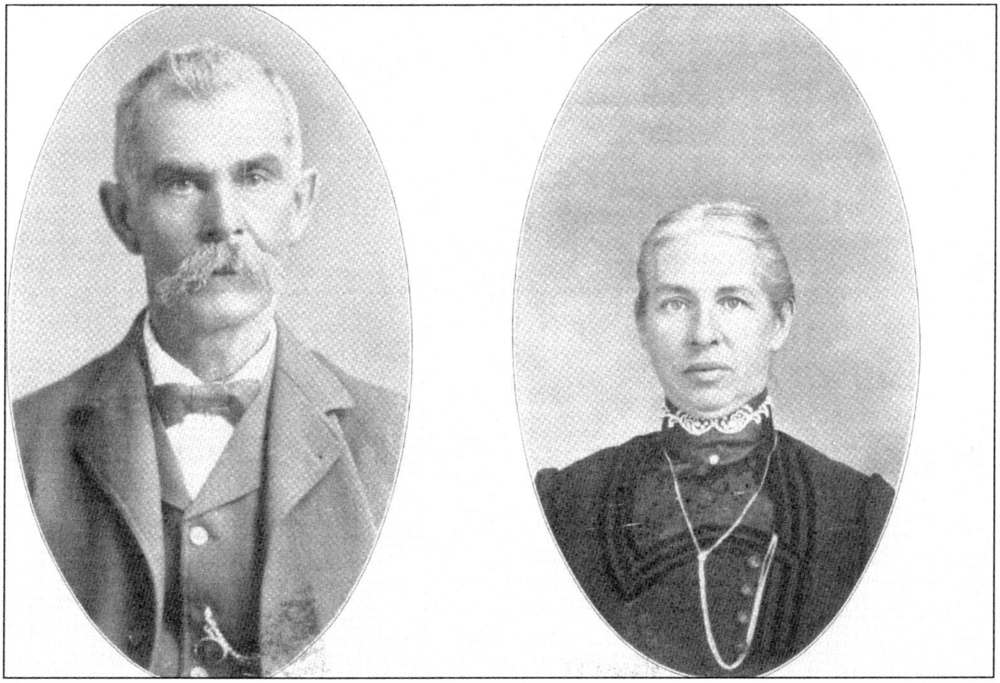

John F. and Louisa Basye came to Idaho and operated a mill at Centerville before moving to Martinsville in 1866. They liked Martinsville and purchased land next to Martin and Smith for their home. Mrs. Smith and Mrs. Basye were very competitive, each trying to cultivate the prettiest flower garden. John F.T. Basye, a son, joined them from California and homesteaded 160 acres north of the Payette River.

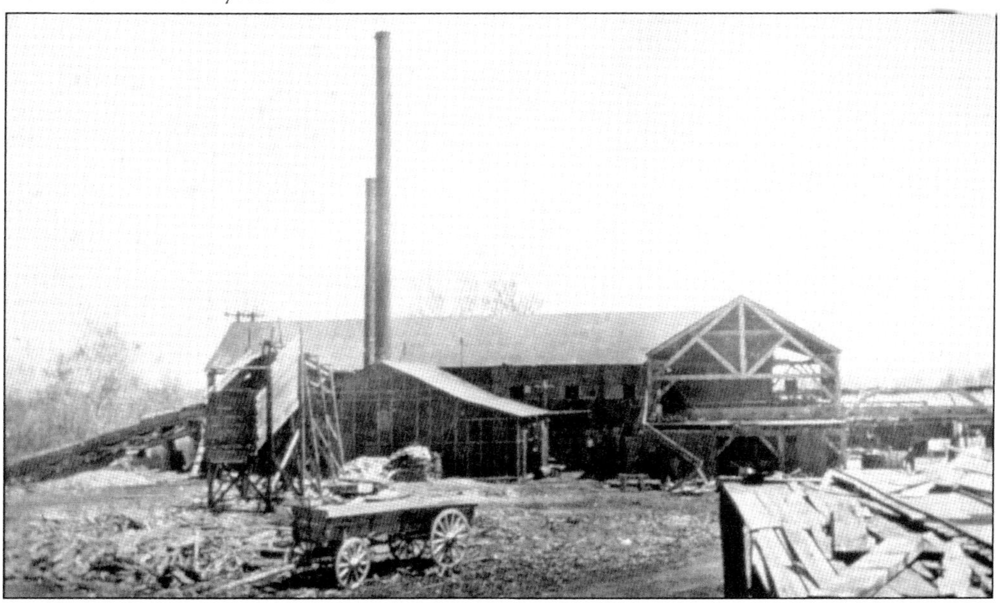

John F. Basye put up a modern mill in 1870 with his son-in-law Samuel Walker. They had a good supply of timber, and demand was high. Jacob Ray Gregg writes in his history of Malheur County, Oregon, that "Malheur homesteaders are hauling lumber from the mills at Emmettsville." The mill filled an important need in the community for building and fencing.

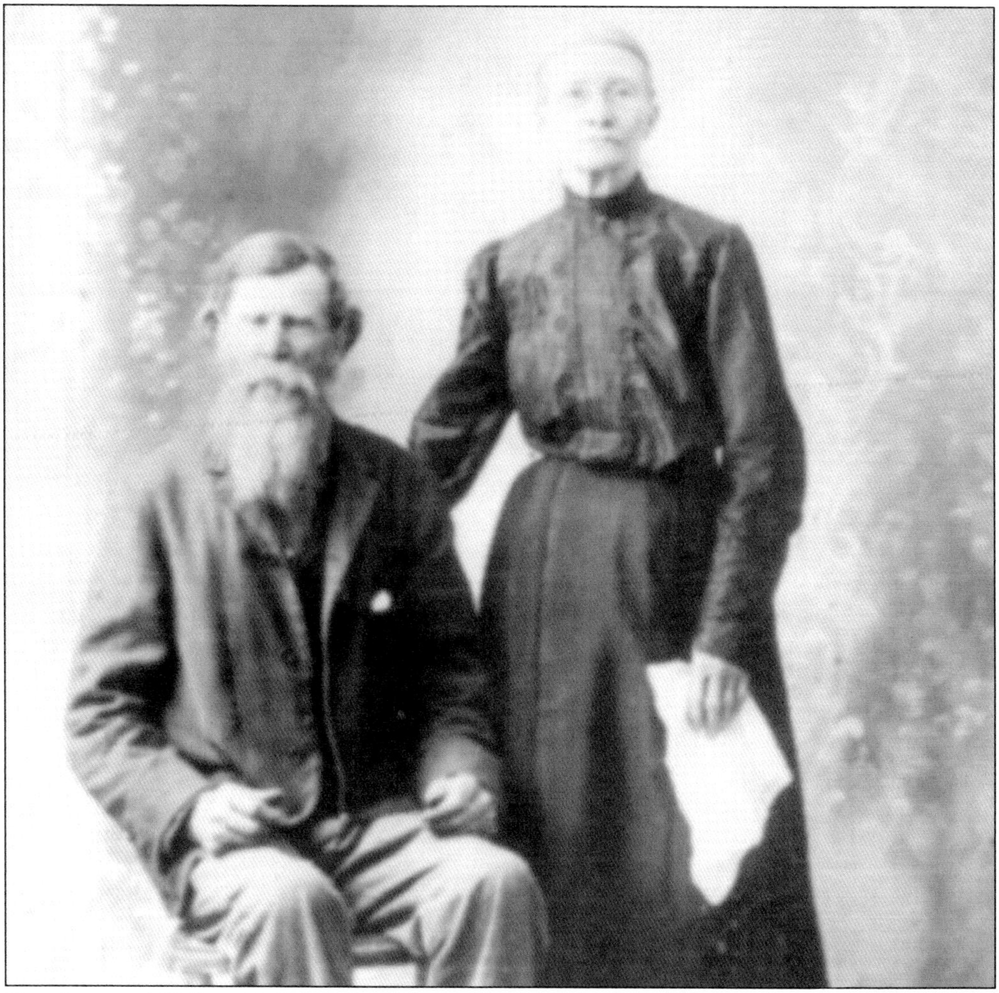

Eliza Jane and William Fuller came to the valley in 1876 and purchased 30 acres in the present city limits. They also acquired an island, which is still called Fuller's Island. Their daughter Annie Fuller Freeman, who was 12 years old when they moved from Missouri, wrote of Emmettsville, "There was no store here then; father had to drive twelve miles with team and wagon west of Emmettsville to Falk's Store to buy staples. About 1878, Aaron Bascom started Emmettsville's first store. A few years before that some of the men got together and built the Shepherd School." She recalled that her "father worked out some shares in the old Emmettsville Ditch when he helped to enlarge it. These shares entitled him to water part of the homestead, and he planted a fruit orchard, a garden, timothy hay and grain."

This image shows four generations of the Womack family. Issac stands at left beside son Walter; Alexander Womack, Emmettsville's first blacksmith, holds great-grandson Elmer. Alex arrived in 1870 and placer mined for gold on Anderson Creek near Martinsville. He earned enough money that he was able to send for his wife and children. The Womacks had a large family of 16 children, and many descendants still live in the area.

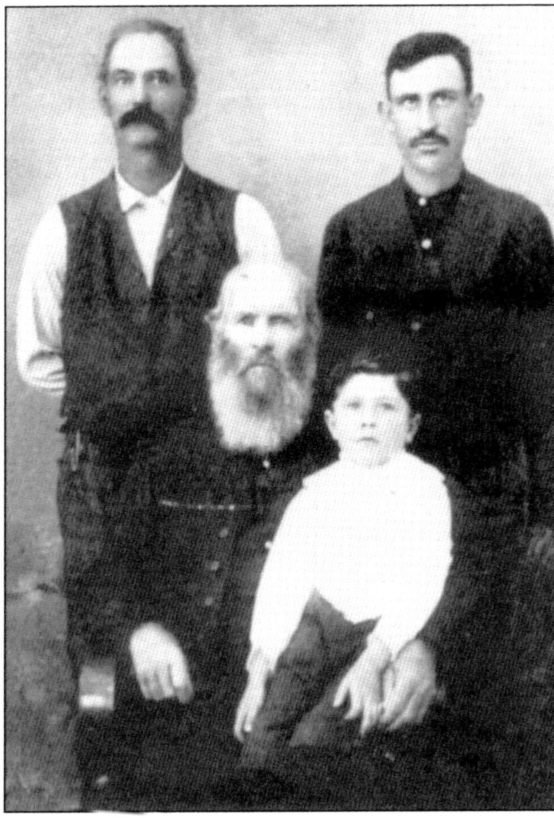

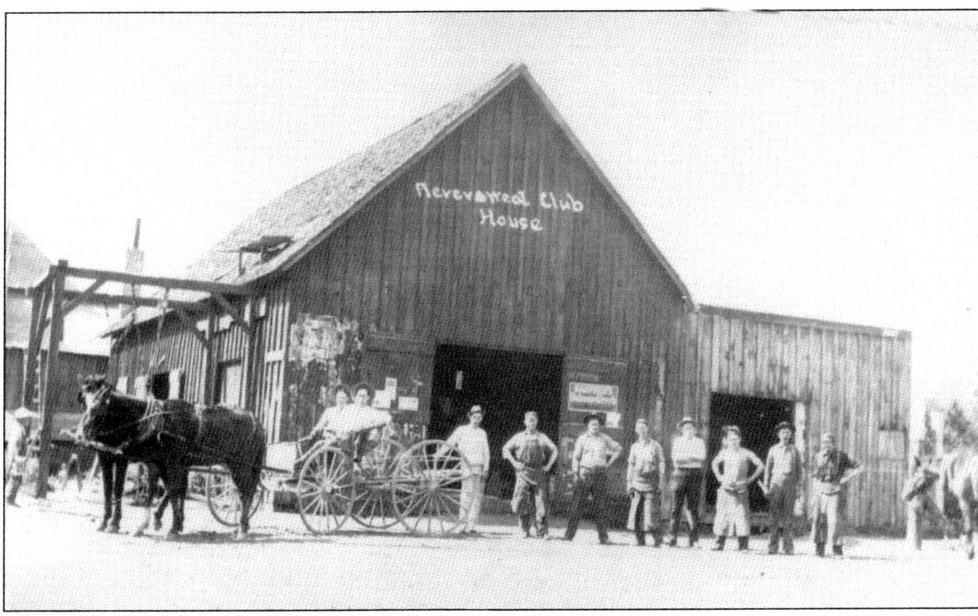

The Womacks' blacksmith shop was located where the train depot stands today. The services of the blacksmith were essential as the freight wagons and the wagons of local people required repair and horses needed shoeing. Blacksmiths were in much demand, and Emmettsville was blessed to have such a good one.

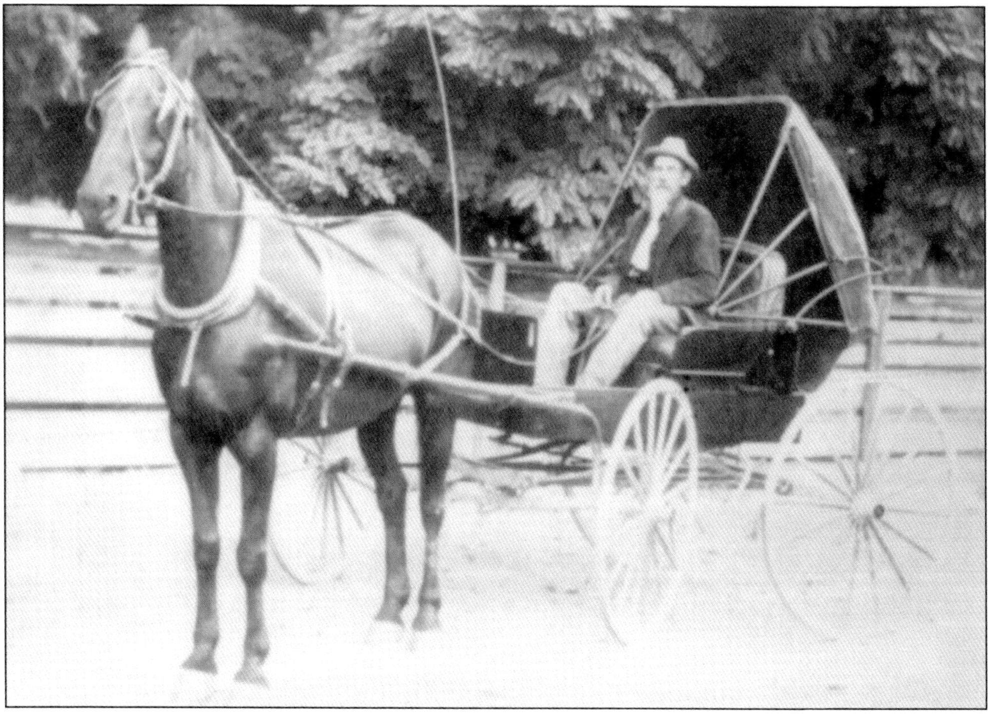

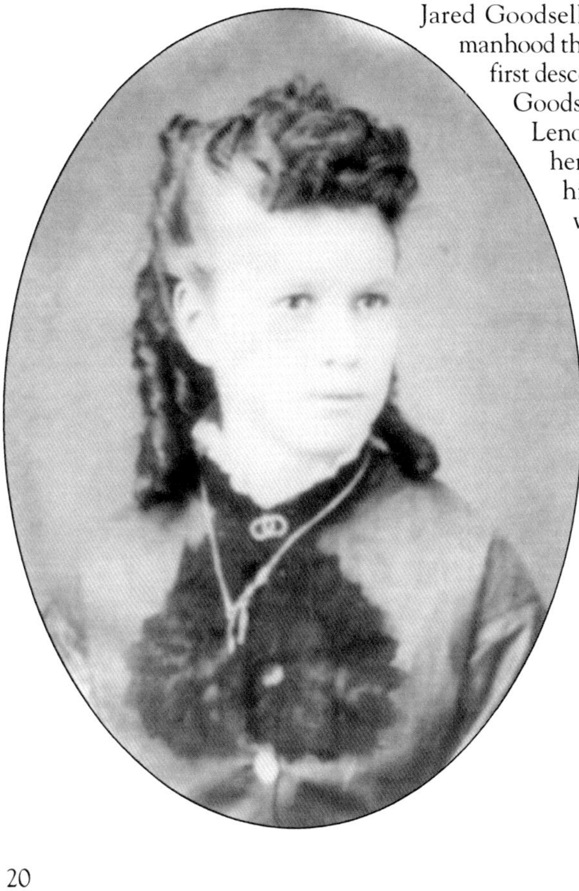

Jared Goodsell was born in New York and grew to manhood there. He accompanied Tim Goodell on his first descent down the treacherous Freezeout Hill. Goodsell married William Burdge's daughter Lenora (right), who came to the valley with her parents in 1862, and he worked with his father-in-law in the sawmill. Goodsell was helpful in establishing the first water rights associated with the Emmettsville ditch. He lent his support to Jonathan Smith and helped him to launch his ditch company by deeding his property to Smith, who had to show ownership. When the water rights were established, the land was then deeded back to the owners. Goodsell's life was ended by an accident when he fell from a wagon. Sons George and Jerry Goodsell lived in Emmett for many years.

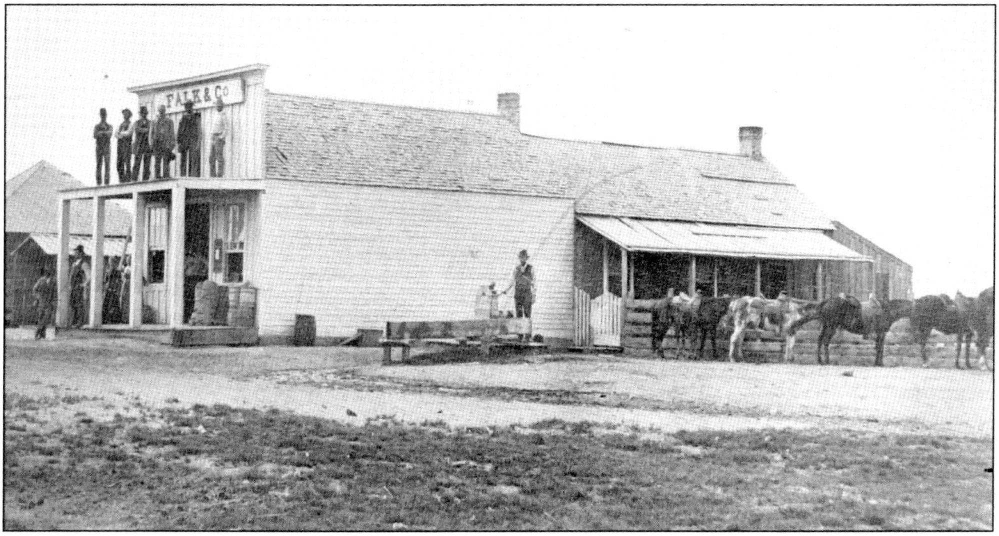

Traffic on the Basin Trail was so heavy that the Falk brothers were able to establish a roadhouse, post office, and general store near the Payette–Gem County line. It was the principle place to purchase supplies and the only place to pick up mail between Boise, Idaho, and Baker, Oregon.

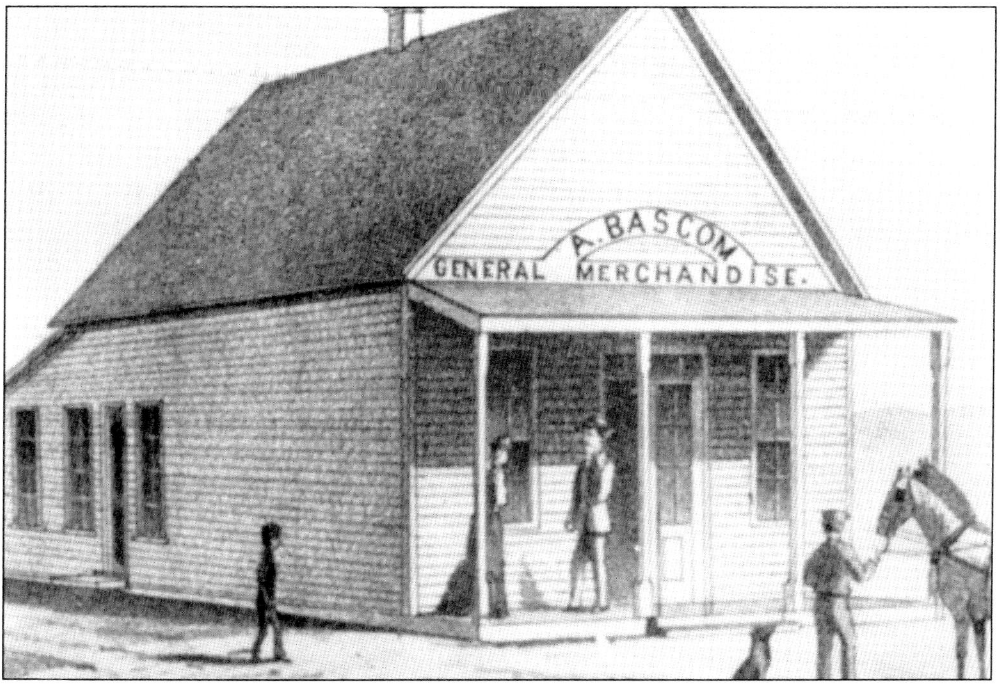

W.A. Goulder, a roving reporter for the *Tri-Weekly Statesman,* was aware of the need for a general store. He knew that money could be made in Emmettsville and that such an establishment would save the people from having to travel to Falk's Store. Soon after Goulder's visit and encouraged by him, Aaron Bascom, son-in-law of the Basyes, opened the first store. Supplies were brought in from Kelton, Utah, by freight wagon.

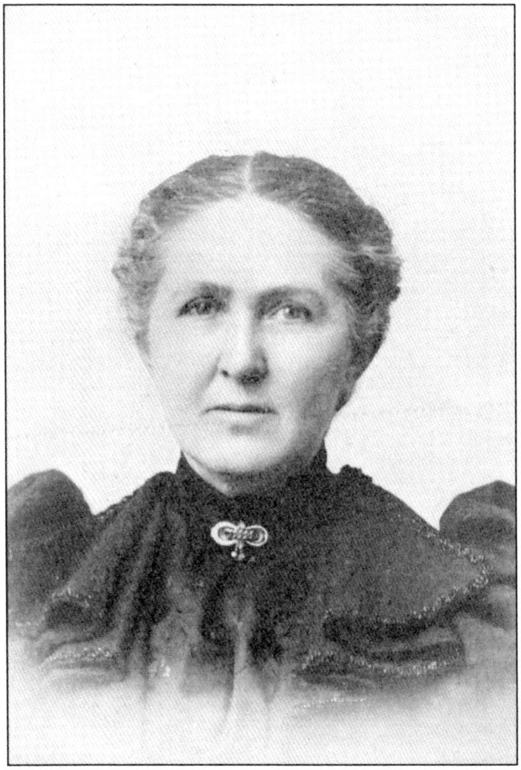

Mr. and Mrs. John F. Daily came to Idaho in 1875 where they were engaged in ranching and stock raising. They had married at Putnam, Missouri. The Dailys farmed in Iowa for a time but decided to come west, where he raised cattle on the Snake River. In 1889, the Dailys purchased a 160-acre farm near Fourth Street. They were able to build a lovely, comfortable, two-story house, which was surrounded with orchards and gardens and a spacious bluegrass lawn with a hedge. It was a beautiful showplace, and the local paper featured it in 1897. Many were interested in planting orchards at this time since railroads provided easy access to the markets and the money return was high per acre.

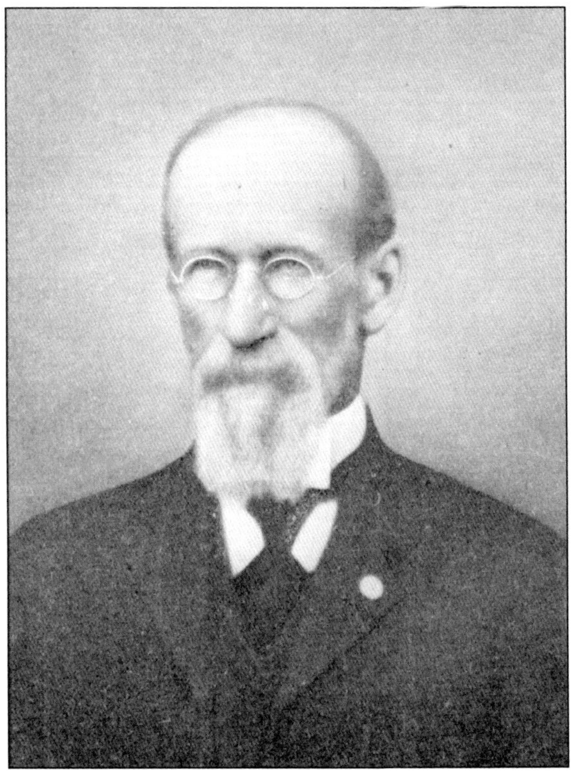

The Riggs family first lived in Boise, then moved to Oregon and settled permanently in Emmett, homesteading along the Payette River in 1871 and engaging in cattle raising. Henry Riggs imported the first bobwhite quail, served in the territorial legislature, and voted to move the capital from Lewiston to Boise. Henry was the father of Boise and Sam Riggs. Boise Riggs was born in and named for the capital city. He was a blacksmith, stage driver, and sheriff.

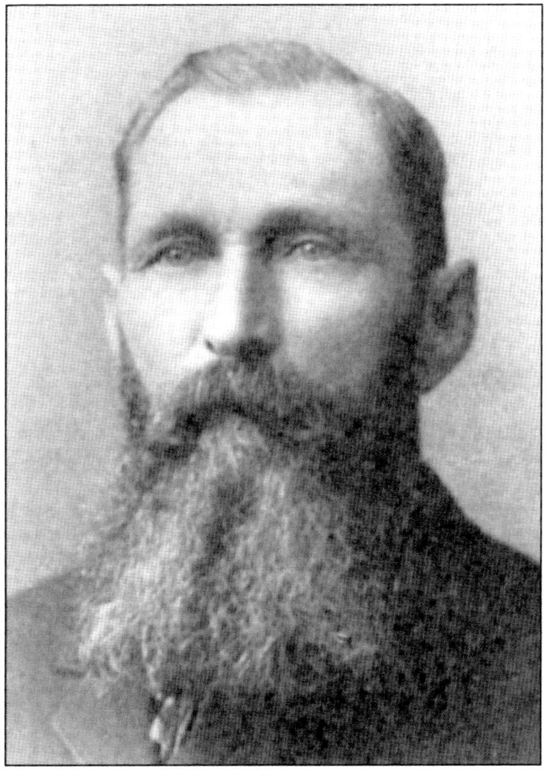

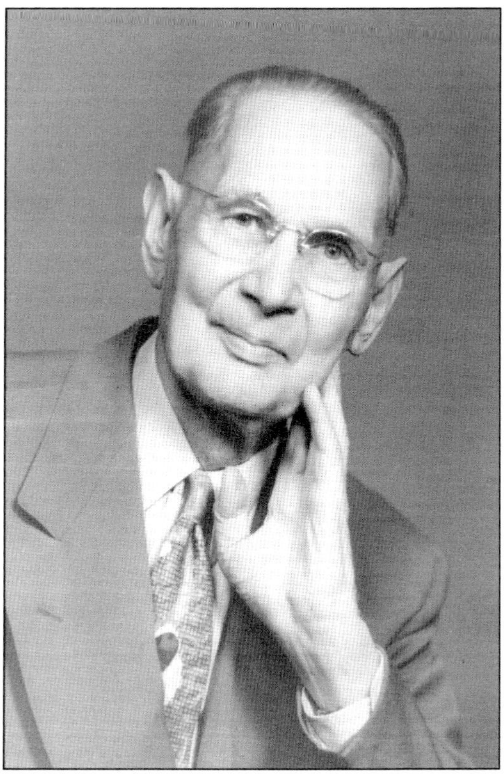

Samuel Riggs (shown at left) said, "We had no educational opportunities to speak of . . . We tried to have three months of school every spring. After I became nineteen, I came to the pioneer school in Emmett for seven months. I learned more there under qualified teachers and an organized school than in all of the other three month terms combined." He was appointed postmaster and was elected state senator from Gem County.

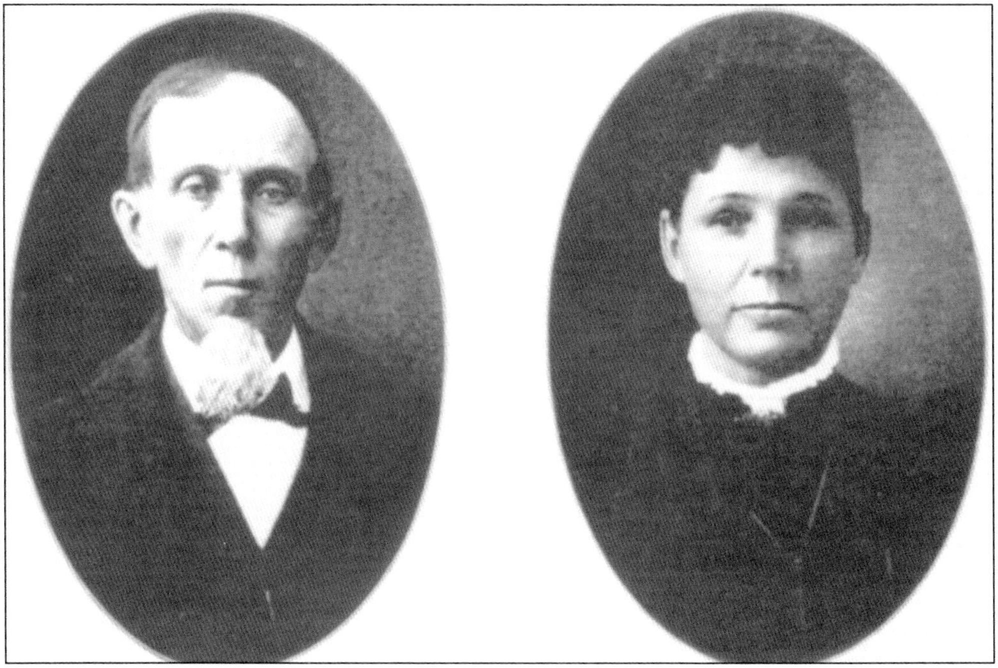

Joseph Degan and his family settled on the south side of the river. They bought the former Gill Stage Station and 160 acres of sagebrush land from David Basye, where they planted one of the first orchards north of Emmettsville. Joseph regularly hauled a load of produce to the basin country. He soon had several wagons to carry his wares.

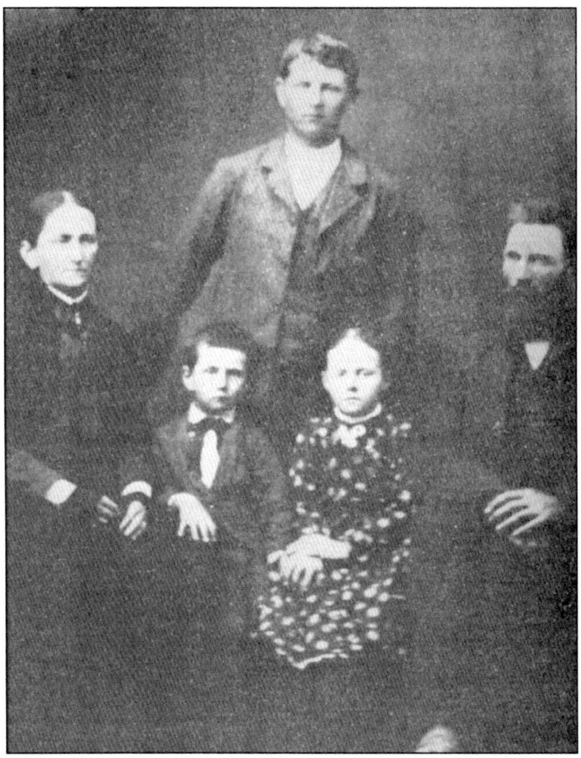

Joseph Shepard served as a Wells Fargo messenger and an early stage driver between Falk's Store and Placerville for a number of years. On June 23, 1877, he wrote to the governor of Idaho Territory, asking for guns and ammunition for the protection of the mail from roving bands of Indians during the Bannock Uprising. Shepard donated land on Fourth Street for a school.

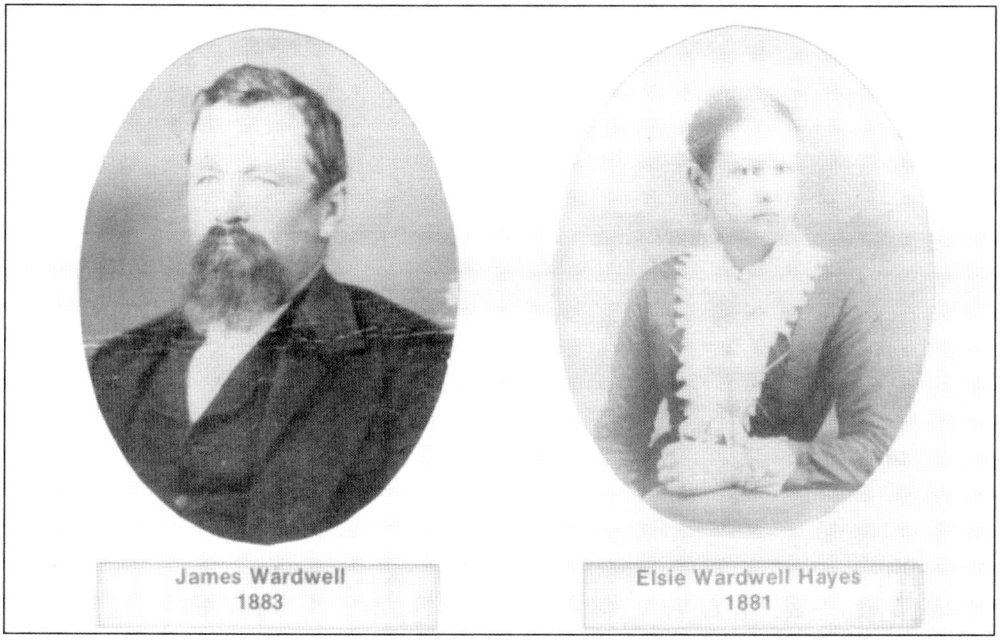

James Wardwell moved his family to Emmett for his wife's health. He filed on 160 acres west of Emmett and built a house. In 1883, he bought 160 acres from James Johnson and had the town of Emmett platted. He also bought the Basye-Walker Sawmill and later sold it to John McNish and Ed Allen. Wardwell's daughter Elsie married Edward Hayes. Wardwell Street and Wardwell School are named for him.

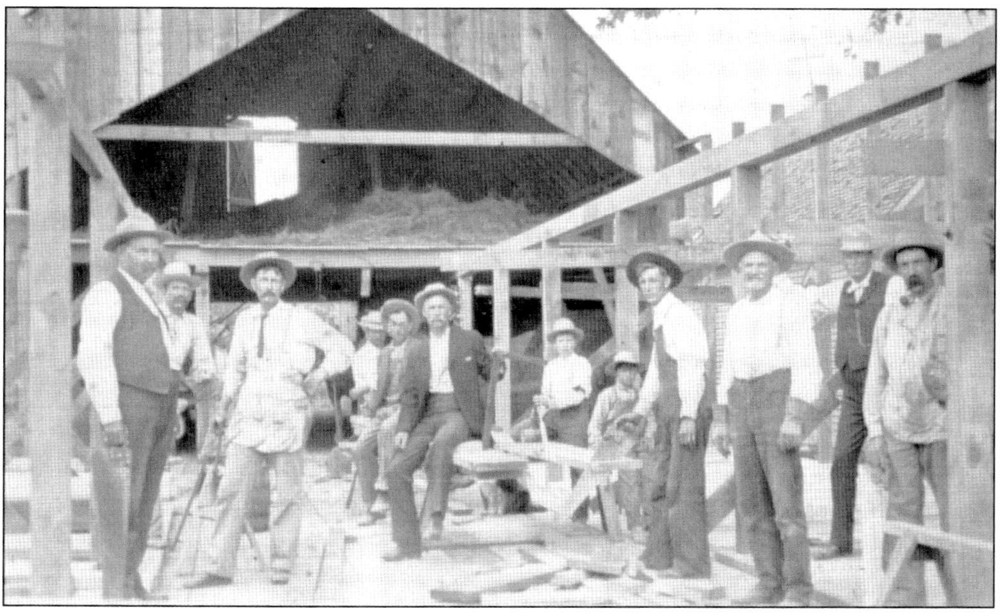

People that came to town from the outlying areas to conduct their business would need a place for their animals. The shared efforts of many hands made the building of the DeMasters Livery Barn, near the corner of First Street and Boise Avenue, pleasant work. These men are, from left to right, Charles P. Bilderback, three unidentified, Frank Carpenter, "Dad" DeMasters, Frank Lowe, Bill Basye, Harry Titus (with saw), Bill Banks, unidentified, and D.W.C. "Clint" Brown.

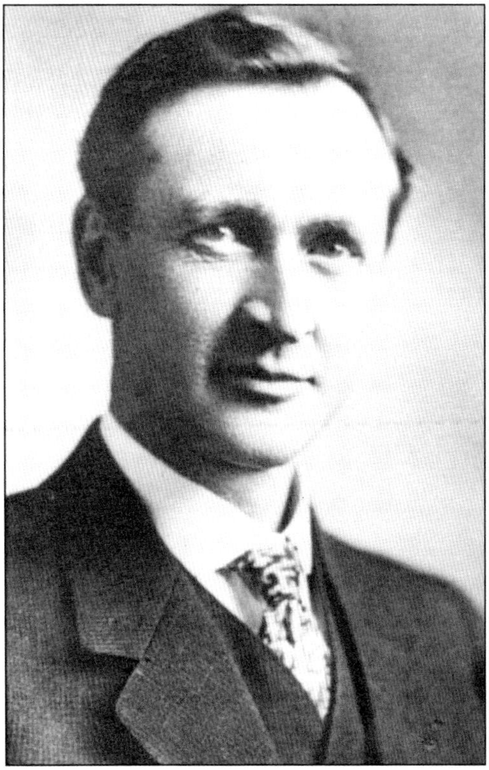

E.K. Hayes owned a mercantile company in Emmett and was interested in many aspects of business. He married Elsie Wardwell, James Wardwell's daughter. Hayes worked diligently to get the town of Emmett incorporated, and he and W.R. Cartwright organized the community's first bank at 137 West Main Street. Ed Hayes was remembered as one who got things done and as a quick thinker.

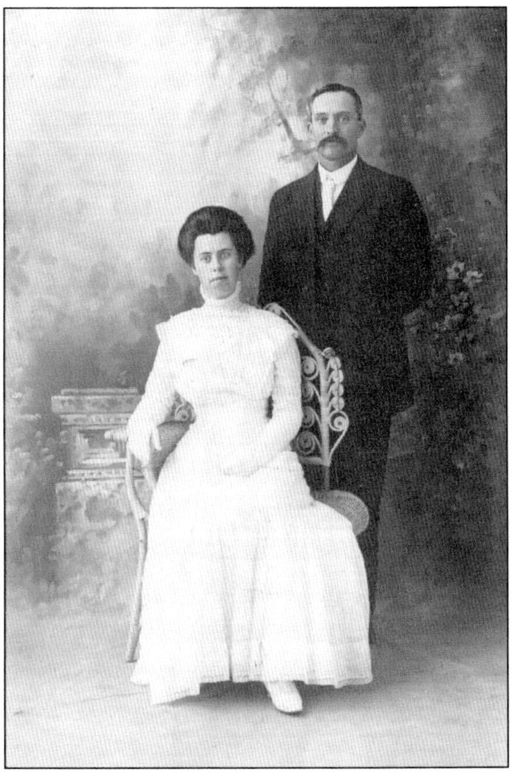

Edwin and Rena Campbell constructed substantial business buildings and attractive, comfortable homes with the firm of Berry and Campbell. They designed and erected the Bank of Emmett building, the Ideal Theater, F.A. DeClark's house at 604 East Main Street, and W.W. Wilton's house with the cobblestone foundation at 621 East Main Street. Theirs were rated as one of the leading contractor and building firms in Gem and Canyon Counties.

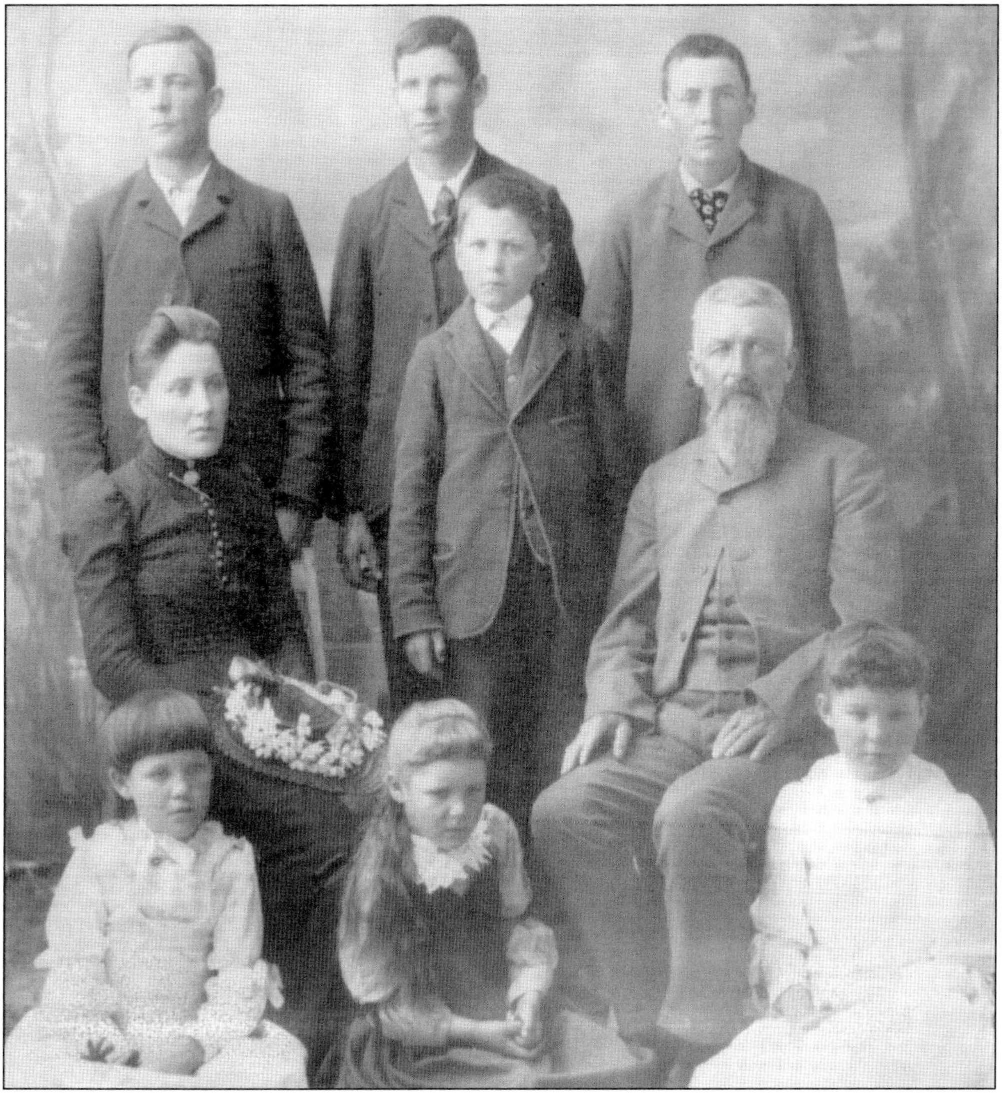

Douglas Knox bought a farm next to the Burdge's. Ella Knox (later Parrish) was brought to Martinsville as a young child. Her father planted the first crab apple and plum trees. The Knoxes were concerned about others and did all they could to take care of the sick and discouraged. Douglas Knox was a public servant throughout his life and served on the school board for 35 years. His daughter Ella helped him raise the rest of the children when his wife passed away. He was known as the father of Emmett public schools, and many of his descendents still live in Emmett.

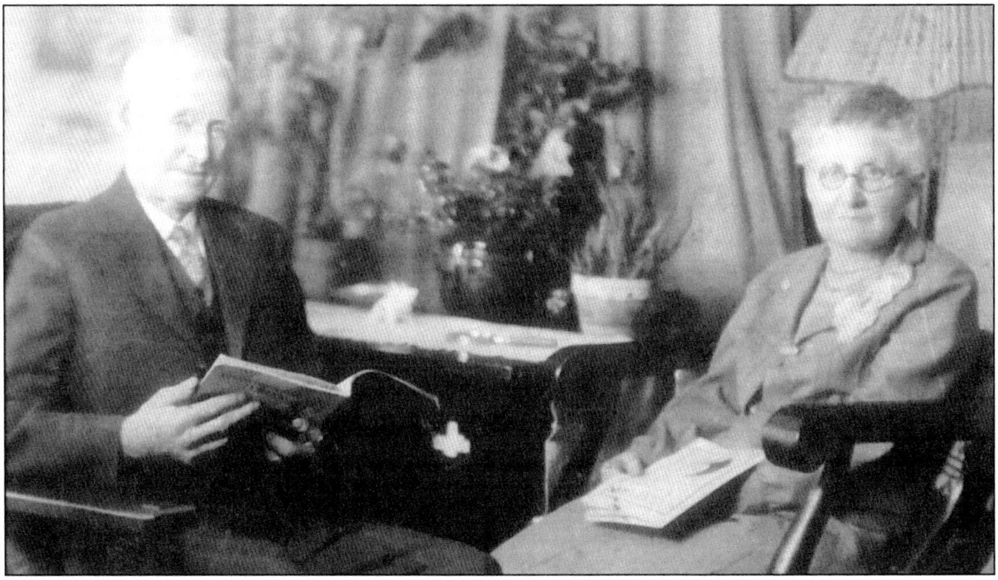

Ella Knox married William Parrish, and they lived with her father and took care of the family. This arrangement lasted seven years until her youngest sisters were able to manage the house. Ella lived her entire life in the community and was appointed county historian by the Idaho Historical Society. She was selected to be Cherry Festival queen for her service and dedication to the community.

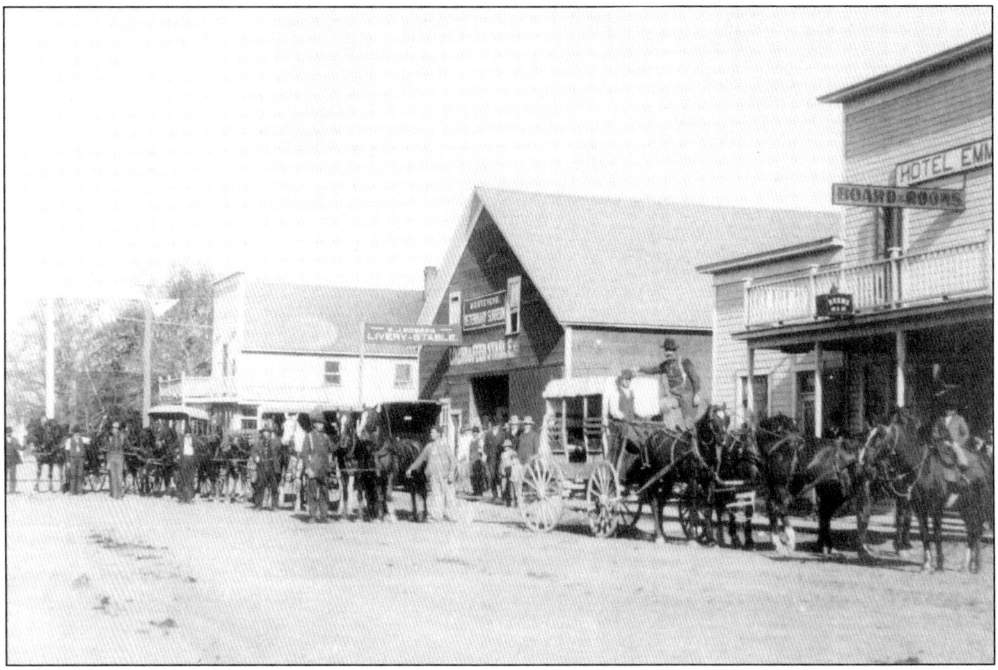

The livery stable displays its horse-drawn conveyances. Boise Riggs, who worked for O.N. Callender Livery, said, "I was often hired to drive a fancy, high-stepping team to Star by customers who wanted to catch the Interurban Street Car there. It was a pleasure to drive that snappy pair of horses." Pictured, from left to right, are the Steinbower building, Gus Amen's Livery Stable, and the Hotel Emmett.

William Curry Burdge excelled at everything he did. According to Ruth Lyon, he brought the first roan Durham cattle and Morgan-strain horses to Idaho. Burdge also had one of the finest outfits to bring him west. He purchased part of the Block House Ranch in 1864; there, he dug a ditch and hired a canal dug on which he built a waterwheel to lift the water for irrigation and to power his gristmill and lumber mill. He hauled some grinding wheels from Eagle and set up his gristmill. The grist wheels are located by the fireplace in the city park. Burdge was able to build a large home in the community, with nine rooms and a large hall of specially selected lumber from his mill. The home was the finest in the area and was used for many special events.

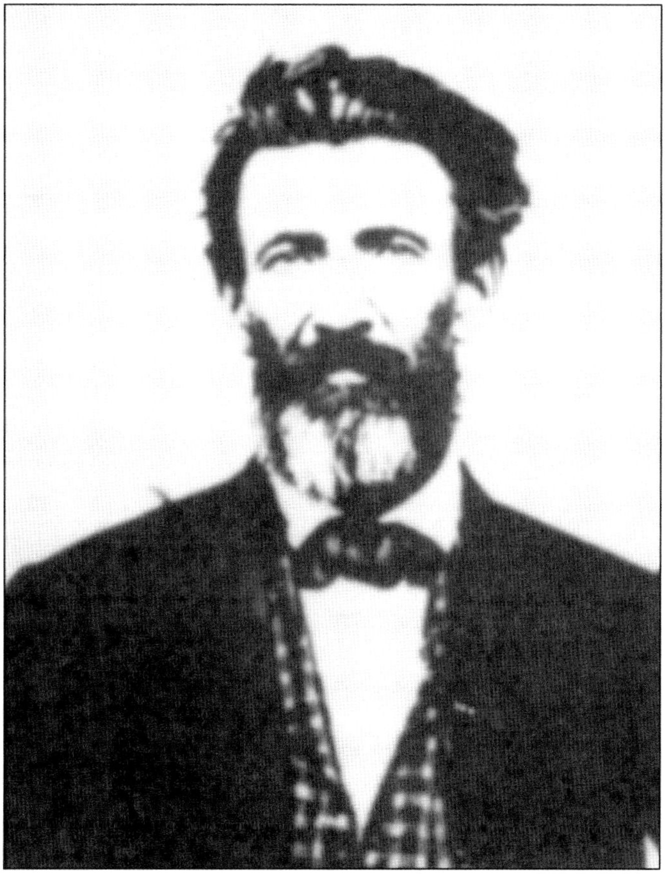

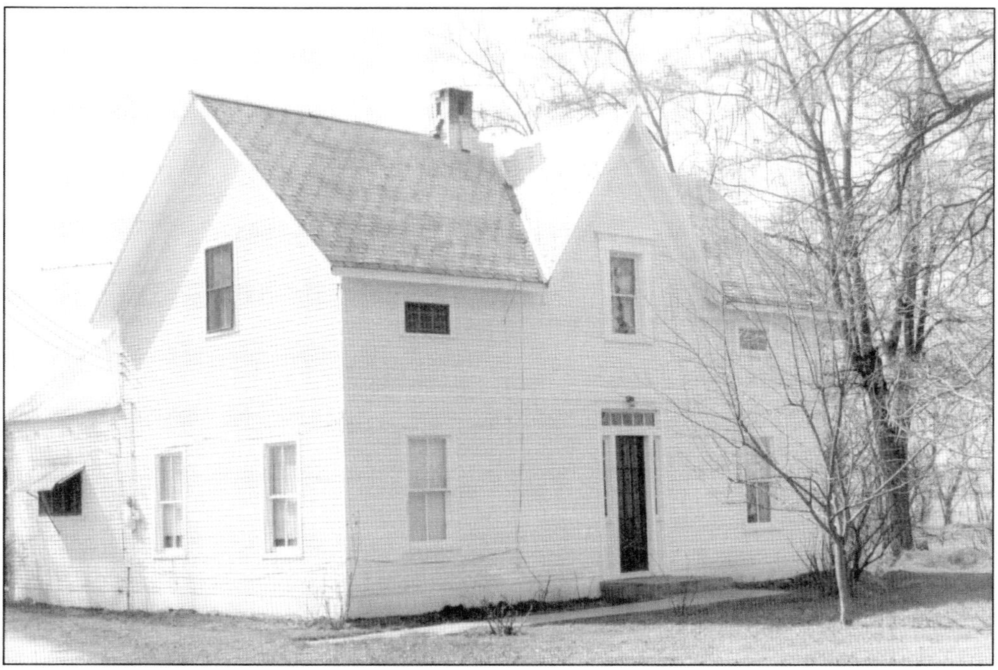

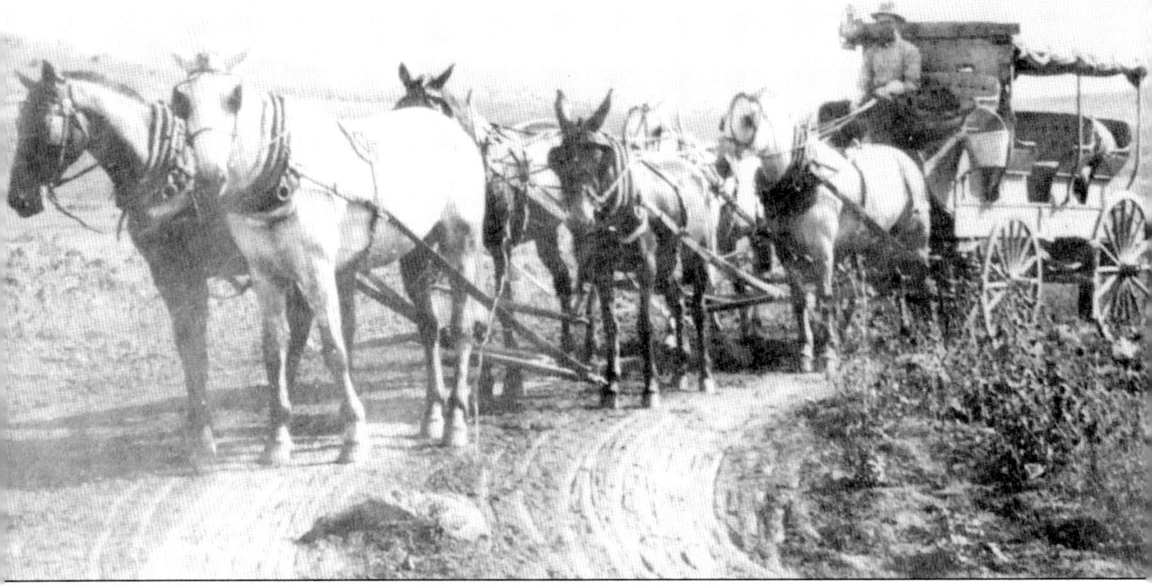

Boise G. Riggs Jr. drove a stage for O.N. Callender from Emmett to Ola in the winter and to Smiths Ferry in the summer. He describes one of his trips: "I started out one winter morning and got along fairly well until I left Sweet. From there on, we had to buck snow, There was as pile of Sears and Roebuck catalogs in the back of the stage. I made it to Squaw Mountain, but the horses couldn't go on. A mailman riding a horse met me there; we unloaded the catalogs and piled them under a big pine tree. I suspect the High Valley ladies were disappointed because the catalogs sort of took the place of a general mercantile store. The rider took the first class mail on to High Valley and Smith's Ferry. There was five feet of snow in High Valley that winter. It was cold sitting in the driver's seat with the wind blowing snow in my face, but I enjoyed the trip back to Emmett. It was mostly downhill, and the horses moved right along."

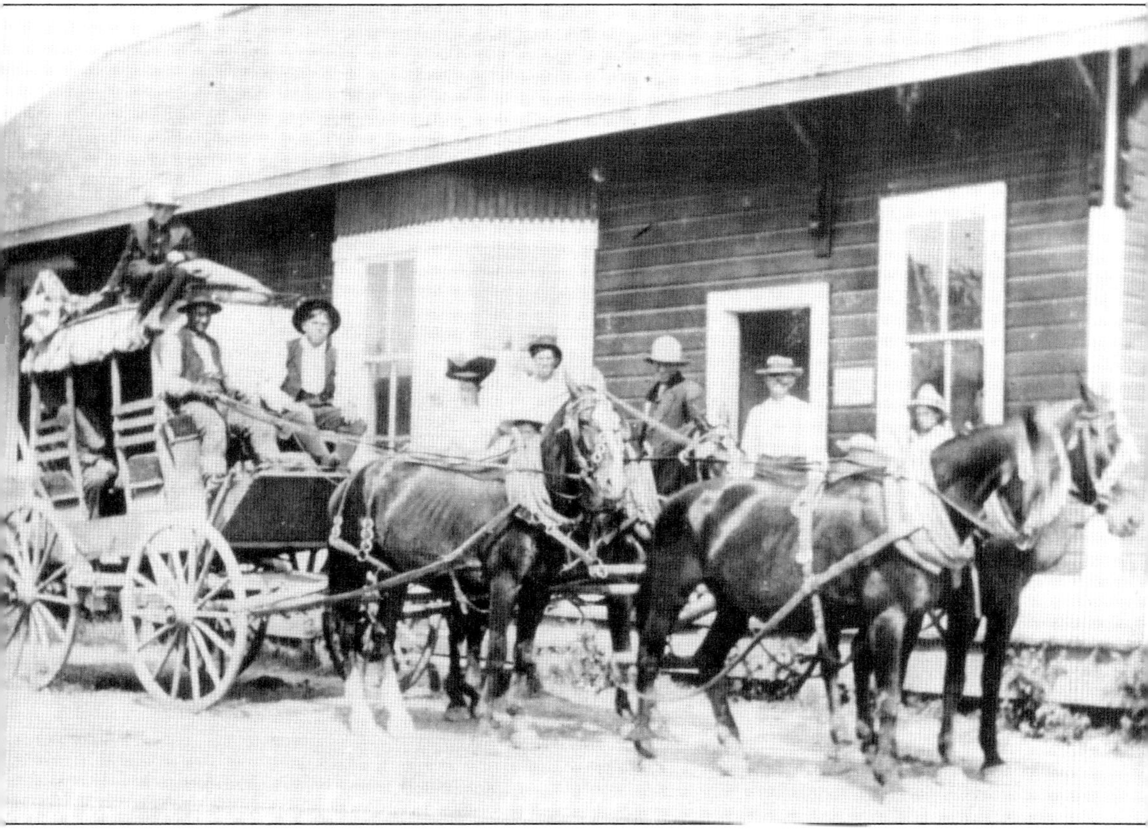

Ed Ingman drove stages for 52 years of his life. He drove for the Thunder Mountain Line and is pictured here in 1905 when Emmett was the end of the railroad line. The stage picked up the mail when the train came from Nampa, and then went to Montour, Sweet, Ola, High Valley, and Van Wyck (near Cascade). The trip could be made in 18 hours if fresh teams of horses were substituted. Edward Ingman is the driver, and J.R. Hughes is sitting next to him. George Flake is on top. The Sweet Community was a supply station and grew because of the Thunder Mountain Stage Line, which provided service from Emmett to Sweet and on to Long Valley. It was a much-needed link to the Thunder Mountain mining district. The stage line was owned by John F. Hall.

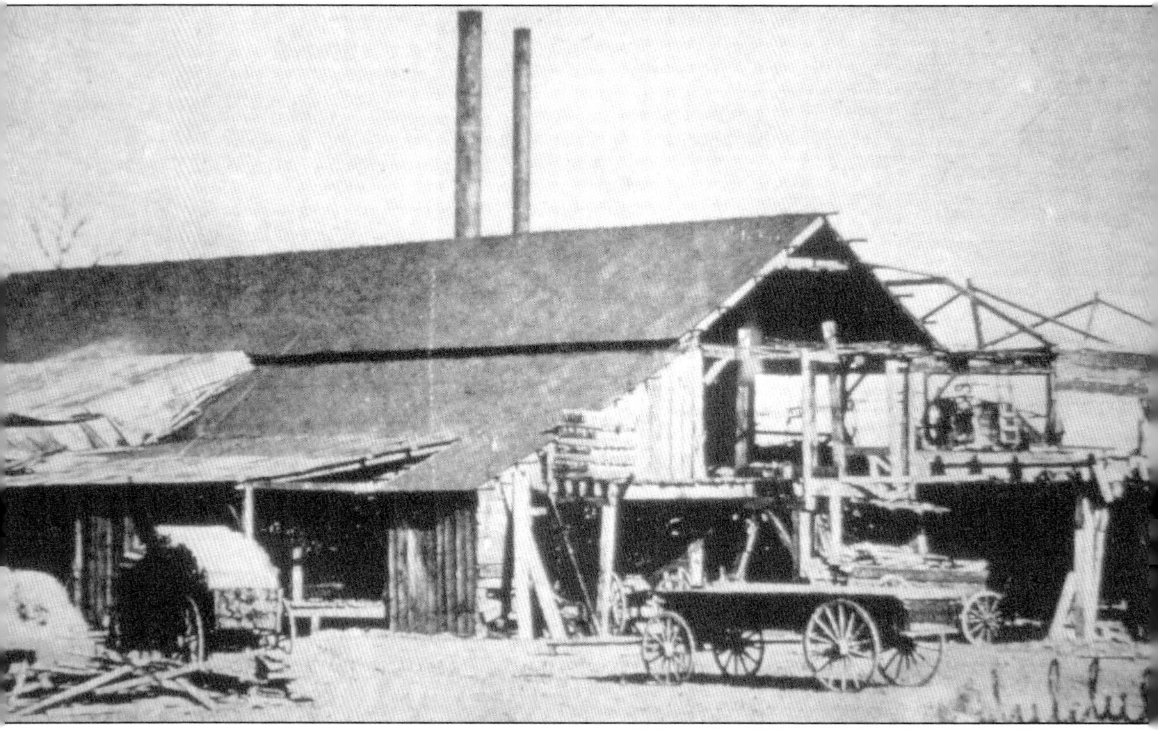

Timber was an important asset in the economy of Emmett as there was much demand for it. The railroad needed ties, the people needed homes, the mines needed supporting timbers, and cattle needed fences. As early as 1870, Basye and Walker constructed the first mill, and James Wardwell bought it in 1883. Wardwell then sold it to John McNish and Edward Allen. In 1902, Hayes investigated the Payette River from Emmett to the lakes and made application to the State Land Board for a franchise to improve the river flow. The franchise was granted, and the river was modified so it was better able to carry logs to Emmett. McNish and his partner also constructed a dam to flush out the logs during the spring log drive. In 1909, the McNish-Allen Sawmill had an output of six million board feet, while the river drive netted 12 million board feet; therefore, about half was sent to the Nampa sawmill by train.

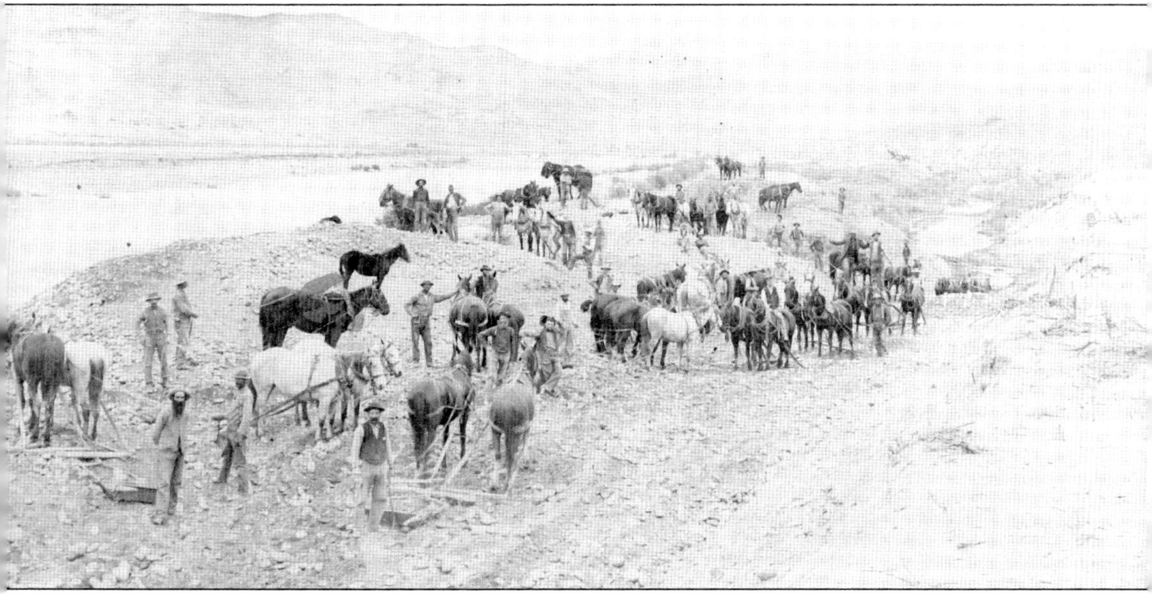

The Last Chance Ditch was four miles long and started a half mile below the present dam. Work began in 1889 and was finished in 1891. According to Ruth B. Lyon, in her book *The Village That Grew*, George Womack clearly saw the purpose of the ditch: "We struggled along and built that ditch when none of us had hardly enough to eat. We had to go over to Boise Valley to buy hay for our teams. Couldn't buy any more and had to rake and scrape 'like all get out' to get enough money to buy that much, all at once. But now, by reason of our frugality and industry, we do not have to go quite so rough. If we would have had to pay ten dollars per acre for a water right and a dollar fifty per acre in cash annual water rent, where would we be? We would be on a rented farm or in the poor house. Past experience has taught us that it is better for farmers to organize companies and dig their own ditches."

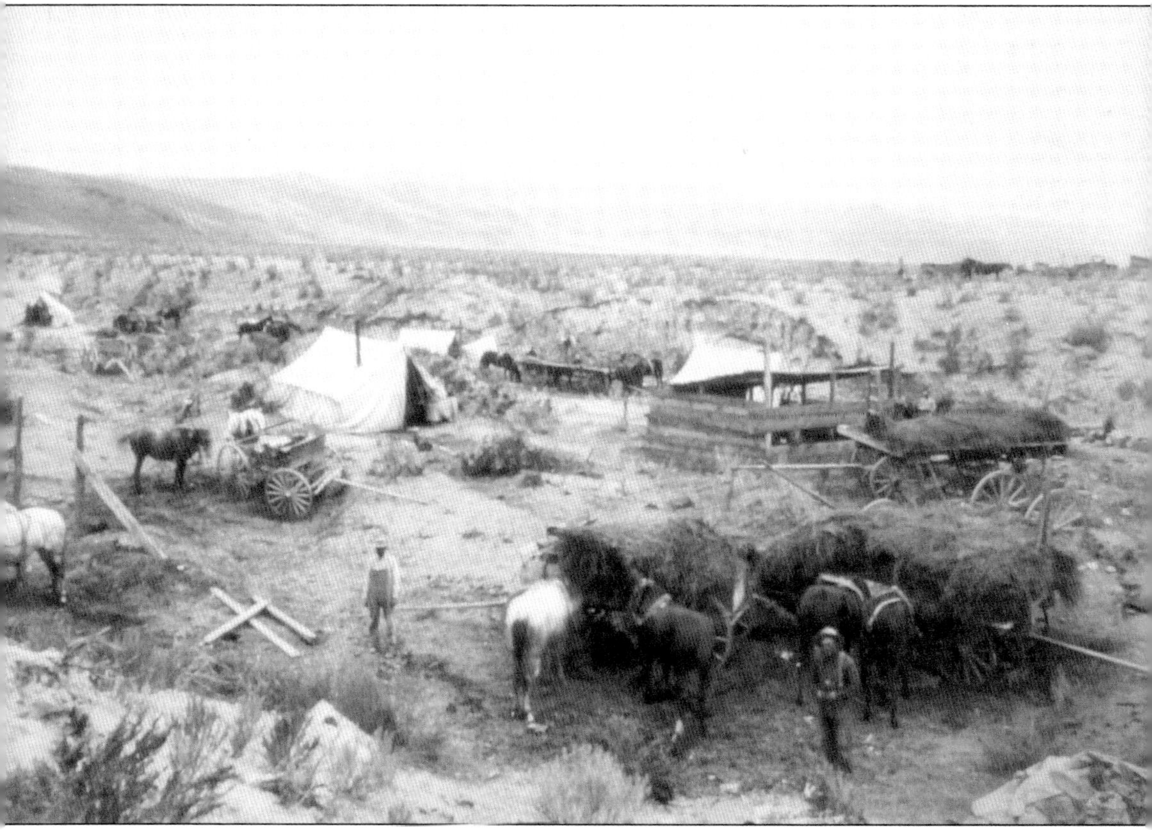

Five years later, in 1889, the Only Chance Ditch Company was formed with the purpose of extending and enlarging the Last Chance Ditch. It was estimated to have cost $16,032. The ditch was made to handle 6,900 inches of water instead of 4,500 inches, and the extension ran south for three miles, watering farms east of Emmett. This development meant that 30 more farmers were able to have a good water right. The Farmers Cooperative Ditch was started in 1892 and extended down to the Payette County line. It had lots of flumes that were not satisfactory. At one point, a flume was deliberately destructed, and there were financial problems. It was a struggle to get water where it was needed as there several breaks in the canal that had to be repaired immediately in order to save crops. Work was done around the clock, and the repairs were made in about three weeks.

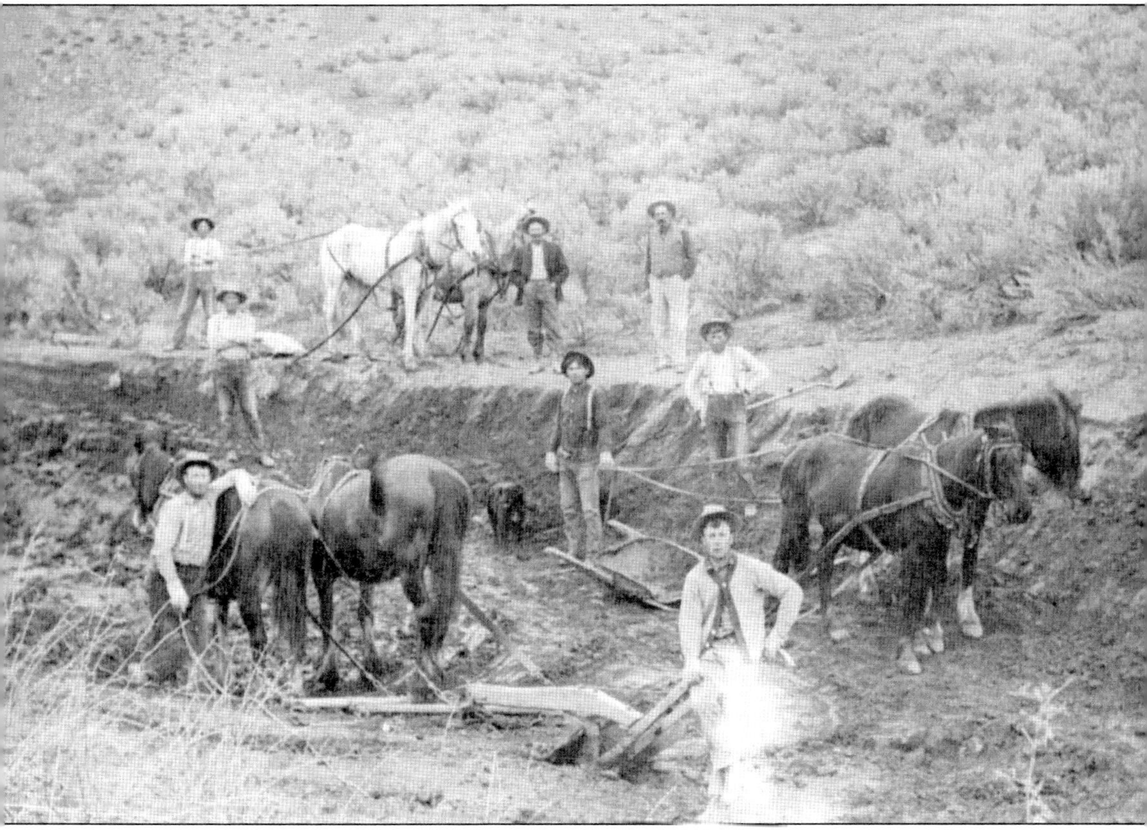

Emmett businessmen and Payette Valley farmers were interested in building a ditch on the bench, and another along the east and south slopes. Businesses were interested in a place to invest their money but did not have the commitment to back the project. It took the townspeople to back such an undertaking. A public meeting was held in Wardwell Hall on January 27, 1895, and was attended by 92 farmers and businessmen. They voted to organize a company as soon as Edward Hedden, a civil engineer for a New York company, could make a survey and a reliable cost estimate. Hedden found that the ditch would cover 20,000 acres on the bench and 40,000 on the slopes. The Canyon Canal Company was organized, and the state board of commissioners approved the application for a water right to construct a dam and a system of canals. Farrison and Kessell were the main contractors, and the estimated cost was $350,000. The contract was signed April 5, 1905, but water did not flow through the canal until April 1908.

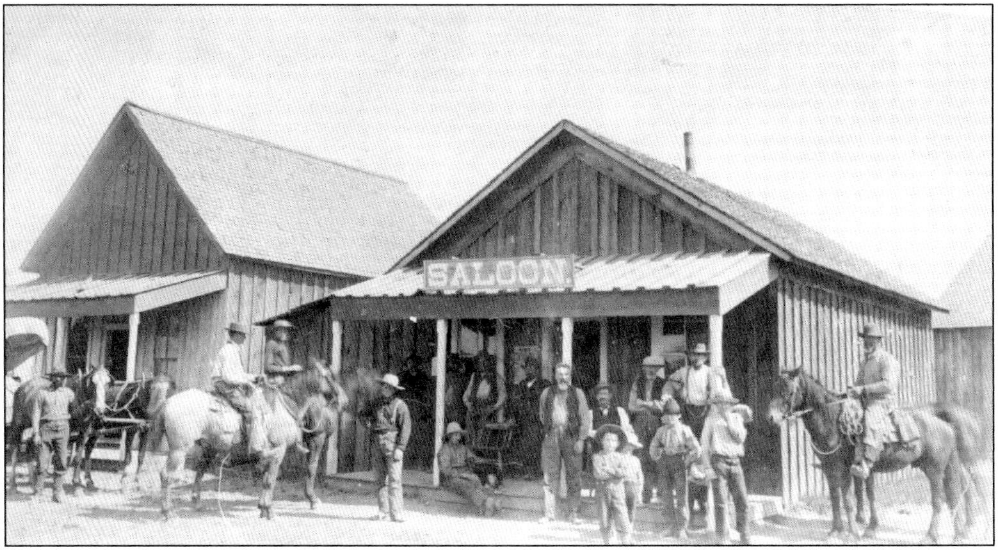

In 1880, the census taker counted 29 miners on Willow Creek, 15 of whom were Chinese. These people were here to make their fortunes and move on. Many had no family with them, so the saloons catered to their needs. Travelers also patronized the saloons, of which Emmett had three at this time.

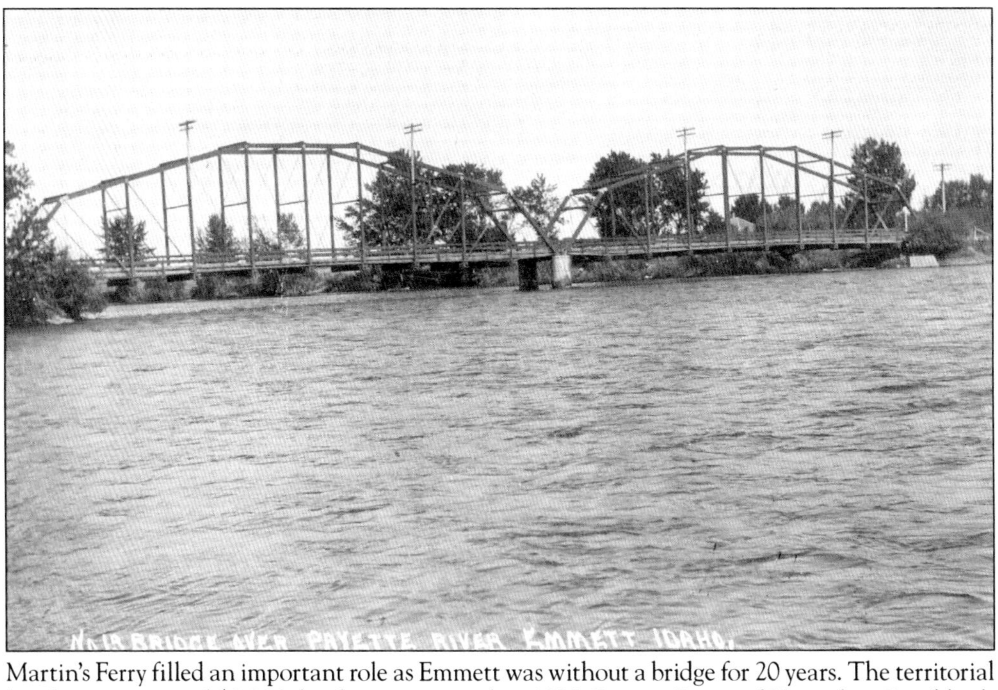

Martin's Ferry filled an important role as Emmett was without a bridge for 20 years. The territorial legislature approved $2,000 for this project and in 1883 George Stone of Horseshoe Bend built the first bridge. In 1892, high rushing water caused damage to one of the spans of the bridge, so in 1893 a more substantial bridge was built.

Three

STEPPING INTO THE FUTURE

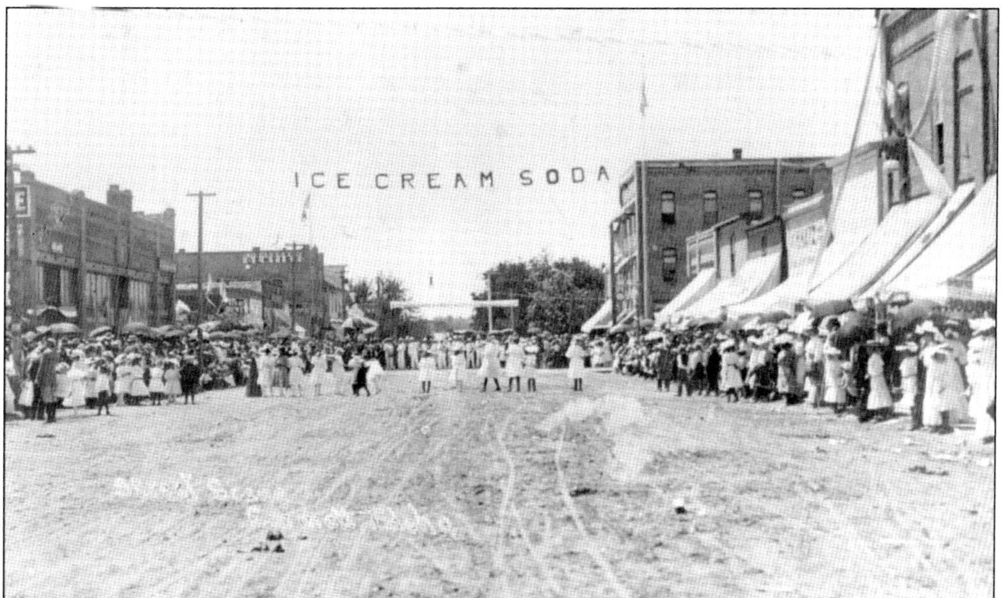

A fire department was housed in the city hall. Electric lights were installed, as were telephones and a waterworks and sewer system. E.K. Hayes built brick structures for businesses on Main Street. Growth and development came to Emmett starting in 1902, spurred in part by the completion of the railroad. This image shows the people of Emmett waiting for the parade to begin on July 4, 1909.

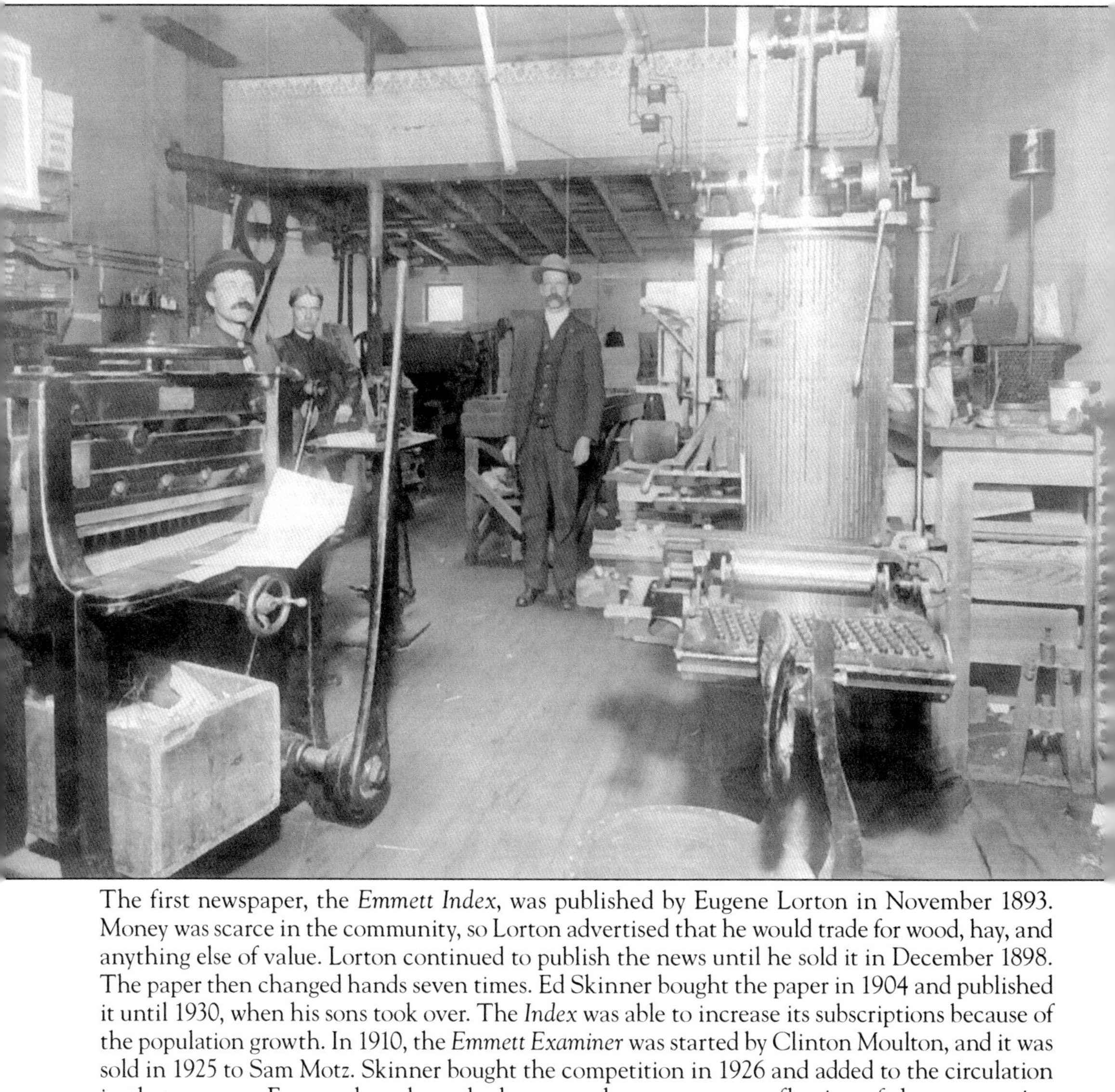

The first newspaper, the *Emmett Index*, was published by Eugene Lorton in November 1893. Money was scarce in the community, so Lorton advertised that he would trade for wood, hay, and anything else of value. Lorton continued to publish the news until he sold it in December 1898. The paper then changed hands seven times. Ed Skinner bought the paper in 1904 and published it until 1930, when his sons took over. The *Index* was able to increase its subscriptions because of the population growth. In 1910, the *Emmett Examiner* was started by Clinton Moulton, and it was sold in 1925 to Sam Motz. Skinner bought the competition in 1926 and added to the circulation in that manner. Emmett has always had a paper that serves as a reflection of the community. Pictured are Ed Skinner (right) and his sons.

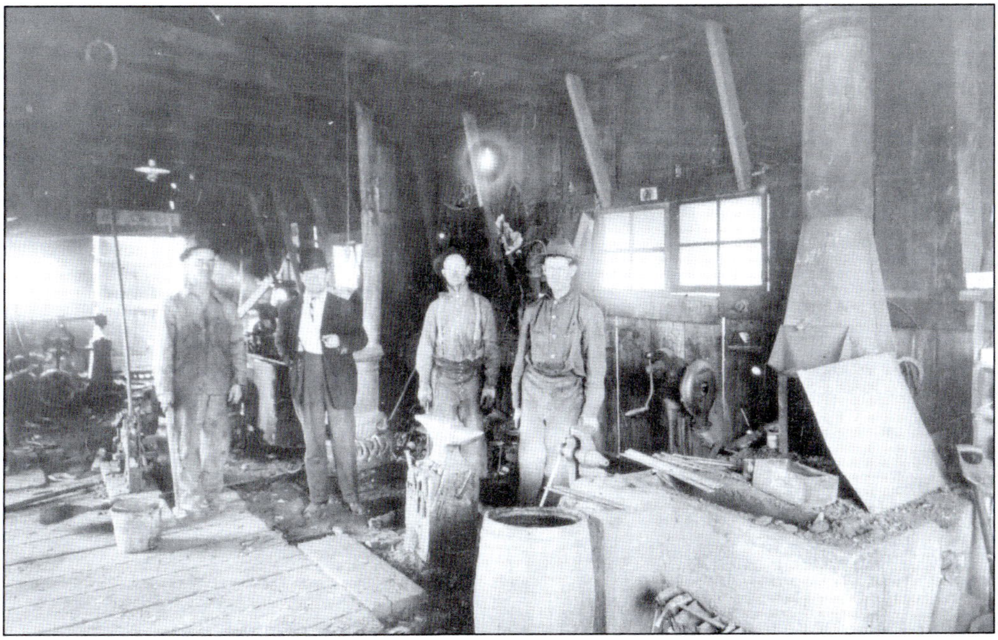

The blacksmith shop of Boise Riggs and Samuel McMillan was located on the corner of Boise Avenue and Main Street. Standing, from left to right, are Amos Kelsey, William Womack, McMillan, and Riggs. The town was growing, and there was need for blacksmiths to help with the work. There were many horses that needed shoeing and many repair jobs that needed to be done.

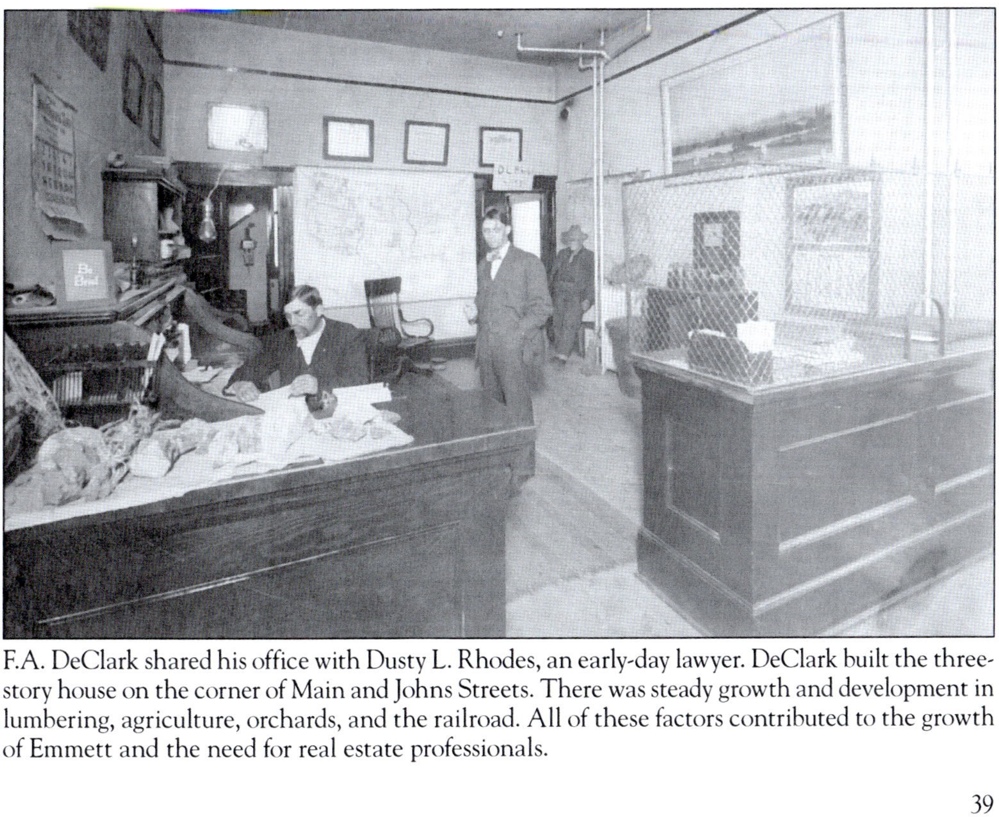

F.A. DeClark shared his office with Dusty L. Rhodes, an early-day lawyer. DeClark built the three-story house on the corner of Main and Johns Streets. There was steady growth and development in lumbering, agriculture, orchards, and the railroad. All of these factors contributed to the growth of Emmett and the need for real estate professionals.

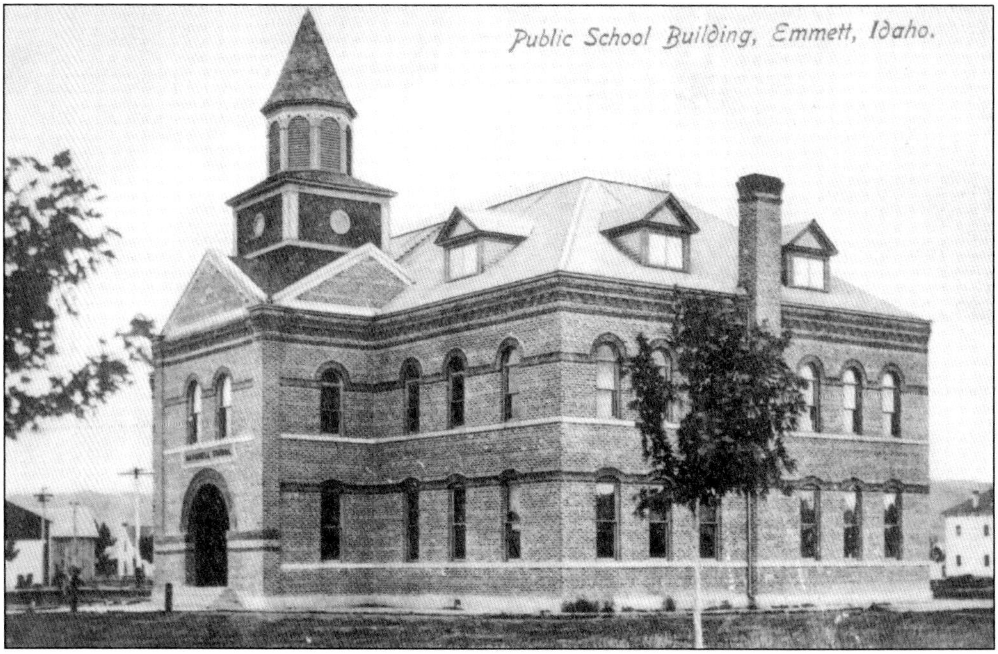

Growth brought more students to area schools. The first Wardwell School was built in 1885; it was later moved one block and renamed Longfellow. The new, brick Wardwell School was erected in 1903 and contained eight rooms so that there would be room for the high school students. This school was located on the present US Bank Block. The townspeople wanted their school to be comparable to those in Boise City.

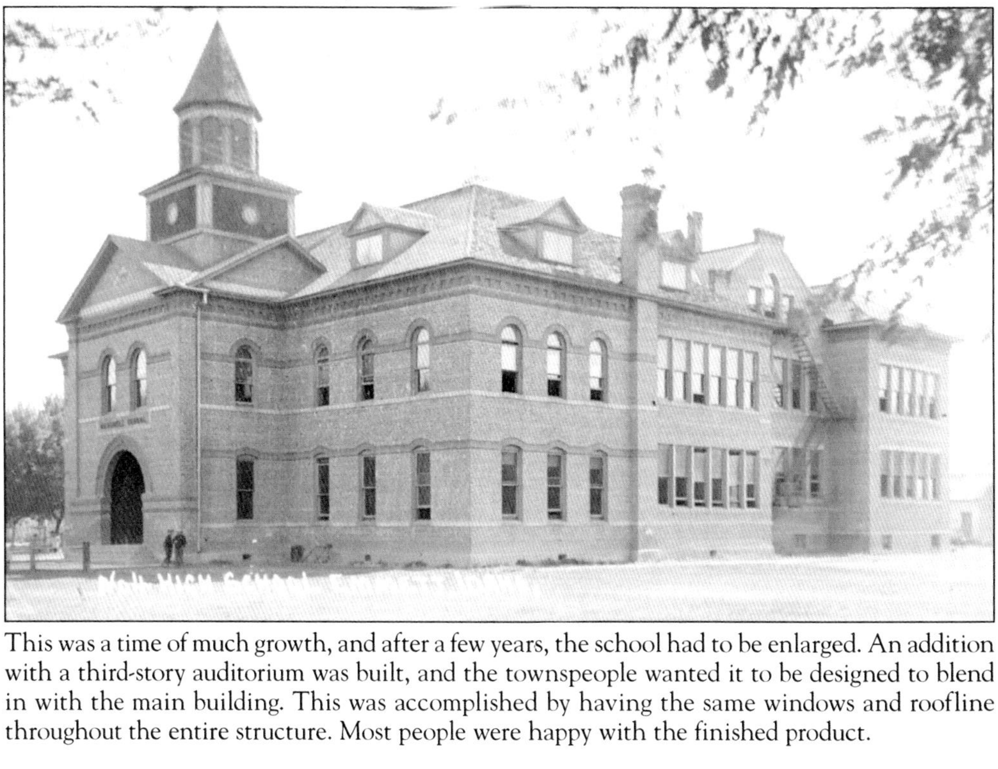

This was a time of much growth, and after a few years, the school had to be enlarged. An addition with a third-story auditorium was built, and the townspeople wanted it to be designed to blend in with the main building. This was accomplished by having the same windows and roofline throughout the entire structure. Most people were happy with the finished product.

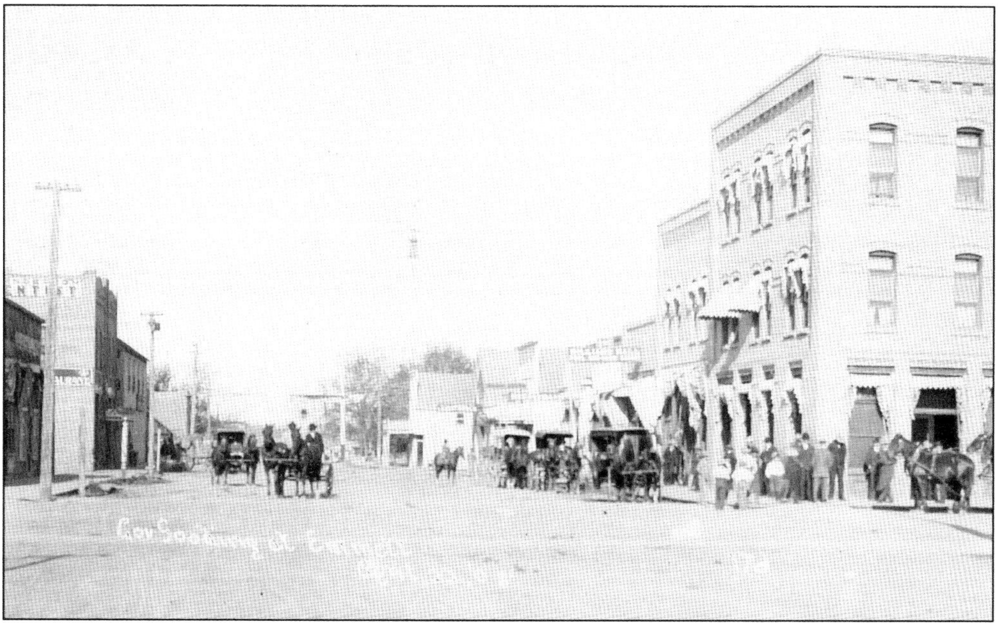

Governor Gooding, officers of the state land board, and members of the state engineering department came to Emmett on April 22, 1908, to commemorate the opening of the Black Canyon Canal. Little did they know that on April 26, fire would consume four buildings on the north side of the block between Main Street and Boise Avenue.

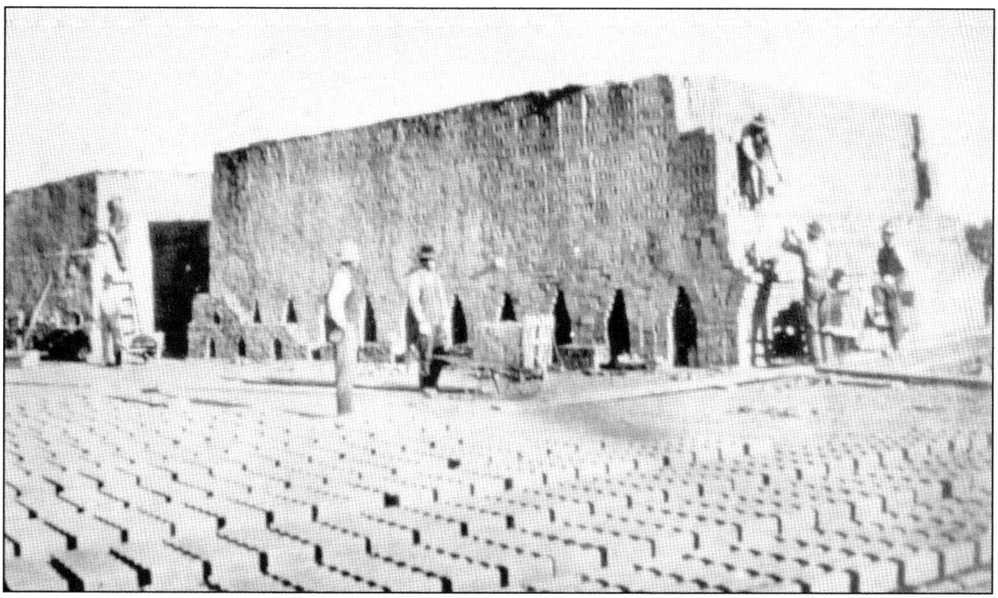

The brickyard was located on South Washington Street and was owned by Frank Graham in 1904. Wardwell School was built of brick, and after the coming of the Idaho Northern Railroad, businesses on Main Street, including the Russell Hotel, the Stewart Building, the Powell Building, and the Odd Fellows Hall were built of brick as well. McNish constructed several brick buildings along the south side of Main Street to the east.

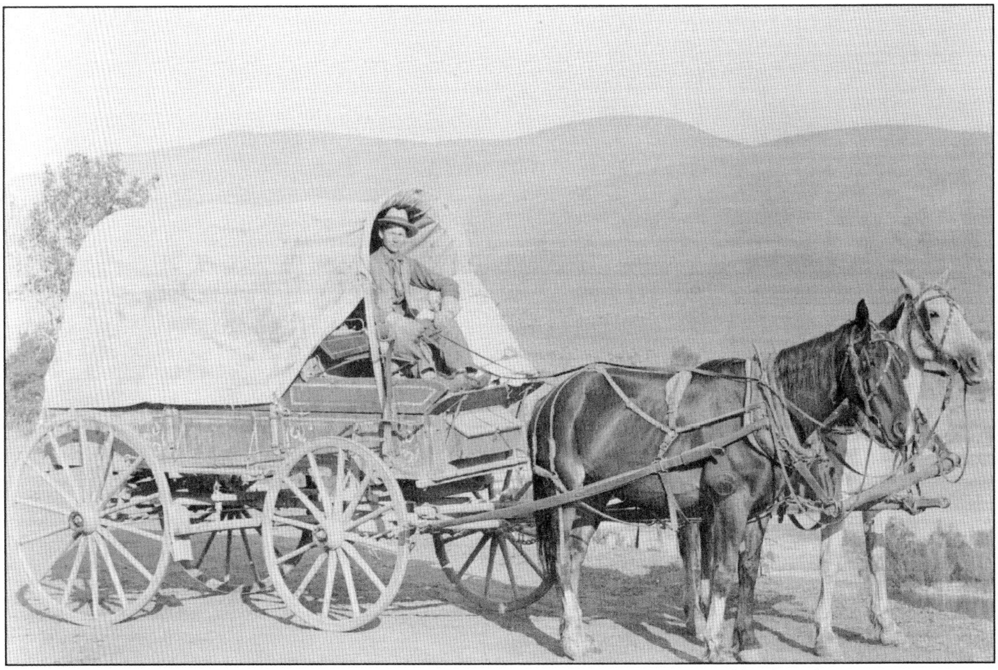

Joseph Degan, an early German pioneer from Missouri, bought the Gills' first homesite. He was an excellent gardener and horticulturist, and he planted an orchard that included berries, grapes, and vegetables. He peddled his produce, chickens, and eggs to the mining camps. Degan was so successful that he owned several wagons and hired drivers to work for him.

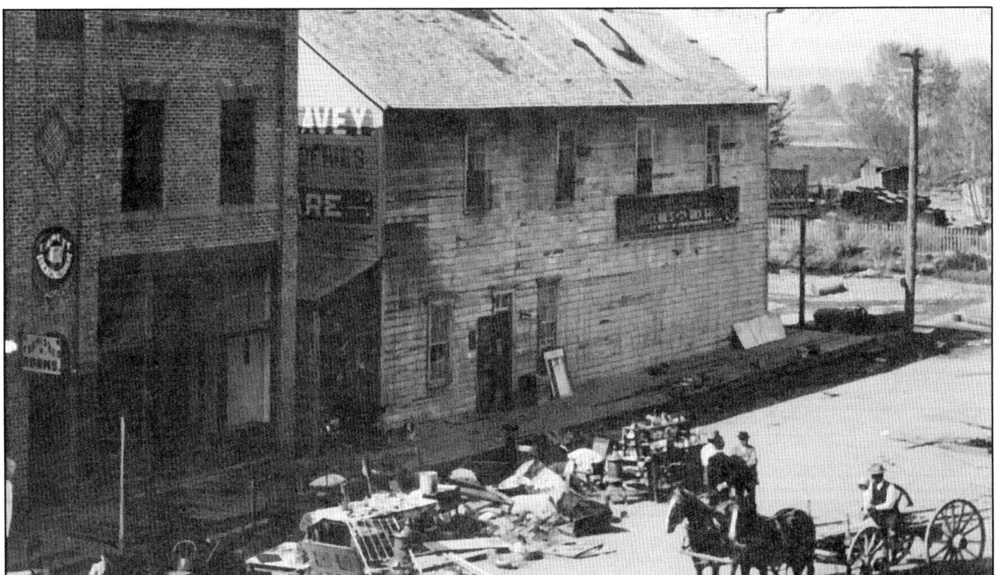

On April 26, 1908, a fire started in the Emmett Hotel and burned the Rogers and Amen Livery Stable, the Red Top Saloon, the Emmett Hotel, and a restaurant. Miners from Pearl were in town and dynamited two wooden structures east of the fire, saving the Bane Building and the Russell Hotel. Women began soliciting for firefighting equipment, and it took only eight months to reach their goals.

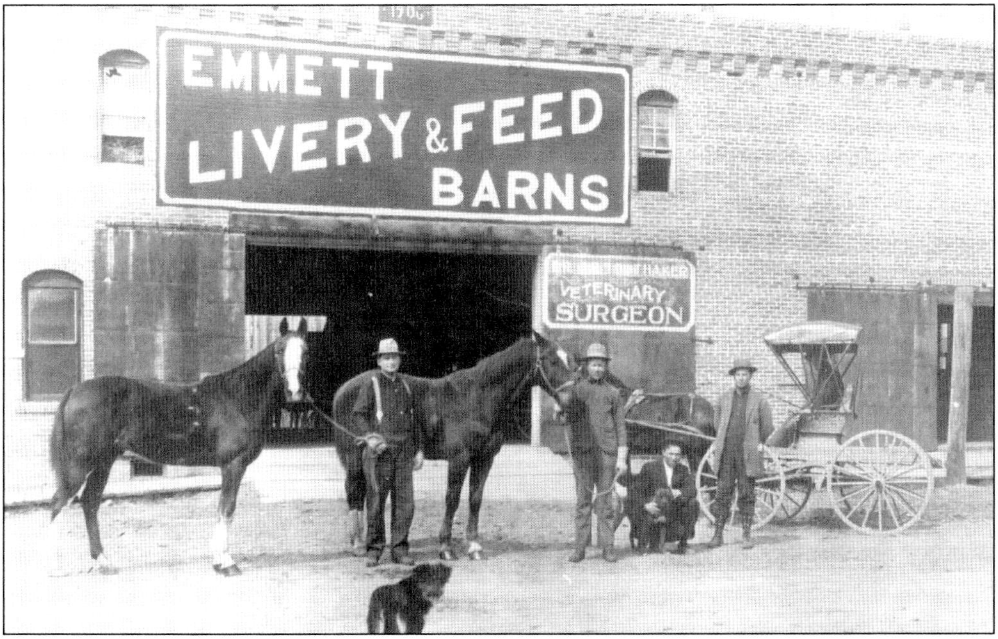

This was the headquarters for the O.N. Callender Stage Line on the corner of Washington and Second Streets. Pictured, from left to right, are Callender, Boise Riggs, Roy Wells (kneeling), and Bill Womack. Transportation is a requirement for development because more goods and services can be offered for the enhancement of the quality of life. This was true during the pioneer era as well as today.

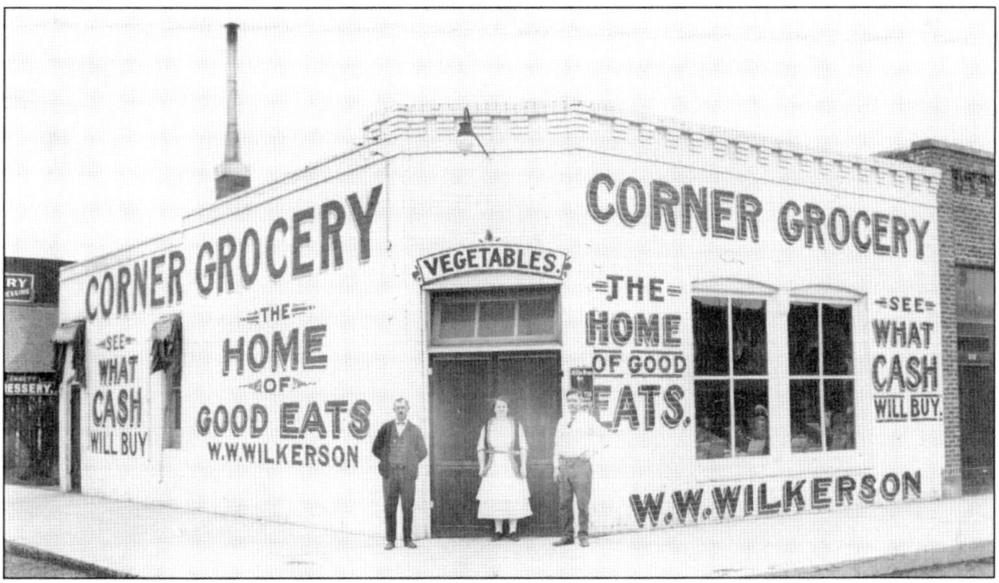

The Corner Grocery was owned by W.W. Wilkerson. Advertising was just as important then as it is now. To get buyers into the store, Wilkerson used the building as a billboard and employed two slogans—"the home of good eats" and "see what cash will buy"—to represent his business. Henry Cutler and Lloyd Lytle were employees. Mrs. Wilkerson is pictured standing between two unidentified men. There has been a grocery on the corner of Main and South Commercial Streets for 50 years. This building is now a flower shop and antique store.

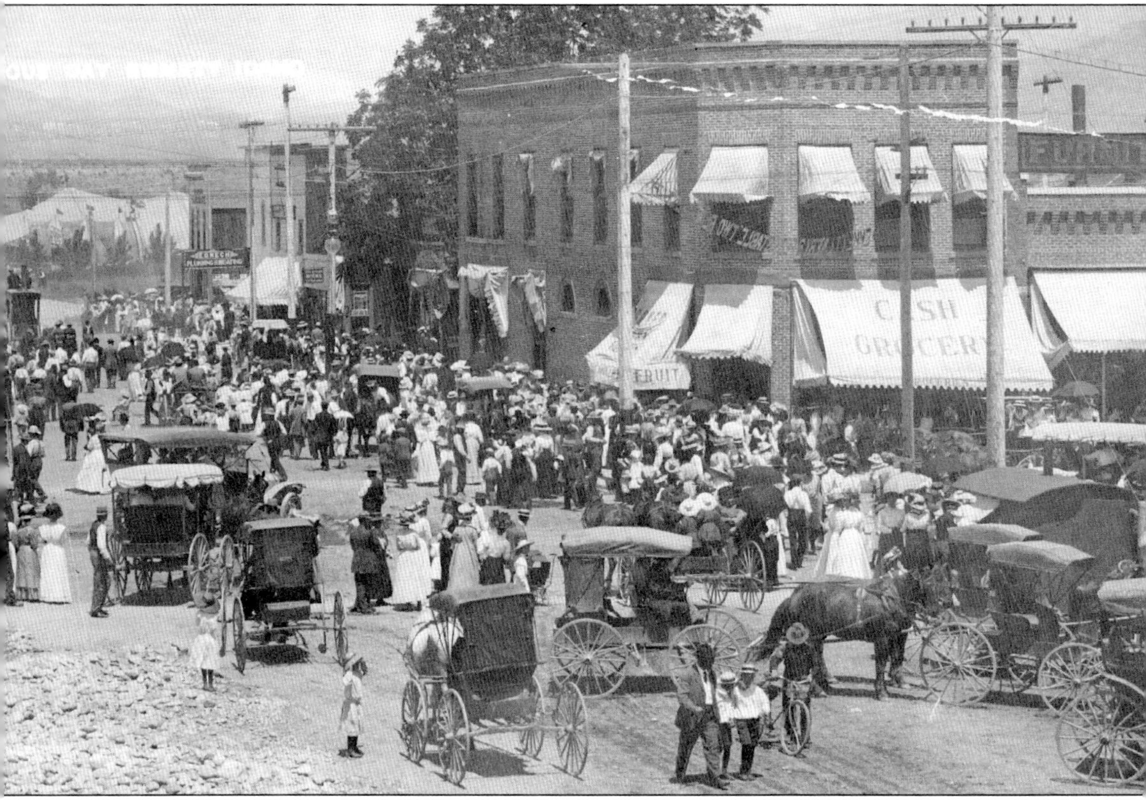

The coming of the circus was a big event for Emmett in 1916. If the entertainment came to town, people could attend, but they otherwise did not have money or time to find entertainment in other places. The circus had a captive audience and was well attended, with the whole town turning out for such an event. Not only were there new exhibits and games to play, but one could also visit with friends and share ideas and entertainment. Another big day of celebration was July 4. It was a day devoted to patriotism. "The Star-Spangled Banner" would be sung, and a speaker would praise the Founding Fathers and talk about the townspeople's responsibility to protect their hard-won freedoms. It was a noisy day as people expressed their patriotism and thanks. Often, the girls would have new white dresses for the occasion.

Charlie Gamage operated a barbershop in the Blackman Building on West Main Street. He was also interested in advancing the goals of Emmett. Gamage served six years as mayor of the city and ten as a member of the school board. He was a member of the famous Alfalfa Quartet and took part in plays. In 1912, a watch was given to him for his work with the boosters.

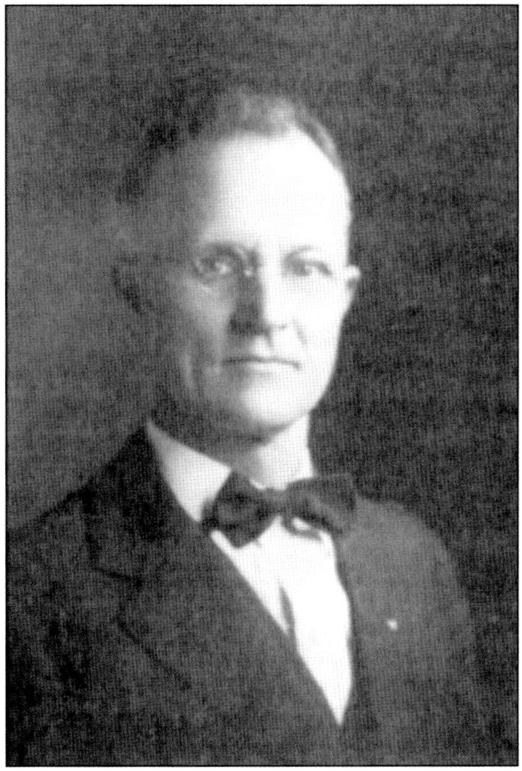

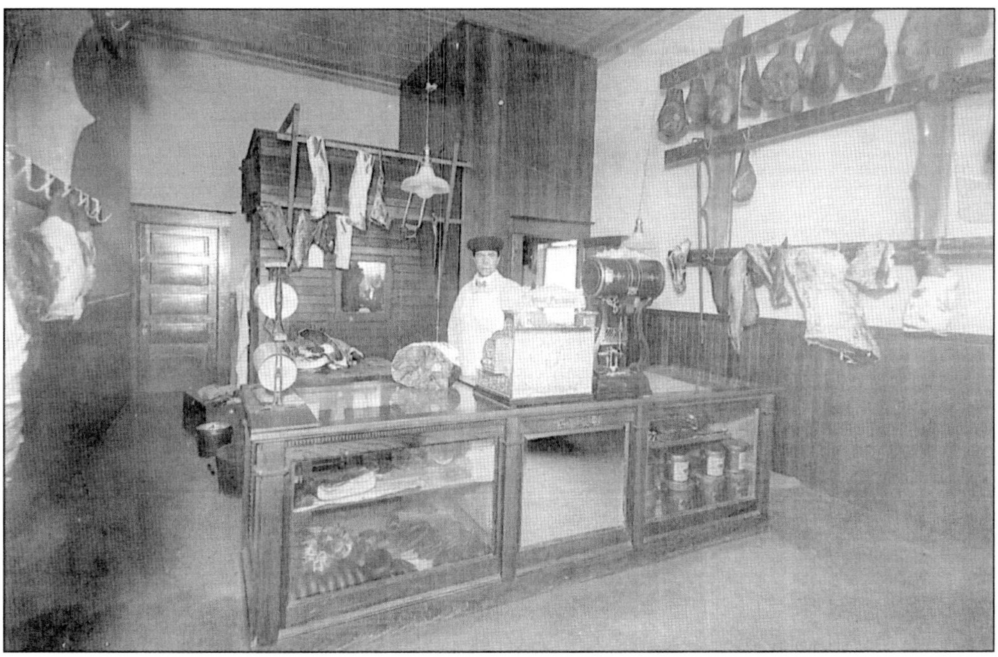

The Burkhard Butcher Shop, which was located in the Steward Building at 117–119 West Main Street, had a large display of meat. At night, the meats would be put in the refrigeration unit to cool. They could also be put on ice in the display case. Most families butchered their own meat at this time.

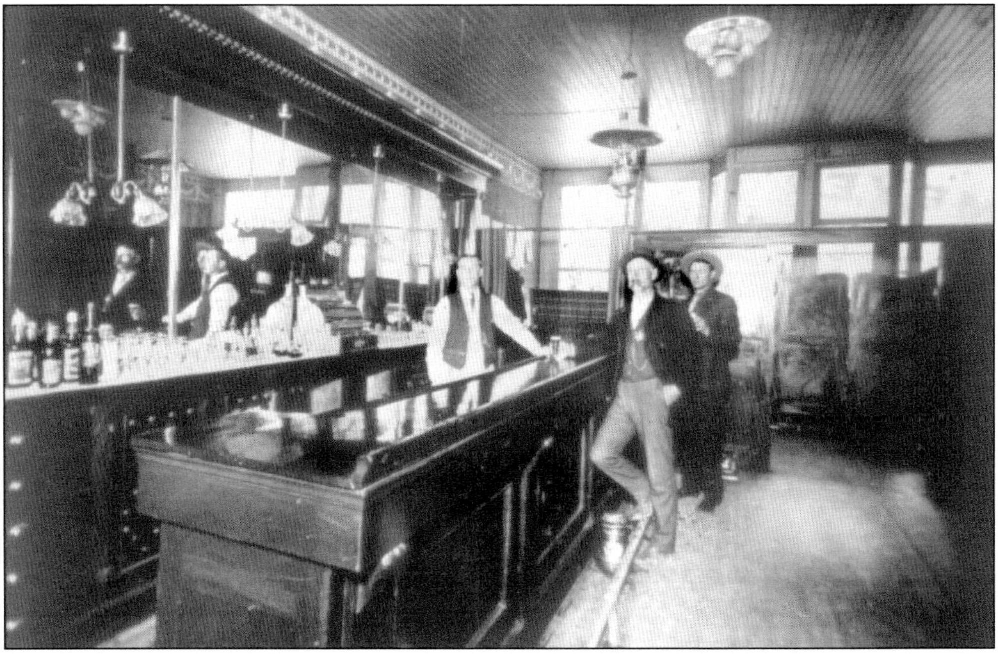

In 1902, an ordinance was passed to hire a marshal, prescribe his duties, and fix his salary. Ed C. Blanchard was appointed as Emmett's first marshal, and he and John W. Martin built the first jail in 1902. This picture, from a very popular postcard that is for sale at the museum, shows Ed Banks (with his foot on the railing) in the Myers Brother Saloon in 1906.

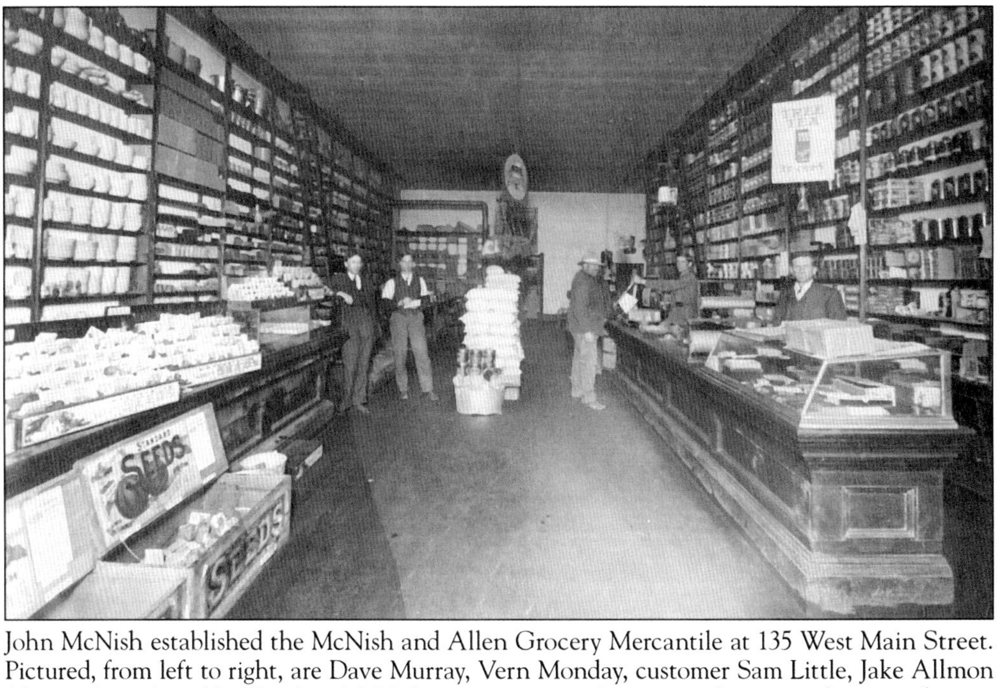

John McNish established the McNish and Allen Grocery Mercantile at 135 West Main Street. Pictured, from left to right, are Dave Murray, Vern Monday, customer Sam Little, Jake Allmon (slicing cheese), and Jay Sanders. McNish was as interested in seeing the town advance as he was in making money. When the Black Canyon Canal would break, McNish and Hawkins would furnish food and equipment for the workers.

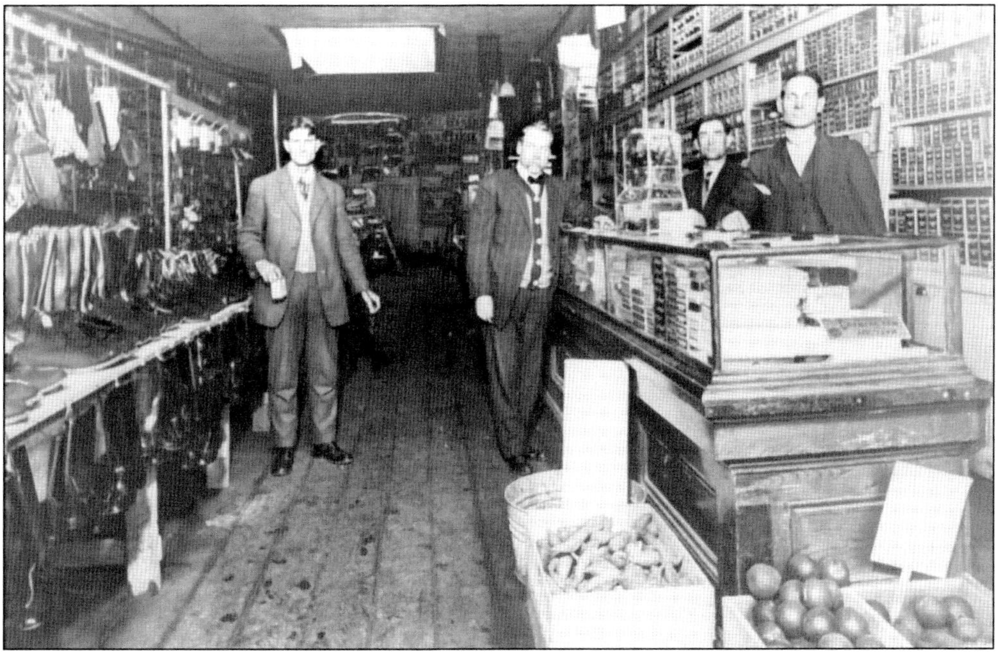

In 1906, E.E. Hunt established his general store. He sold hay and grain as well as coal, which he kept in a long, wooden box that sat outside near the front door. It was at 116 East Main Street, which is on the north side of the street where Copy Plus is now located. Pictured here in 1910 are, from left to right, Samuel Riggs, Will Langroise, F.L. Williams, and E.E. Hunt.

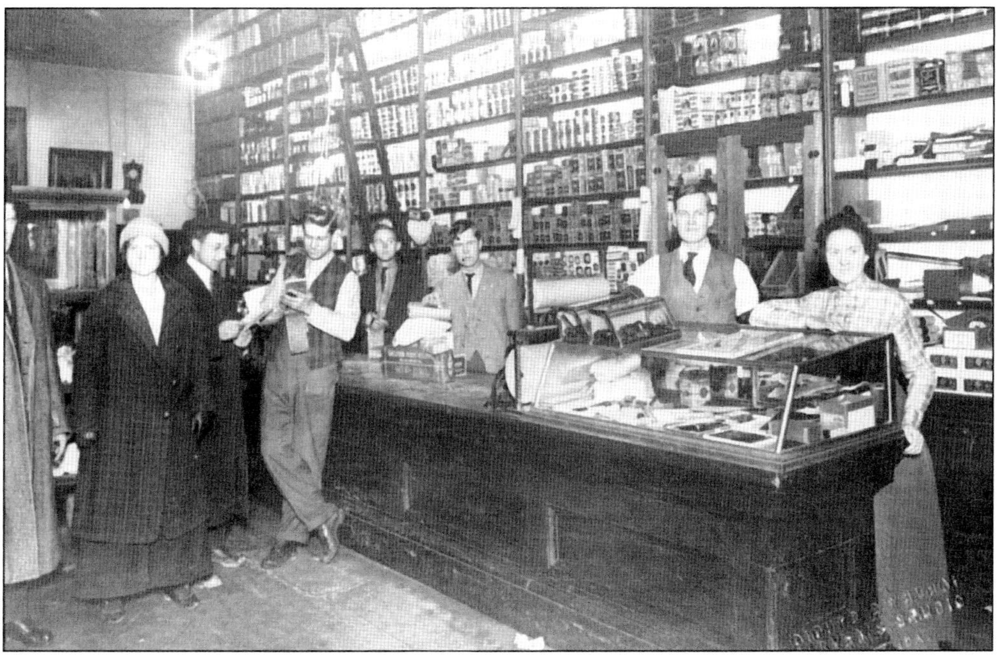

The McNish store was located at 133–137 West Main Street. Dry goods were located in the west half of the building, and groceries, in the east side. This picture taken in 1915 shows, from left to right, Boise Riggs, Carol Keithly, Ray Newcomer, Jacob Allmon, Merton Cook, Ross McPherson, Vern Monday, and Grace Cook.

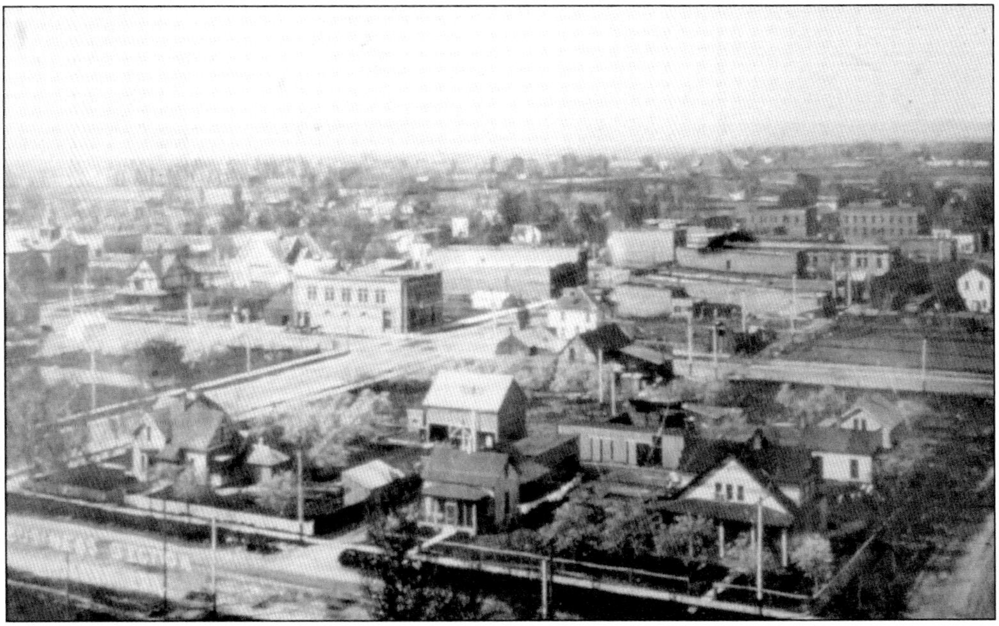

This is the business section of town in 1909. A telephone line from Caldwell to Emmett was installed. Next, the people wanted electricity. When the Pearl mines closed in 1906, the power was diverted to Emmett, and a power plant was also built on the Boise River. With power, a municipal water system was installed in the city, and a sewer system was added. Finally, sidewalks were poured.

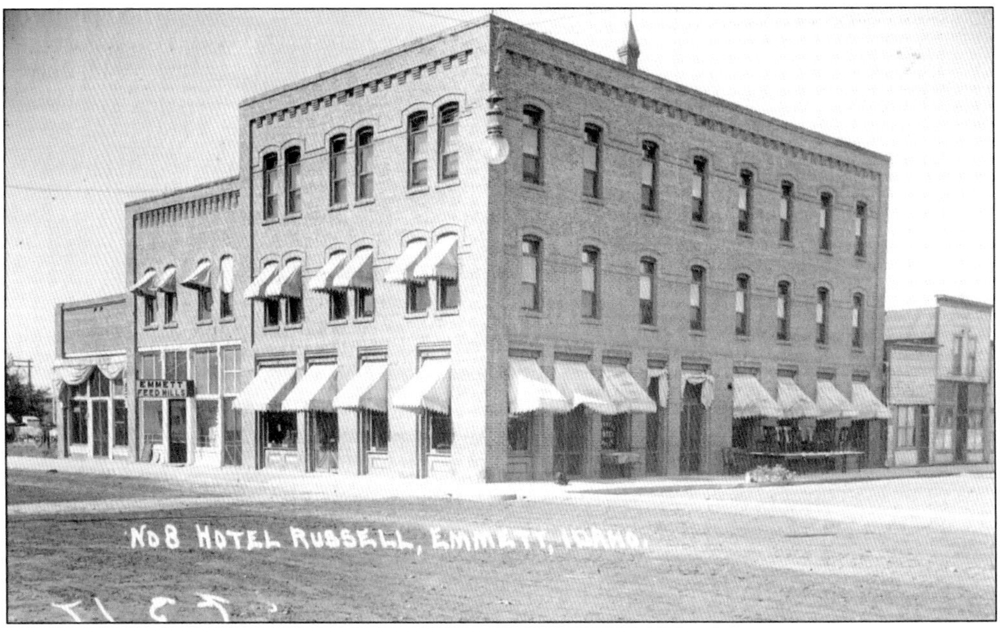

Businessmen encouraged William Russell to build an upscale hotel. Three stories and furnished with the latest oak furniture, it was close to the depot so that drummers and visitors coming to Emmett on the train would have easy access to hotel accommodations. Local people ate there and were impressed with the food and elegance. The hotel had two cooks and used fine linen tablecloths and napkins.

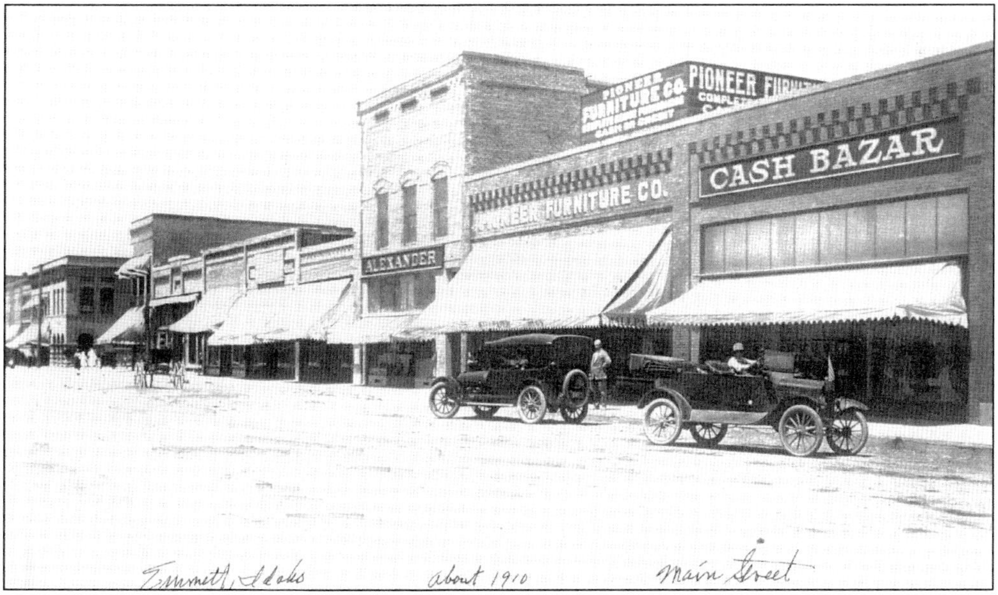

By 1910, there were many stores located on Main Street, including a Cash Bazaar, Pioneer Furniture Store, Alexander's, the Golden Rule, Gamage Barbershop (which had three chairs), Davis Drug Store, the Bank of Emmett, the Brunswick Billiard Parlor and Hotel Thommen, the First National Bank, and the McNish and Allen Mercantile Store. The population of Emmett had reached 1,351 people.

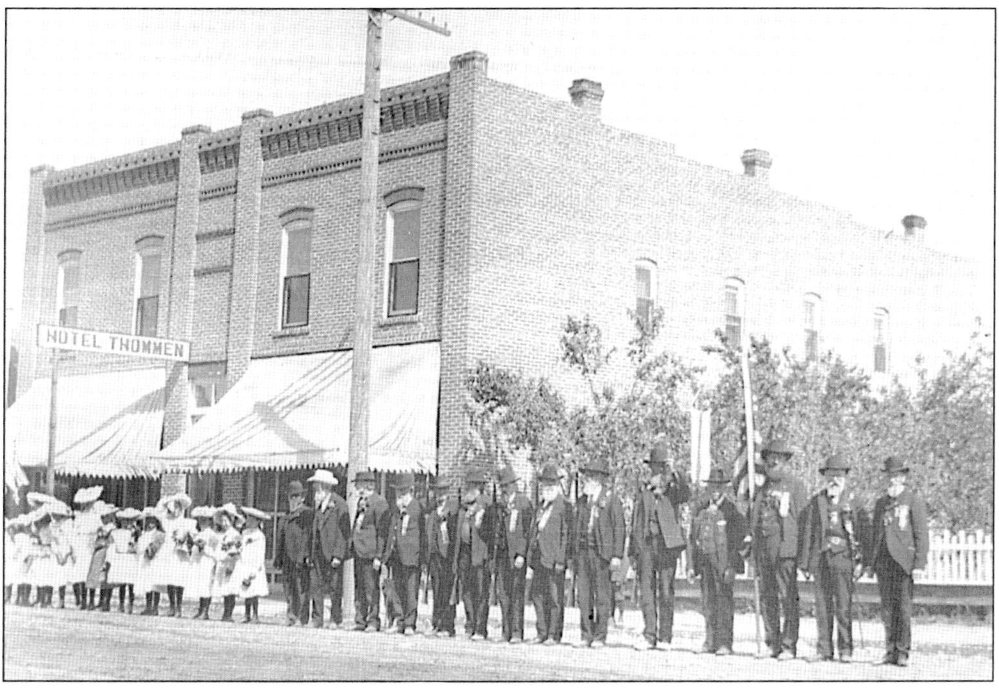

In 1903, August Thommen owned a hotel on Main Street, a pleasant place with a reputation for excellence in food and comfort. The hotel occupied the second floor, and businesses were housed below. Charlie Gamage had his barbershop in this building. Baths could be purchased here, as could haircuts and shaves.

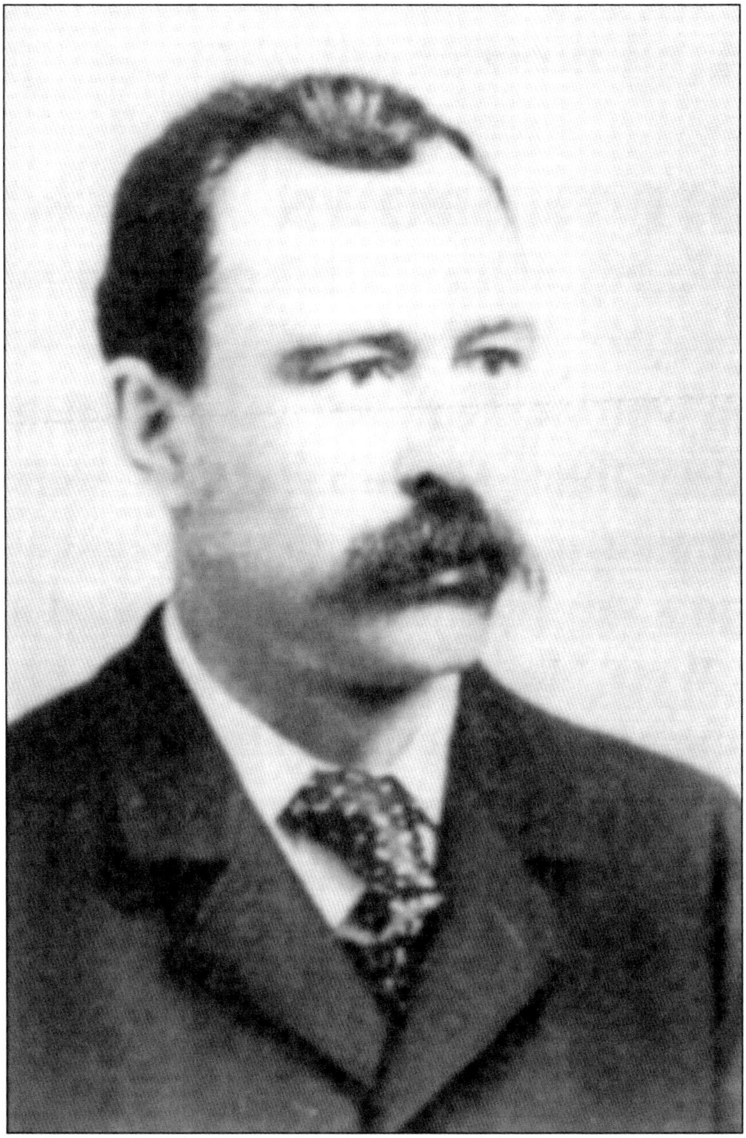

John Jacob Salskov had words of great appreciation for John McNish: "Now, that John McNish was the man who did more for the town and this valley than anybody else I know of. He grubstaked a lot of homesteaders, miners, sheepherders and lumbermen who would have never made it without his help, and he was active in about every betterment cause that came along for many years. If it hadn't been for his putting a lot of his own money into the Black Canyon Canal Project, this valley might still have been half sagebrush. And to think that we don't even have a street in Emmett named after him!" Adam Klingback remembered when he was 17 and took up a squatter's claim on the butte with his brother. McNish backed them over the protest of his partner. Sure enough, they paid him back the next year and traded with him as long as he was in business. McNish was a good judge of character.

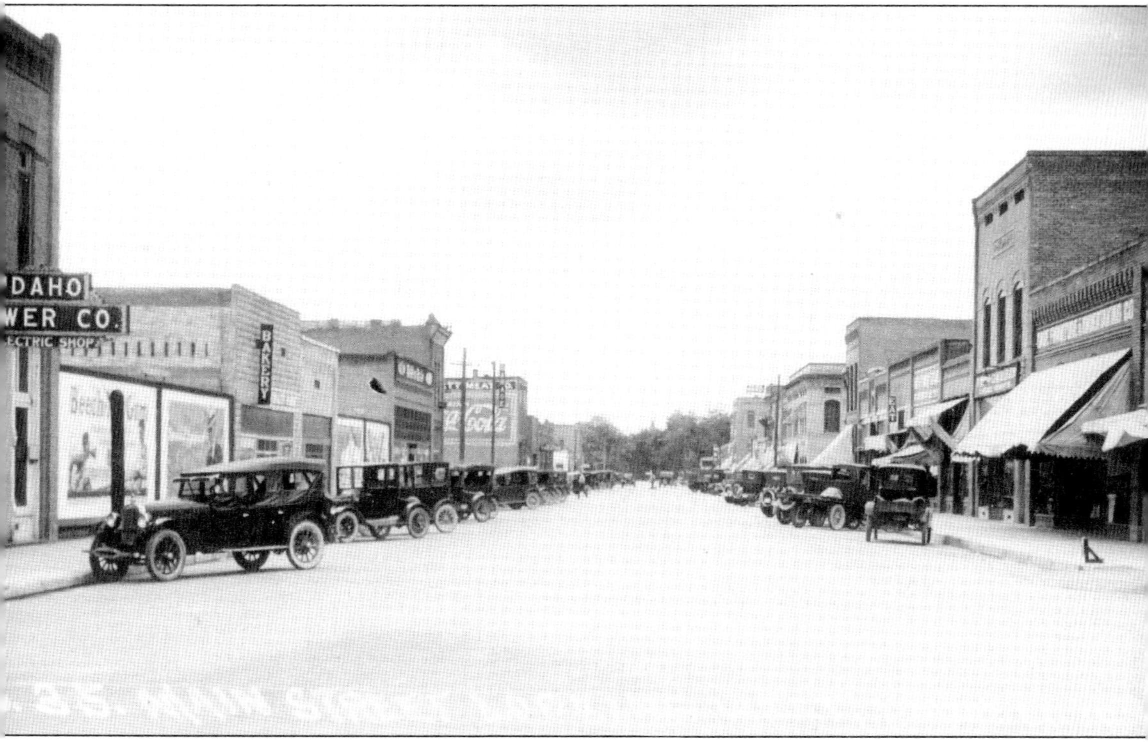

This picture was taken in 1922, and the view is looking west from the funeral chapel. According to Leonard J. Arrington in his article "Idaho and the Great Depression," the industries of agriculture, mining, and lumbering commanded high prices because of World War I, which had caused expansion in each of these areas. Suddenly, the war was over, and demand was gone, which caused a severe depression in 1921. Recovery never took place. Wheat sold for $2.50 in 1919 and brought only $1.30 in 1929. Potatoes sold for $1.51 a bushel in 1919, and in 1922, they sold for only 31¢ a bushel. Then came the Depression of the 1930s. The price of wheat dropped to 26¢ a bushel. Cattle dropped to less than $20 a head, the lowest average price since the 1890s. Sheep sold for $2.25 per head, and there was no demand for lumber. These were hard times. In June 1922, it was announced that the secretary of interior, Albert B. Fall, had allowed $600,000 for the Black Canyon Dam. This project was just what the economy of Emmett needed.

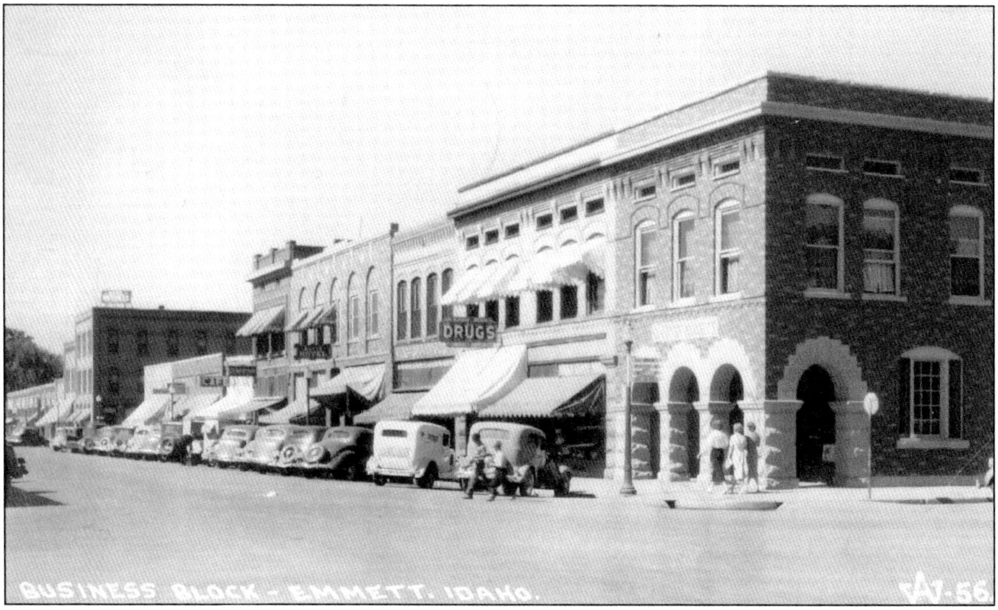

The Bank of Emmett was located on the corner, in the building with the arches. This is the business section of town, which housed the President Cafe, the post office, Golden Rule, and the Emmett Department Store. The economy was improving, and Roosevelt's New Deal was providing jobs for those who needed employment in 1936.

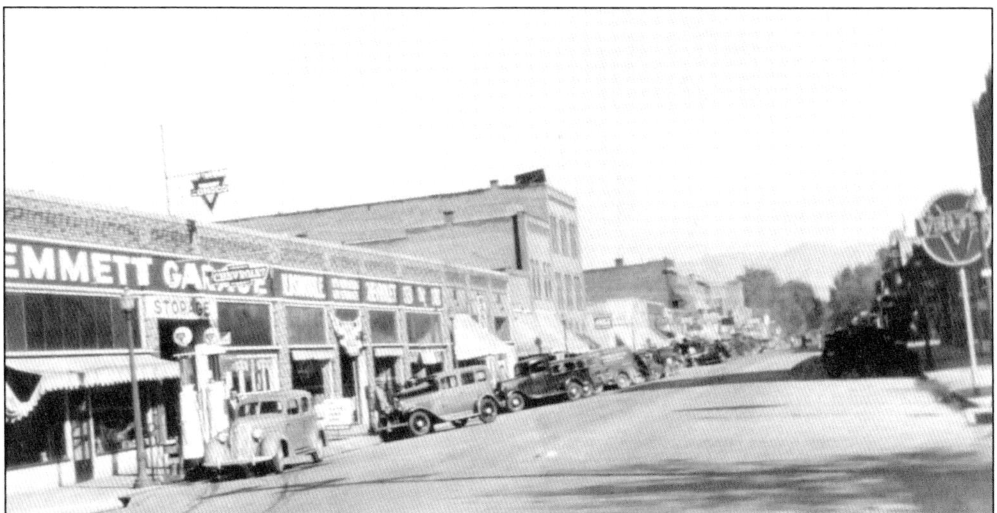

The Emmett Garage began on Commercial Street and was later moved to this location on Main Street, where it remained for many years. Chevrolet and Oldsmobile cars were sold here in 1936. Most of this building burned in 1976, and the site today is a vacant lot. The tallest building on the left is the Russell Hotel.

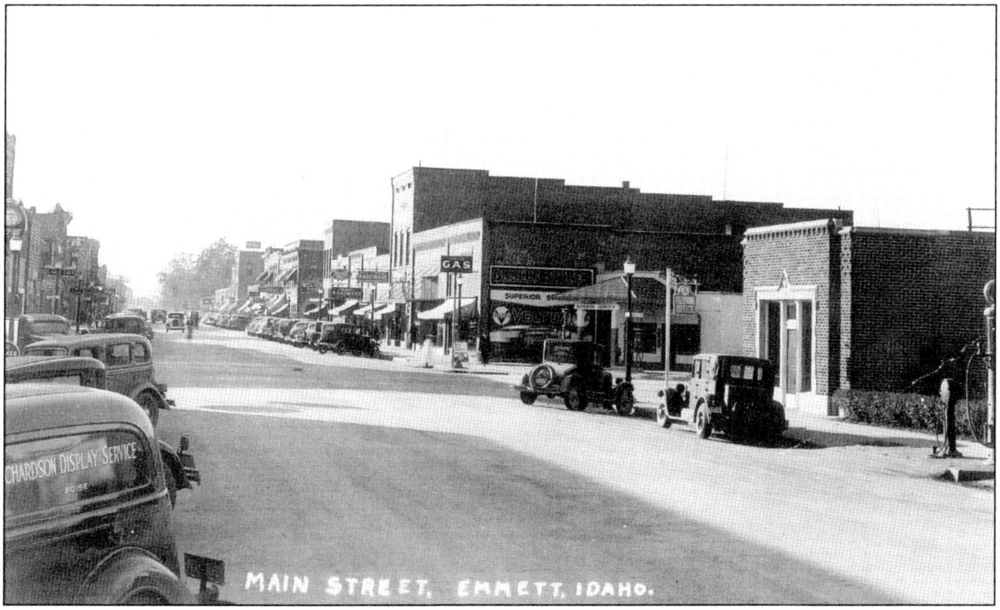

The business district of Emmett is shown here in a 1936 view looking west from Hayes Avenue down Main Street. It was on a good, solid foundation for the pioneer businessmen. McNish had championed the rights of the community for many years, and he served as a banker for pioneer residents before the first bank was established. Everyone knew and trusted him. Pictured, from the tallest building in the middle, the Masonic Building, to the right, are the White Building, Crammer's Hardware, Veltex gas station, and Bell Telephone.

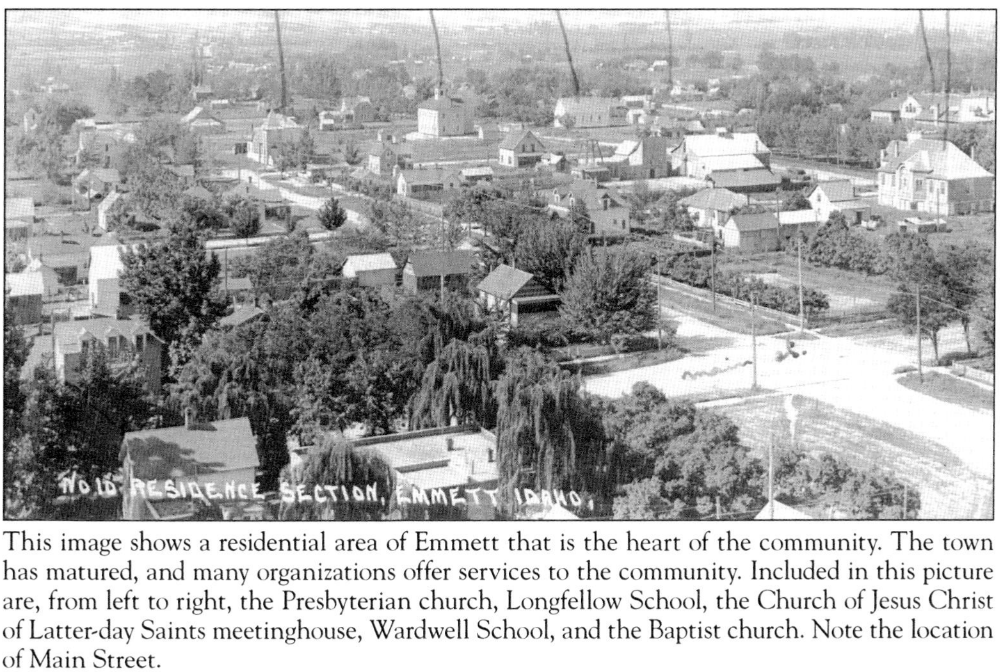

This image shows a residential area of Emmett that is the heart of the community. The town has matured, and many organizations offer services to the community. Included in this picture are, from left to right, the Presbyterian church, Longfellow School, the Church of Jesus Christ of Latter-day Saints meetinghouse, Wardwell School, and the Baptist church. Note the location of Main Street.

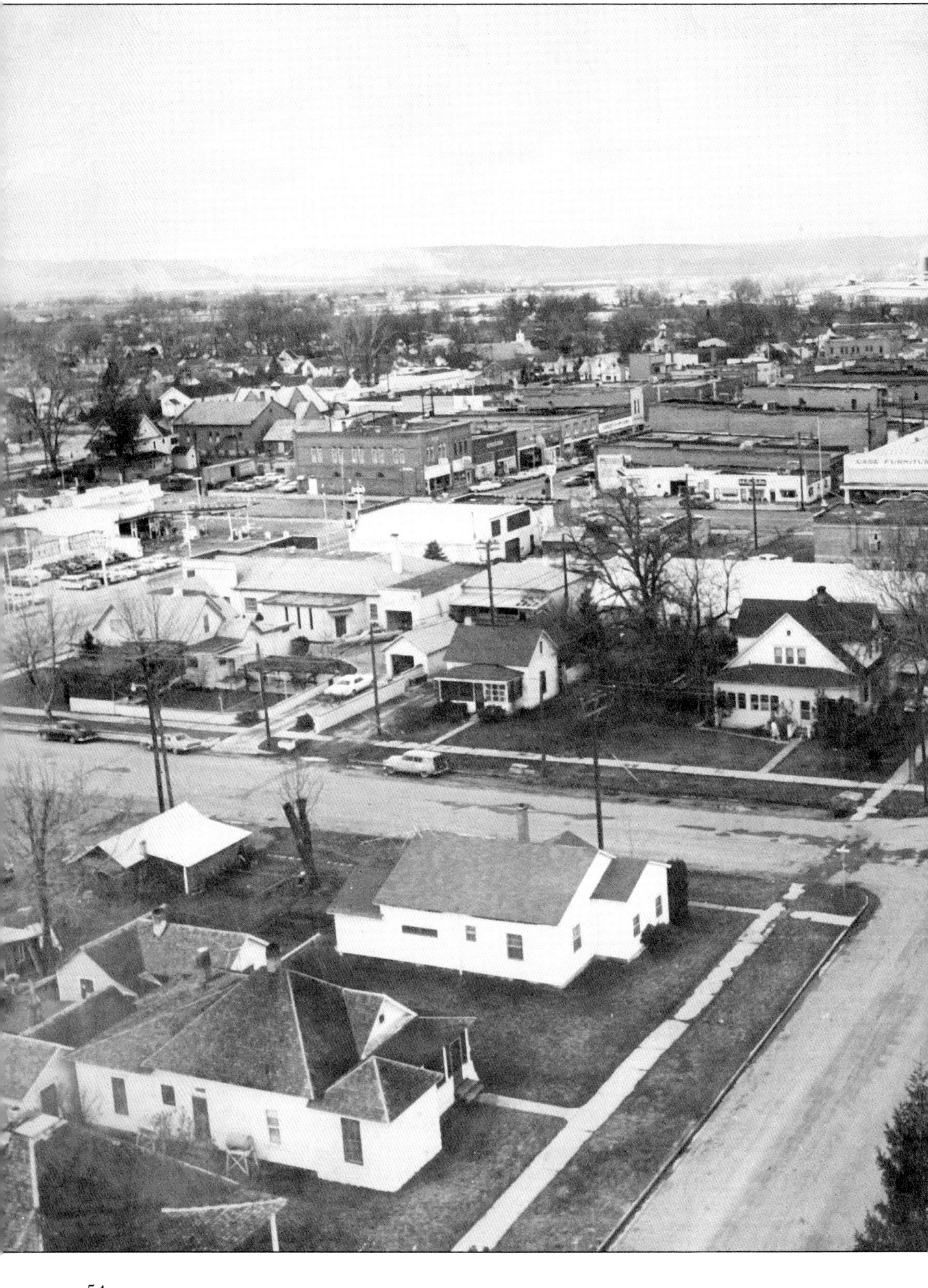

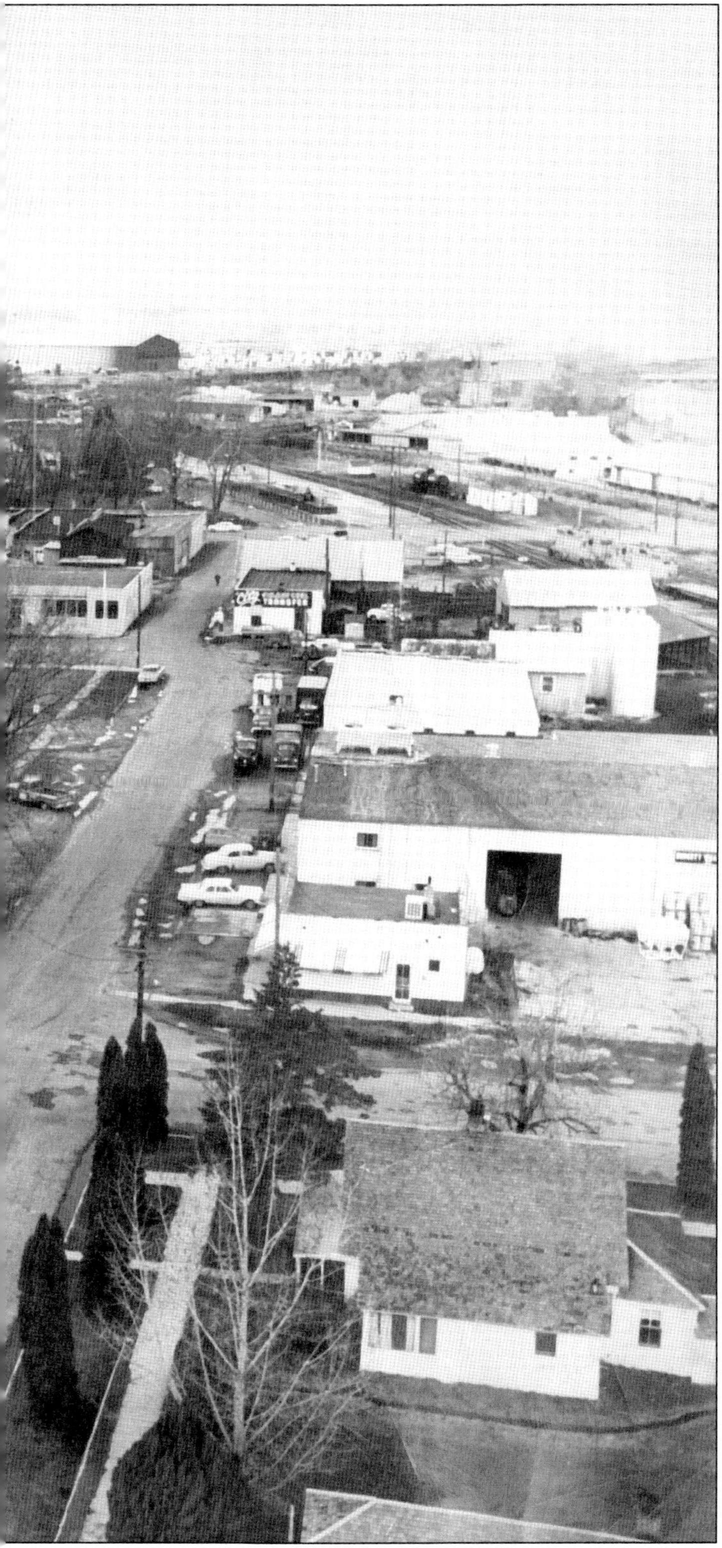

A photograph of Emmett shows the prosperity and orderliness of the town. People had individual homes with well-kept yards and gardens that surrounded the community. In 1917, the Boise Payette Lumber Company built a large sawmill just west of Emmett, and the Black Canyon Dam was completed in 1924, providing a constant flow of water for 50,000 acres of rich farmland. Boise Cascade Mill, in the background, supplied steady employment for anyone needing a job. The fruit industry was well established, offering part-time employment to provide extra monies to individual households. It was a time of peace, security, and prosperity. Most places were within walking distance, and youths could still find summer jobs working with fruit, hauling hay, or moving irrigation pipe, and there were tennis courts, the swimming pool, and softball for recreation.

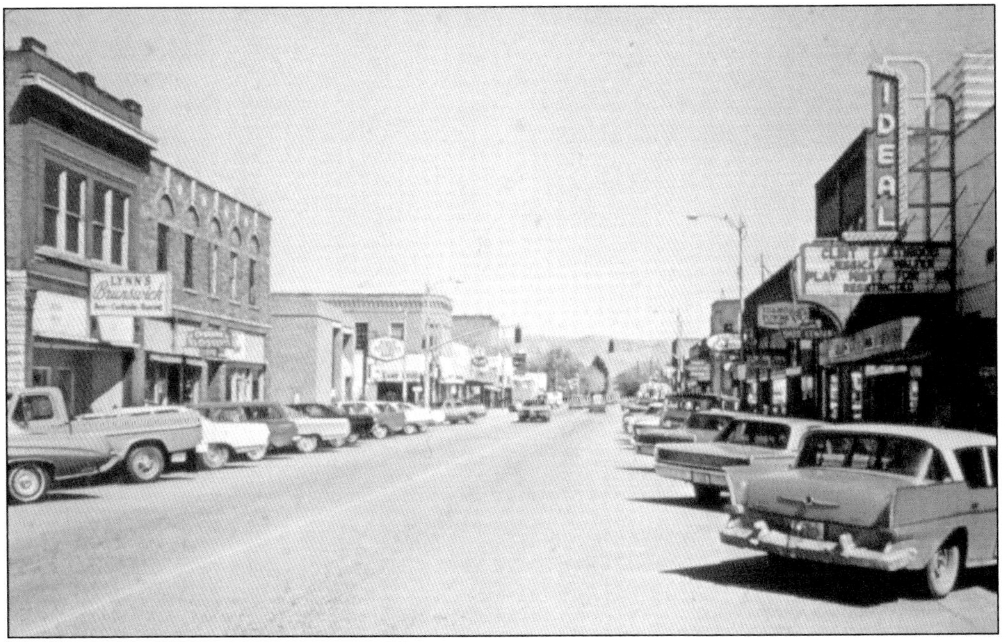

This view is looking east on Main Street in 1972. It has been a struggle to keep the existing buildings occupied. The Golden Rule Department Store on the southwest corner of West Main and South Washington Streets burned. The Albertsons grocery store moved from Washington Street to Highway 52 in 2002. Thrift stores have been very successful, as have barbershops, beauty parlors, and antique stores.

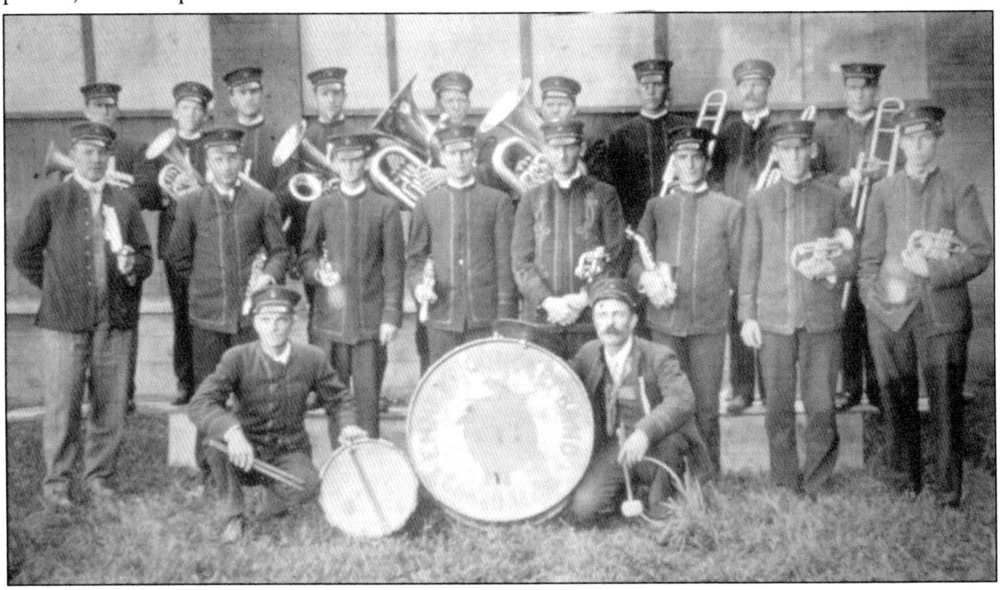

Emmett Concert Band received the highest honors at the Idaho State Fair. Pictured, from left to right, are (first row) Frank Tarleton (snare drum) and Sam Motz (bass drum); (second row) unidentified, Harry Brown (clarinet), George O'Connell (clarinet), Vern Monday (clarinet), Clint Martin (trumpet/director), Elva Coonrod (saxophone), Elva Bell (trumpet), and Byron Turner (trumpet); (third row) Lewis Burton (alto), Harry Bell (alto), Jay Stoner (alto), Claude Bucknum (baritone), Phil Whitsell (trombone), Tom Hance (trombone), and William Womack (trombone).

Four

Agriculture, Cattle, and Sheep

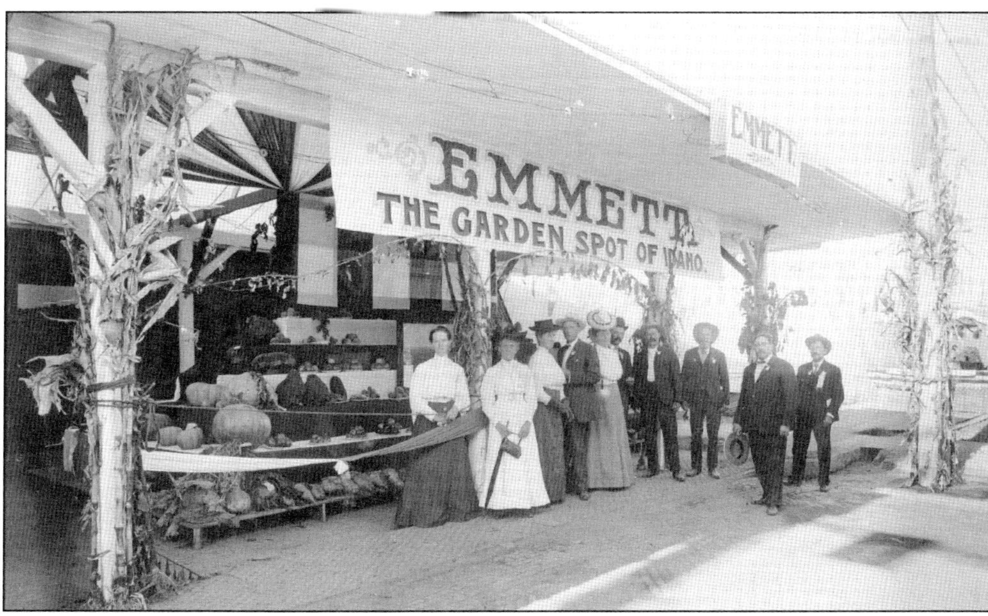

"Emmett: The Garden Spot of Idaho" was the theme for Emmett's display at the Caldwell Fair in 1912. It is still the "garden spot," and many nurseries have located in the Emmett Valley. Pictured, from left to right, are Clara Crouch, unidentified, Mary Kesgard, unidentified, Mrs. Frank McCrossen, Frank McCrossen, Jack Little, J.W. Cook, and two unidentified men. Emmett has become the bedroom community for those who want a rural lifestyle.

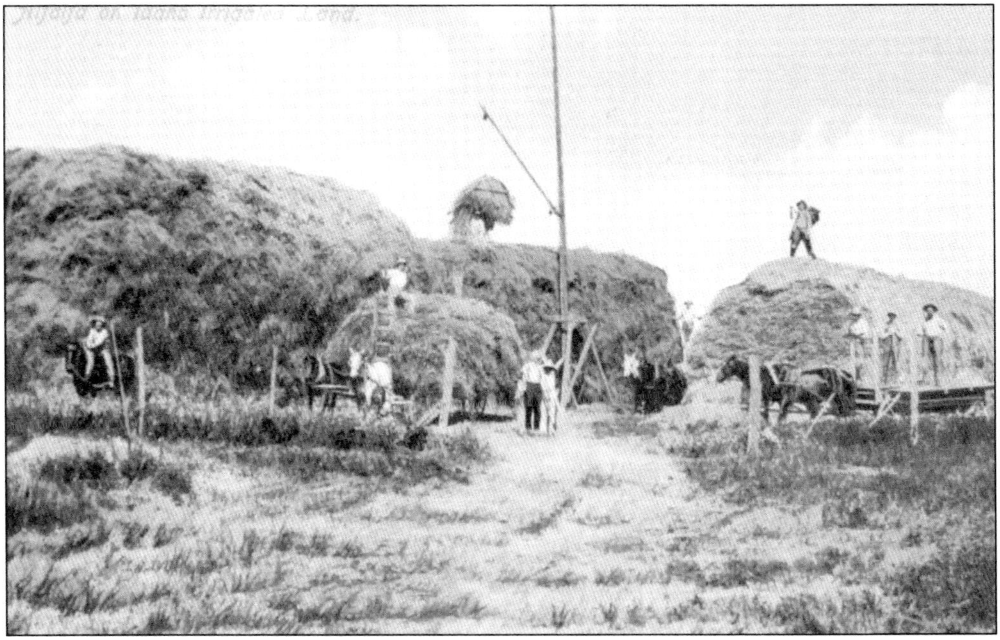

One of the main crops in Gem County is hay. Here, the hay is being harvested and stacked with horses, a derrick, and manpower. Today, alfalfa is harvested with huge machines. Bales are 1,000 pounds each and are handled with a front-end loader on a tractor. In 2007, according to the Gem County Extension Service, 54,608 tons of hay were harvested.

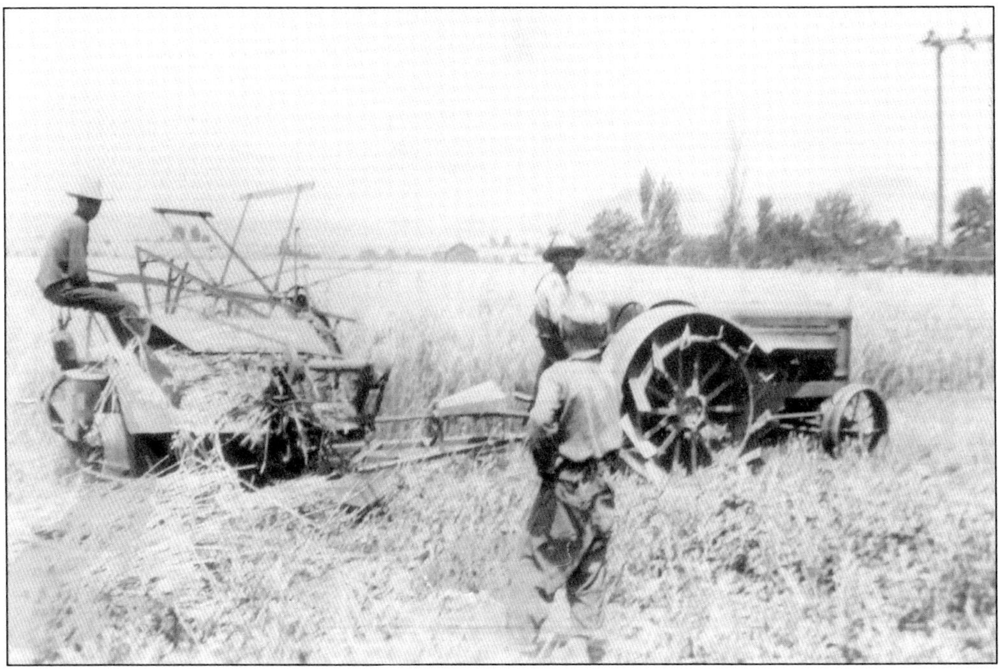

John Klingback is driving the tractor, and Eldon Klingback is riding the binder in 1936 at the John Peterson farm in east Emmett. The boy in the foreground is Roger David Peterson. The grain was cut and tied into bundles that were hauled to the thresher, where the grain was separated from the straw. It took a crew to get the job done. (Courtesy of Ruth Cutbirth.)

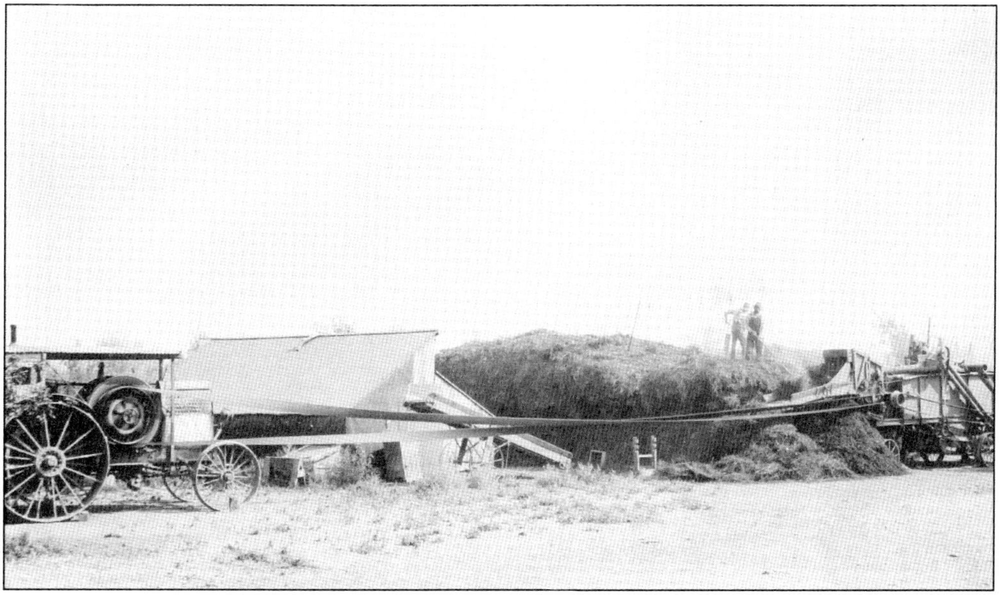

Above, Al White's threshing machine is set up and powered by the tractor on the left. Men on the stack are feeding grain into the thresher. Below, Al White is moving his machines to a new field. Machines made the work much easier; before, the grain had to be separated by hand in a long, laborious process. Today, combines cut and thresh the grain in one pass of the field. In 2007, according to the Gem County Extension Service, 180,027 bushels of wheat and 40,684 bushels of barley were harvested. Today, wheat is the easiest crop to grow.

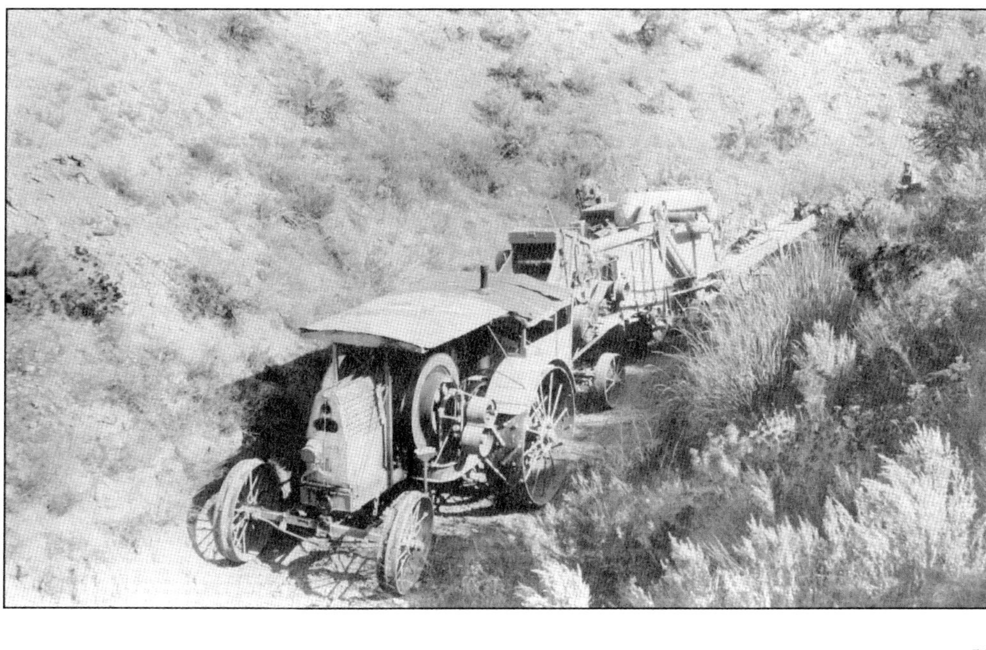

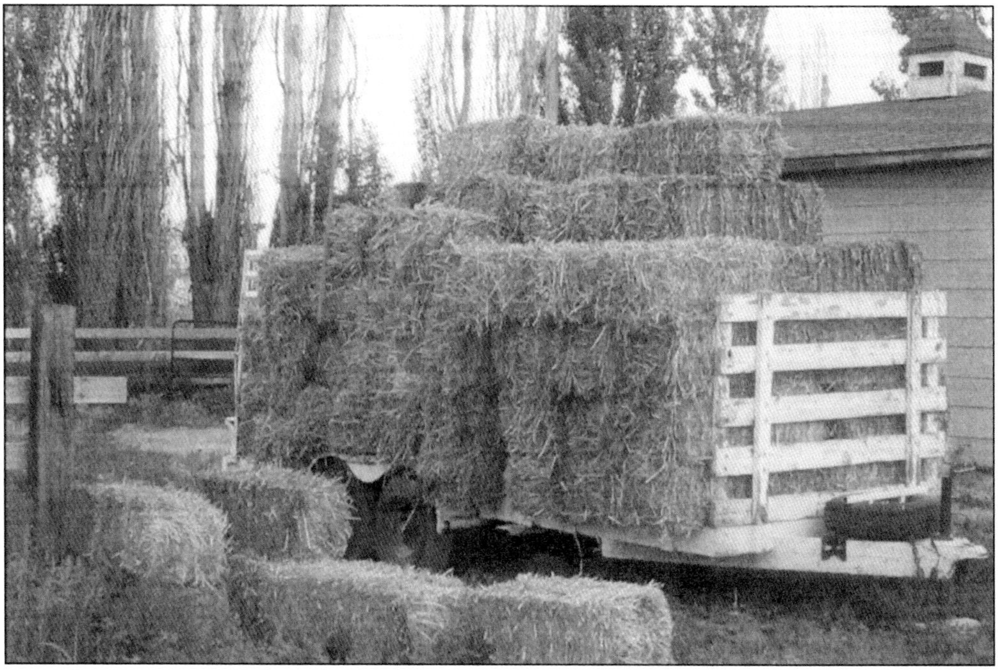

In 2007, Gem County had 318 farms that were between 10 and 49 acres in size and 247 that were between 1 and 9 acres in size. Many of these small acreages have horses that need hay, so there is a demand for small bales of hay like those shown here.

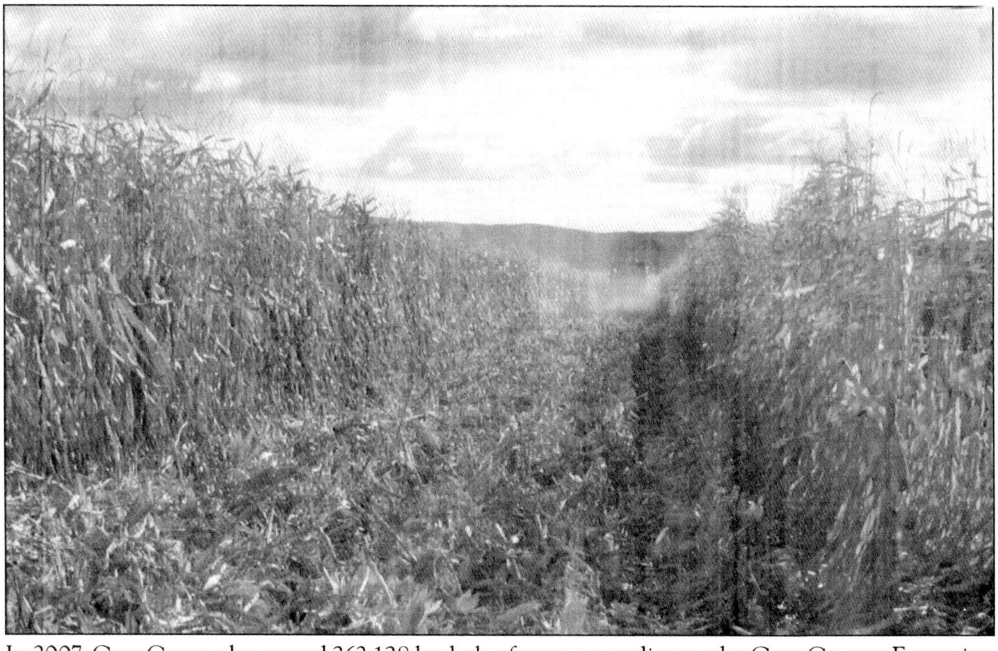

In 2007, Gem County harvested 262,128 bushels of corn, according to the Gem County Extension Service. When Stokely-Van Camp was operating, farmers could grow sweet corn for the cannery. Corn grows well in Gem County and is important in the rotation of crops. The same crop is not grown year after year because that would foster diseases. The main crops in Gem County are grain, corn, hay, and dry beans.

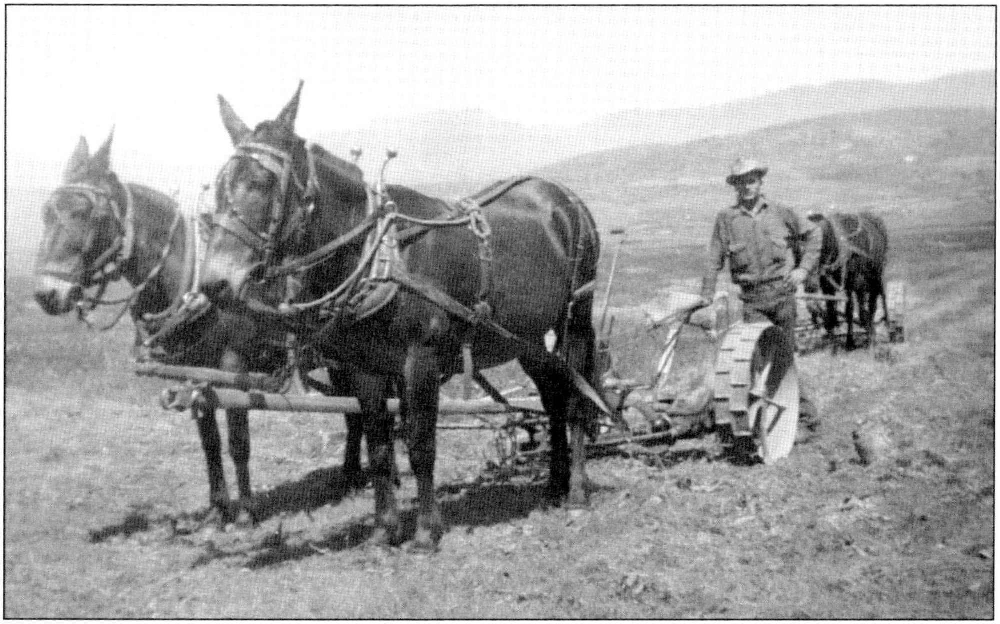

Lewis Beemis is mowing hay with mules on the Van Deusen Ranch in 1947. Van Deusen began in the sheep business as a feeder. He came to Idaho to buy sheep for his company and recognized the opportunities to go into business for himself. He and his brother John bought the sheep and the ranch from the former owners, and two other brothers joined them. They had one of the largest sheep and cattle businesses in Idaho. H. Dudley Van Deusen became president of the Bank of Emmett. They had thousands of acres of land and large numbers of sheep and cattle. Andrew Little bought the ranch from the Van Deusen brothers; however, it is still known as the Van Deusen Ranch.

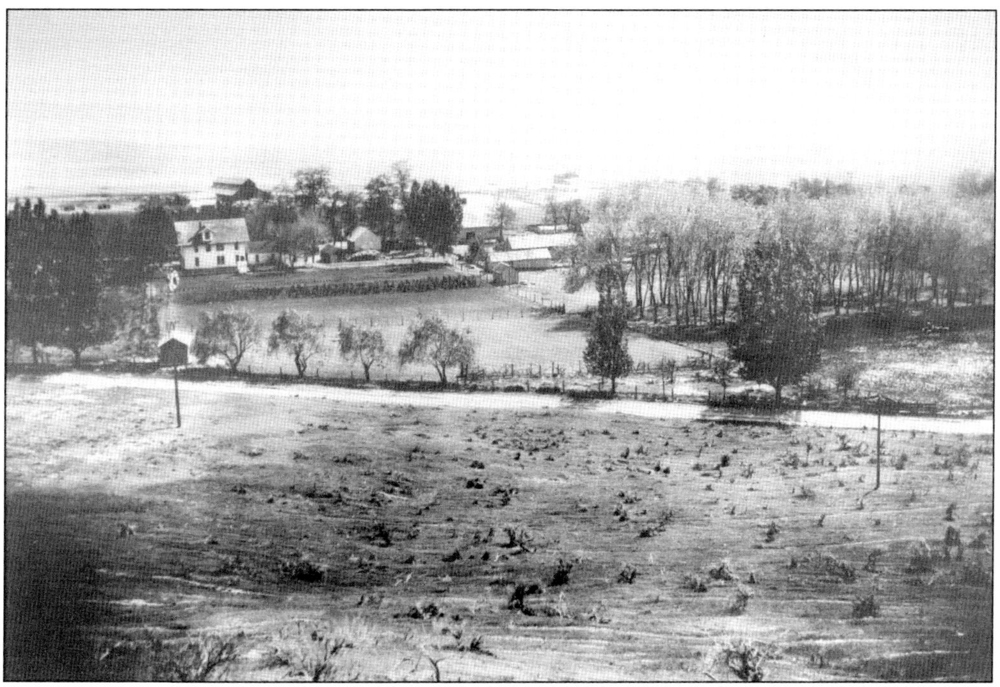

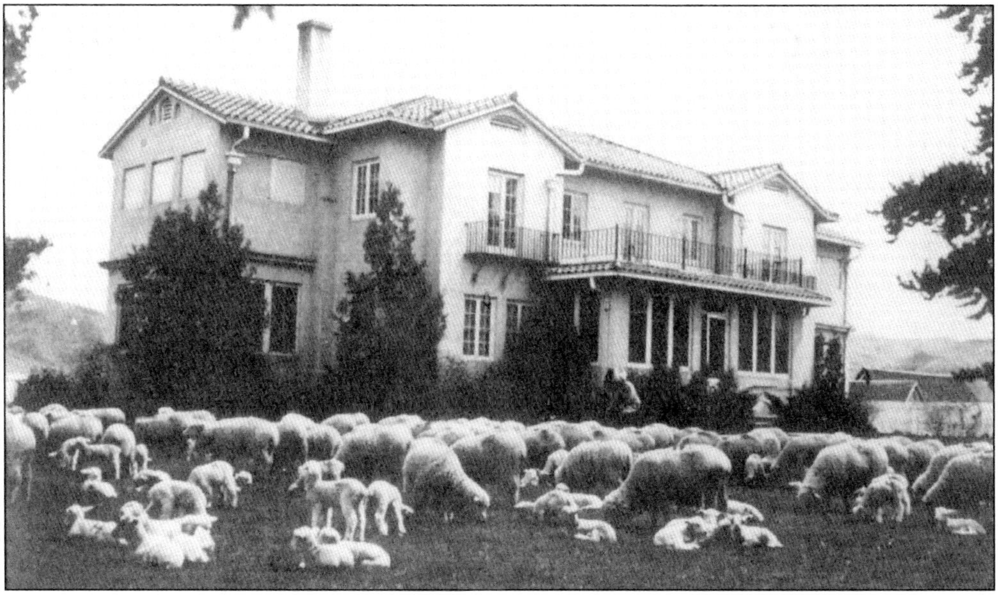

Andrew Little came to Gem County in 1894 and was employed by the Robert Aikman Ranch. He walked 22 miles from Caldwell to work as a sheepherder. From that humble beginning, he built a large empire with his close attention to detail. He built this mansion in the style of a Scottish manor house on Substation Road, and it is still lived in today.

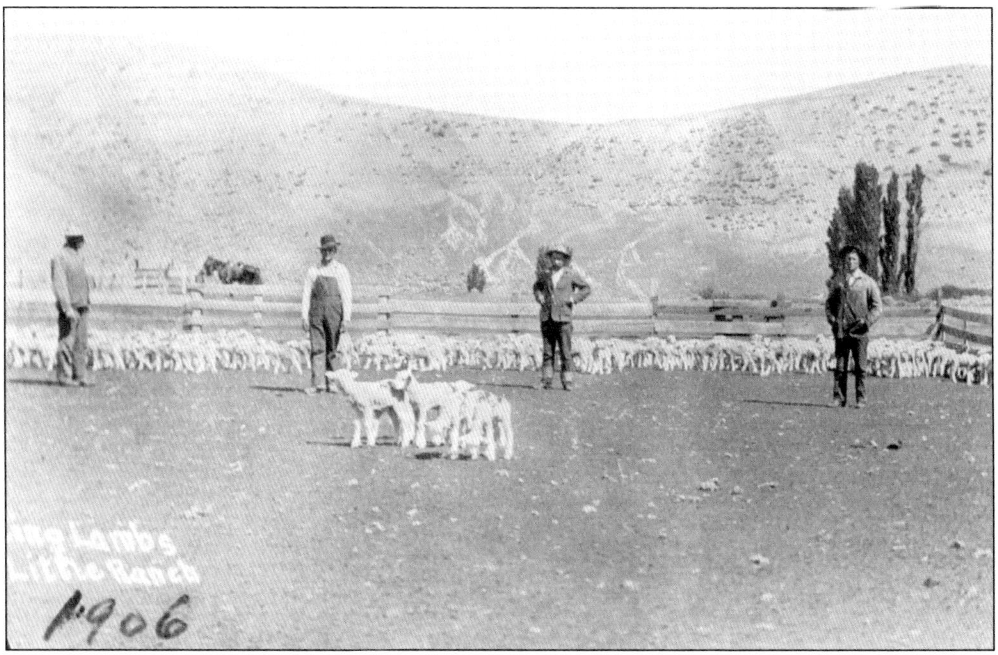

Little hired between 350 and 400 people to manage his 6,000 acres of irrigated farms and tend his sheep, which numbered as many as 100,000. He was careful to buy good breeding stock so that he had a good end product. Little hired his employees for the entire year; that way, he had dependable people he could count on whenever they were needed.

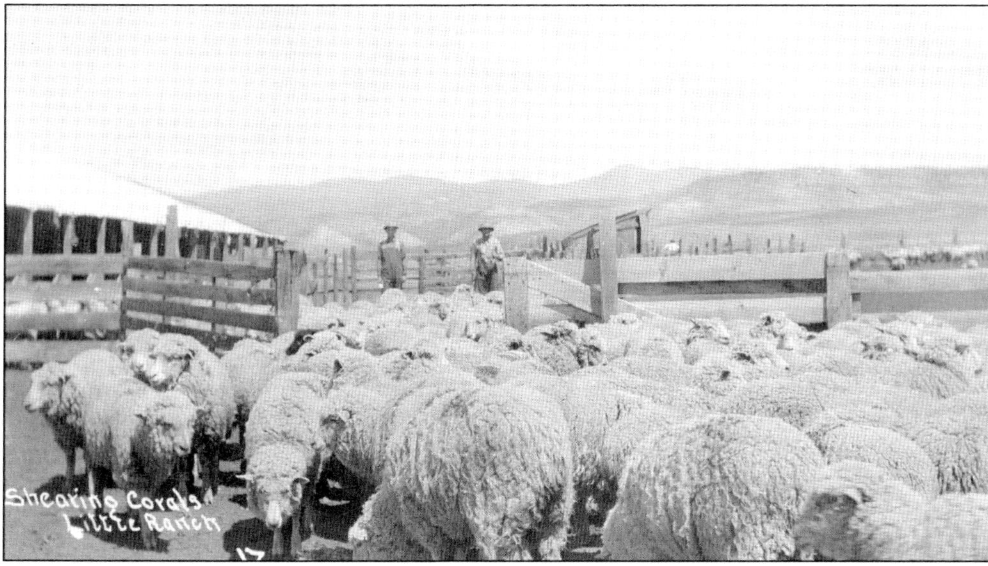

Little was called the "Sheep King of Idaho." A large portrait of him now hangs in the Saddle and Sirloin Club of Chicago. He is the only Idahoan, and one of the few men in the West, to have this honor. He controlled 7,000 acres of grazing land for his animals, and he organized wool sales so that the buyers sent their bids to him and cut out the middlemen. In 1935, he had 700,000 pounds of graded wool for sale, and the sale took place in Emmett. The bids for that year were low, so he did not accept any but sold at a later date. Little Land & Livestock still exists today in Gem County.

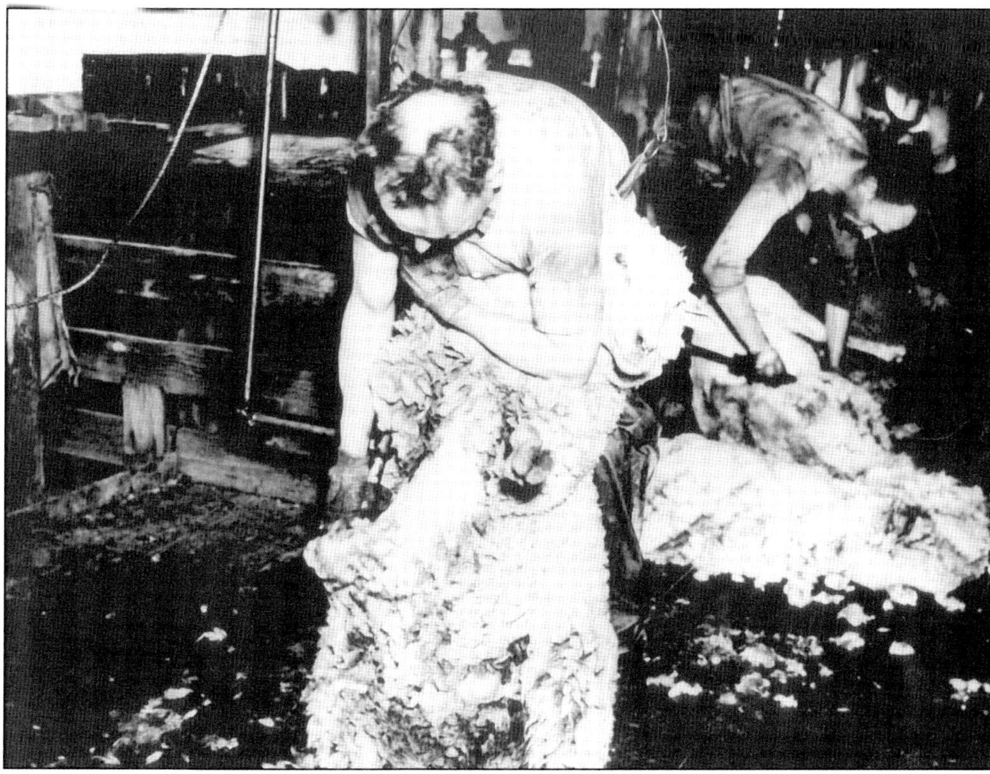

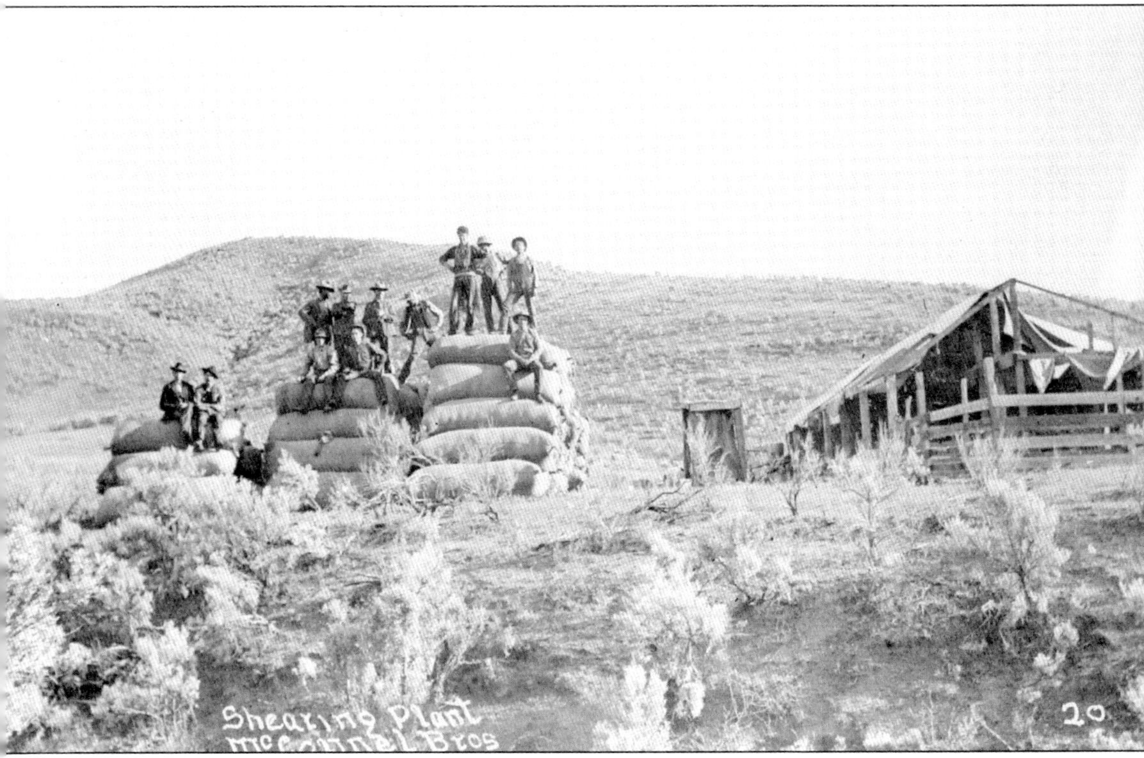

In 1900, there were many well-known sheep operations in existence in the Emmett and Squaw Creek areas that ran a total of 125,000 sheep. The main sheep growers were Andrew Little, Bullard and Johnson, the Knox brothers, James Little, Jack Little, Alex Cruickshank and sons, William Woody, the Van Deusen brothers, and the McConnel brothers at Montour. The hillsides and the high mountain valleys had good forage for these animals, and they prospered. There were also many acres of federal land that could be utilized for feed. Large bands of sheep were trailed from Idaho to market in the Midwest. These large bags hold 400 pounds of wool each. There was a good market for wool, and the shearers made good wages. (Courtesy of the Idaho Historical Society, No. 1986-27.42.)

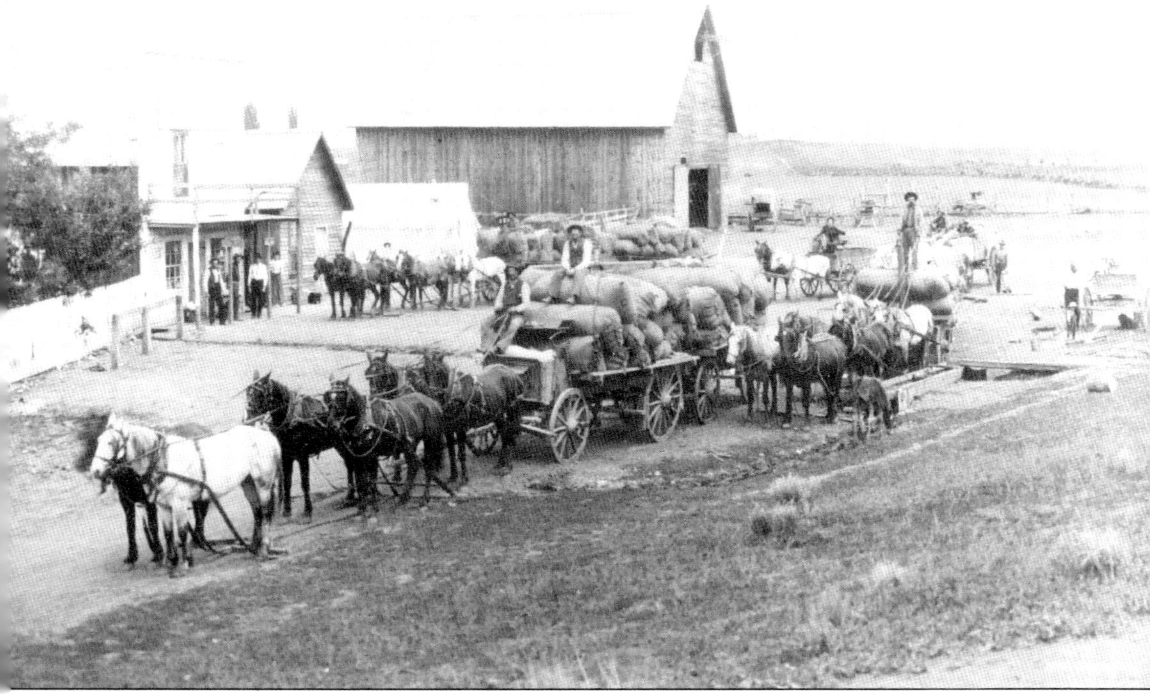

James Ballantyne first came to America in 1863, leaving his bride and daughter in Scotland. Lured by gold, he went to Denver, where he was stricken by typhoid fever. The Freemasons paid for his stay in the hospital there and also paid his way to Canada to recuperate. He returned to Scotland for his family, which included his mother, sister, and brother-in-law. He booked passage on a ship to Portland, Oregon, where he settled his family on a small farm that he visited two or three times a year. He left his family and walked to the basin, where he established a mining claim. He returned to Oregon for his family and eventually settled them in Ola in 1869. In addition to mining, he raised sheep. He donated the land and built the Methodist church in Ola, which is now the Ola Community Church.

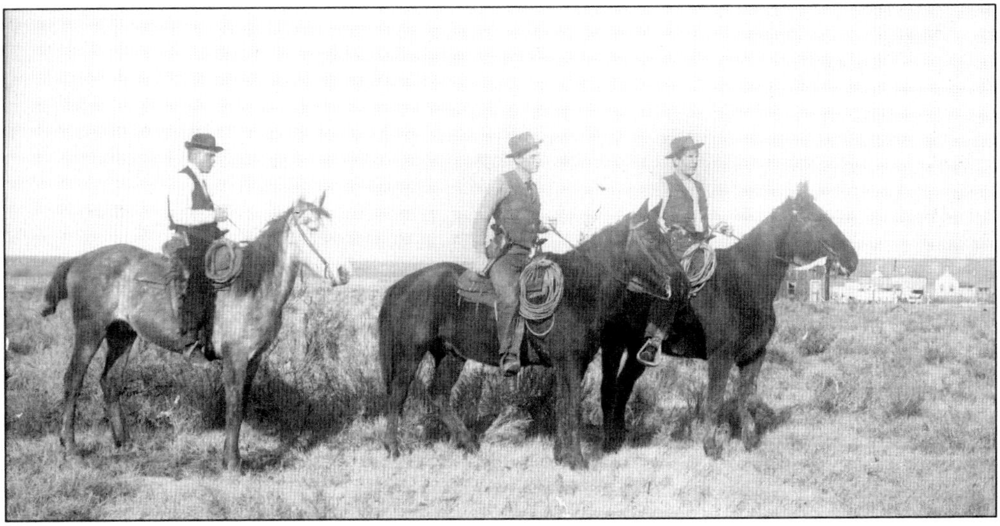

George Anderson (left), who lived near the town of Letha, is shown above with Henry Boquet (center) and Hugh Bishop, son of Sarah and Edson Bishop, who were homesteaders near Falk's Store. The easiest way to bring the meat to the people was to have a cattle drive. Branding was one of the important operations that took place before turning the animals loose on summer rangeland. It is estimated that by 1860, the count for cattle and sheep was nearly one million. When the livestock business began in Idaho, cattle were cheap in California and Texas because of oversupply, making it easier for the settlers to establish the cattle business in Idaho.

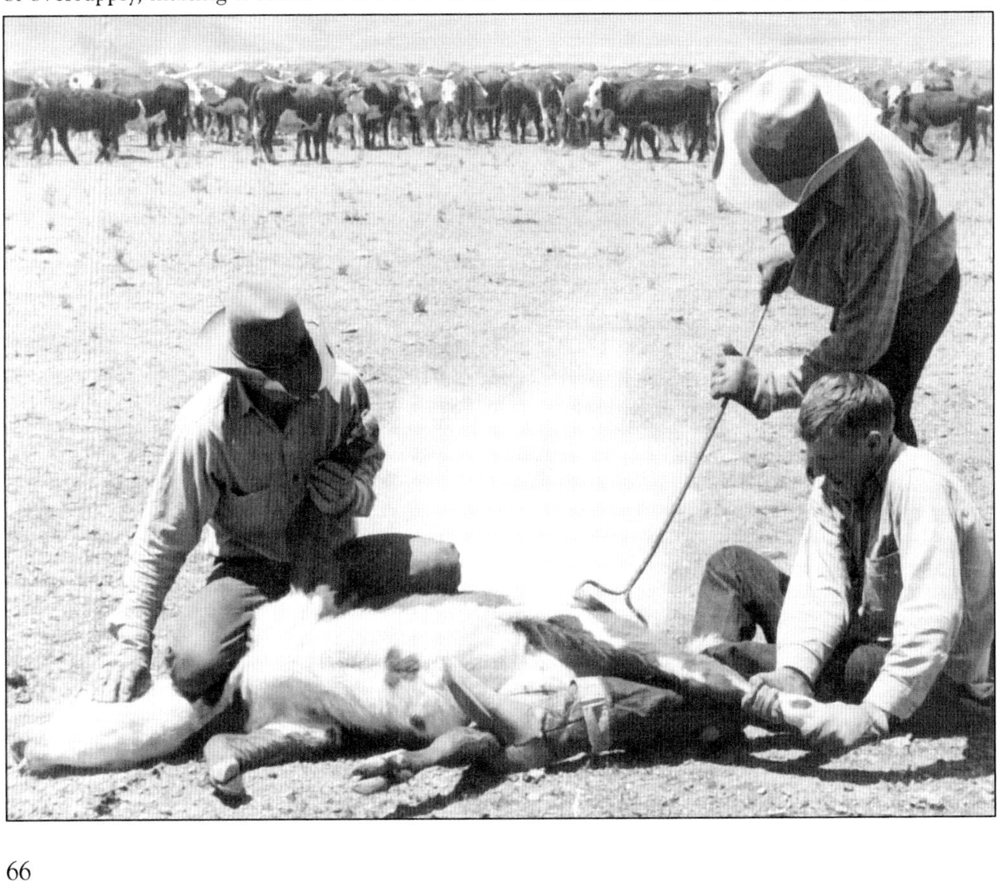

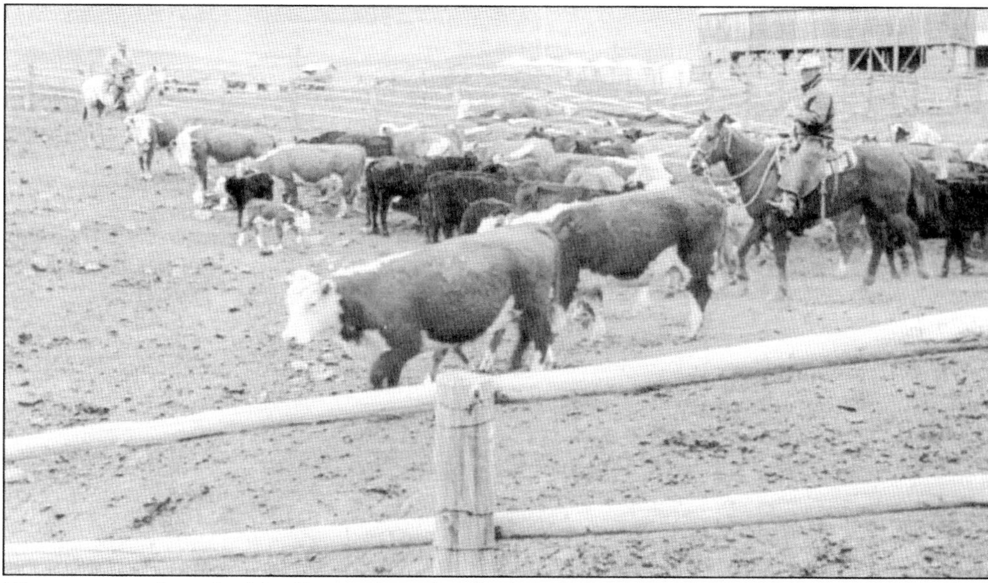

Theses are cattle at the Van Deusen Ranch, which is 10 miles north of Emmett. It was important in the feed supply to have cheap grazing land for summer pasture. In the fall, the cattle were brought back to the valley for wintering. The winter of 1889–1890 was so severe that thousands of cattle died, and many cowmen went broke. In the void, the cattlemen discovered it was cheaper to start over with sheep than with cattle. Most of southern Idaho became dominated by sheep, so there was serious competition for forage. Soon, overgrazing caused much destruction, and established stockmen petitioned for creation of forest reserves in Idaho and other states to eliminate competition and halt range decline. This ground is rocky but produces enough good feed to raise cattle. (Both, courtesy of Kennie Lyn Klingback.)

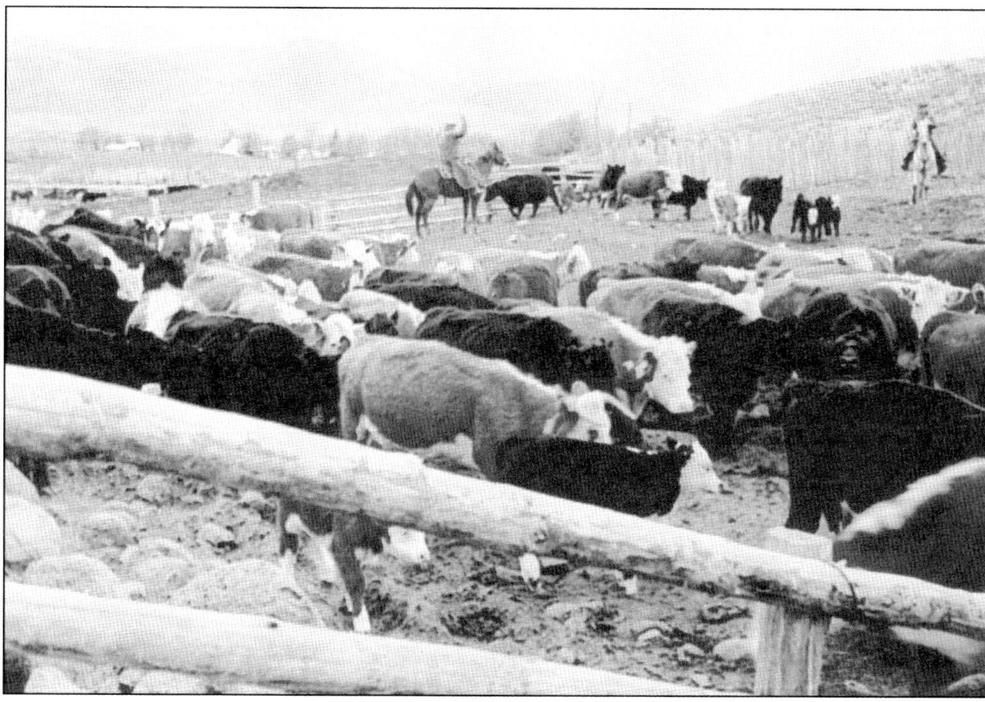

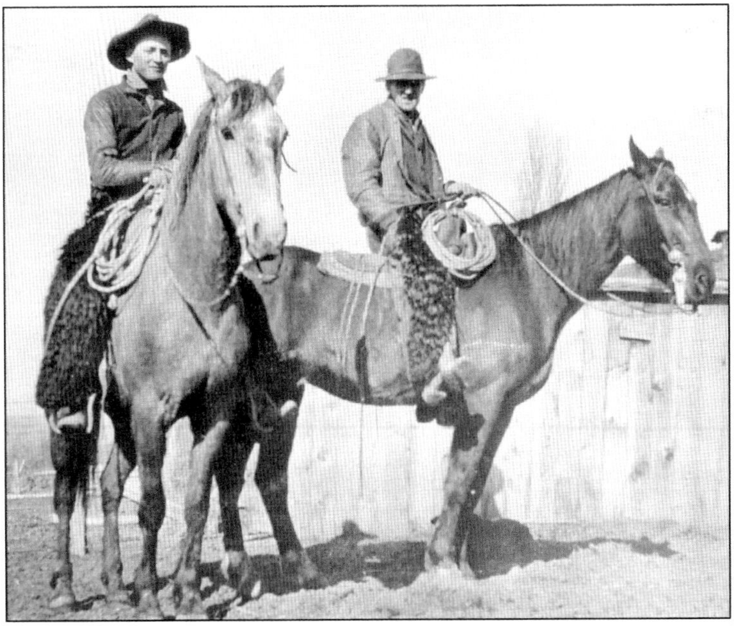

Harry Knox (left) and Albert Martin are shown in the Squaw Creek area in 1919. The region was hilly and rocky and had a shorter growing season than Emmett, but there was plenty of feed to raise cattle, which could then be trailed over to Placerville to market. Statistics from the Idaho Department of Agriculture show that there was a steady increase of cattle from 1870 through 1900.

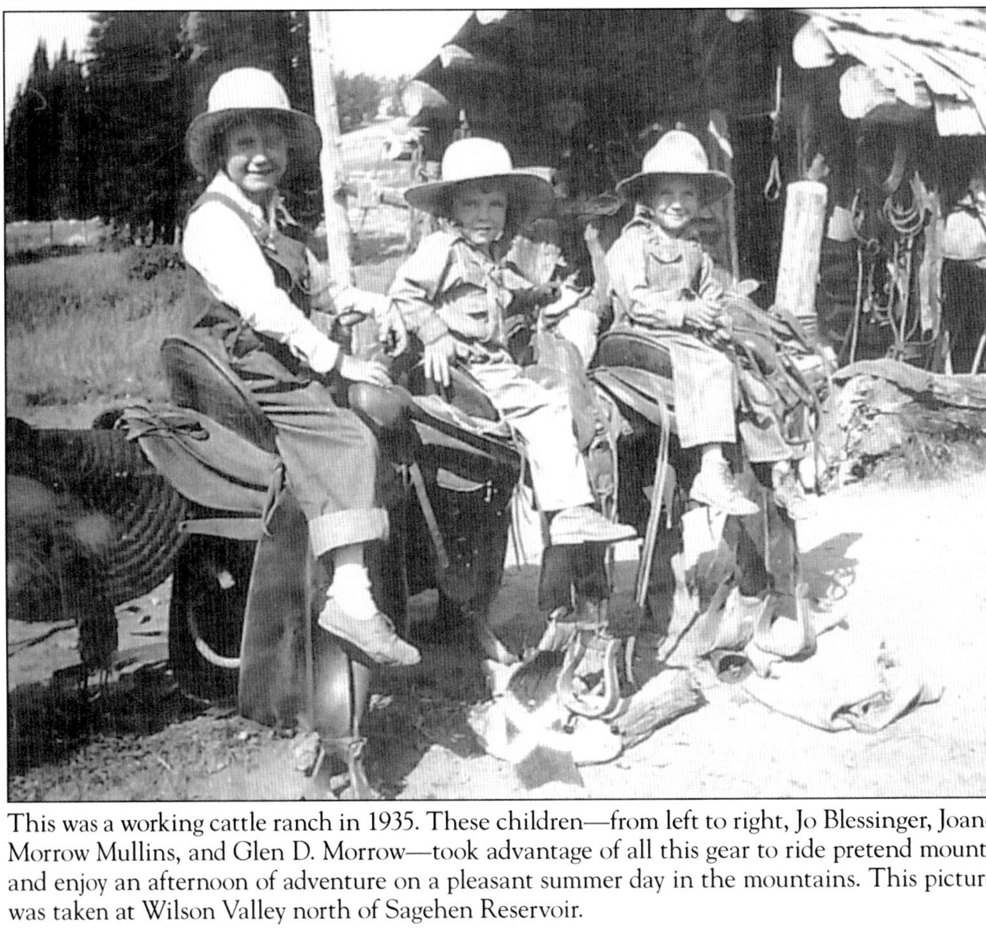

This was a working cattle ranch in 1935. These children—from left to right, Jo Blessinger, Joane Morrow Mullins, and Glen D. Morrow—took advantage of all this gear to ride pretend mounts and enjoy an afternoon of adventure on a pleasant summer day in the mountains. This picture was taken at Wilson Valley north of Sagehen Reservoir.

Five

RAILROADS

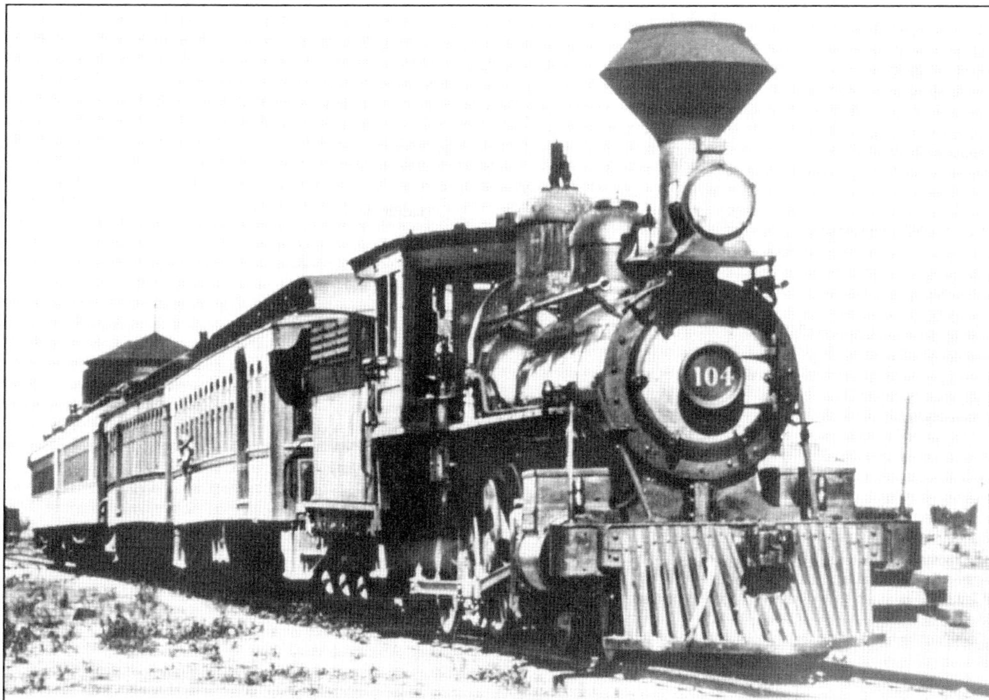

MARCH 1902
IDAHO NORTHERN'S SPECIAL TRAIN CELEBRATING IN EMMETT THE COMPLETION OF THE IDAHO NORTHERN RAILWAY TO EMMETT.

The Idaho Northern Train was extended to Emmett 1902 with the influence of Col. W.H. Dewey. Dewey needed to transport mining equipment to his mines at Thunder Mountain. It was a great day for the people of Emmett; they would now have means to send their products to market, and the upper country could be developed. The population increased from 300 to 1,000 people in one year. .

The Payette Valley Railroad

OPERATES DOUBLE DAILY PASSENGER TRAINS BETWEEN EMMETT AND PAYETTE VIA LETHA, FALK'S STORE, GESS, NEW PLYMOUTH AND FRUITLAND

THIS RAILROAD TRAVERSES THE HEART OF THE FAMOUS PAYETTE VALLEY WHICH SHIPPED LAST YEAR

1008---CARS OF FRUIT---1008

MORE THAN HALF OF ALL THE FRUIT SHIPPED FROM THE STATE OF IDAHO

Don't fail to make a trip to Payette and return through

Idaho's Paradise Valley

It was not long before another rail line, the Payette Valley Railroad, came to Emmett. It was built in 1906 by the Payette Valley Railroad from Payette to New Plymouth, Idaho, a distance of 11 miles, and was extended 18 miles to Emmett in 1910 by the Payette Valley Extension Railroad. Some fruit growers used the Payette Valley Railroad to ship fruit to market.

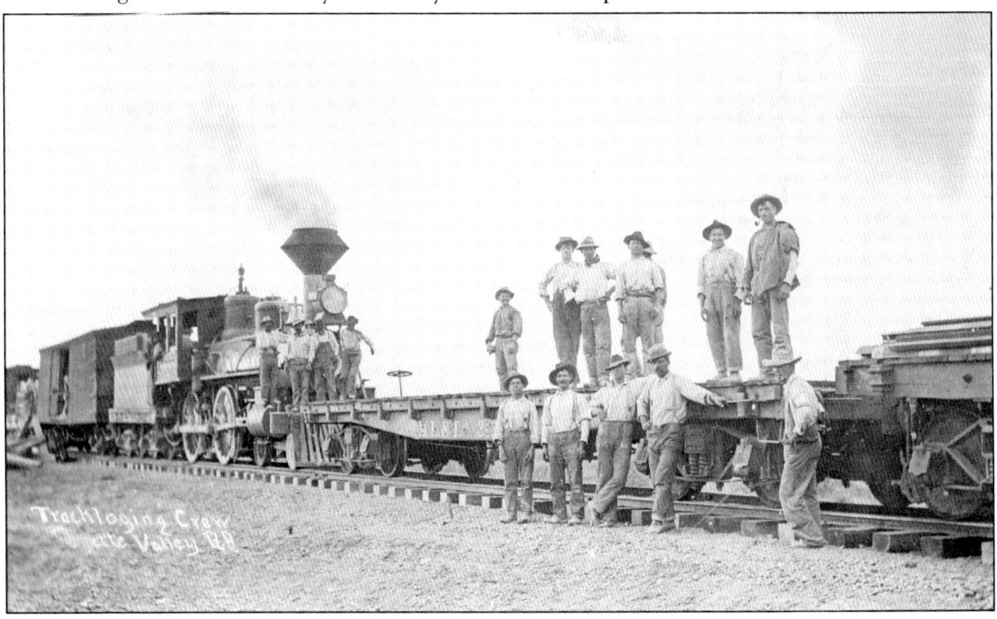

Local people were hired to build the railway into Emmett. It took four months to finish that section of track and cost $100,000. The mayors of Emmett and Payette had a celebration when the tracks were joined, with bands from both towns present at the ceremonies. The Oregon Short Line acquired these lines by purchase on August 5, 1914.

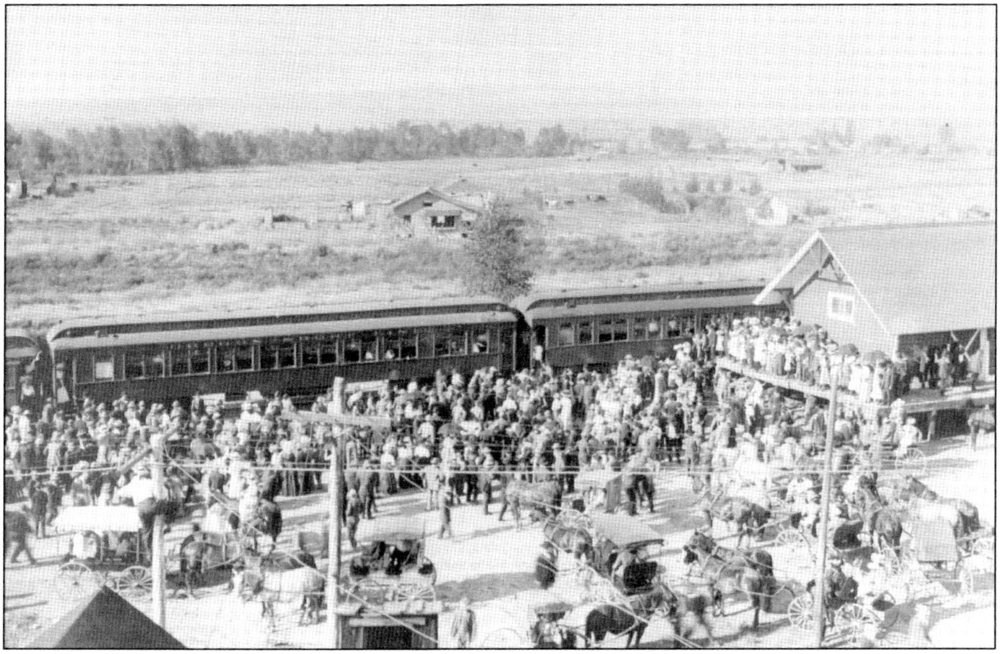

It was a day of celebration when the Idaho Northern rolled into town in 1902. A trial run was made, and when the train ran through the swamp west of town, the track sank out of sight. The engine and the car had to be pulled along until they reached solid ground. The track was taken up, and pine pilings were driven down to make a solid foundation for them.

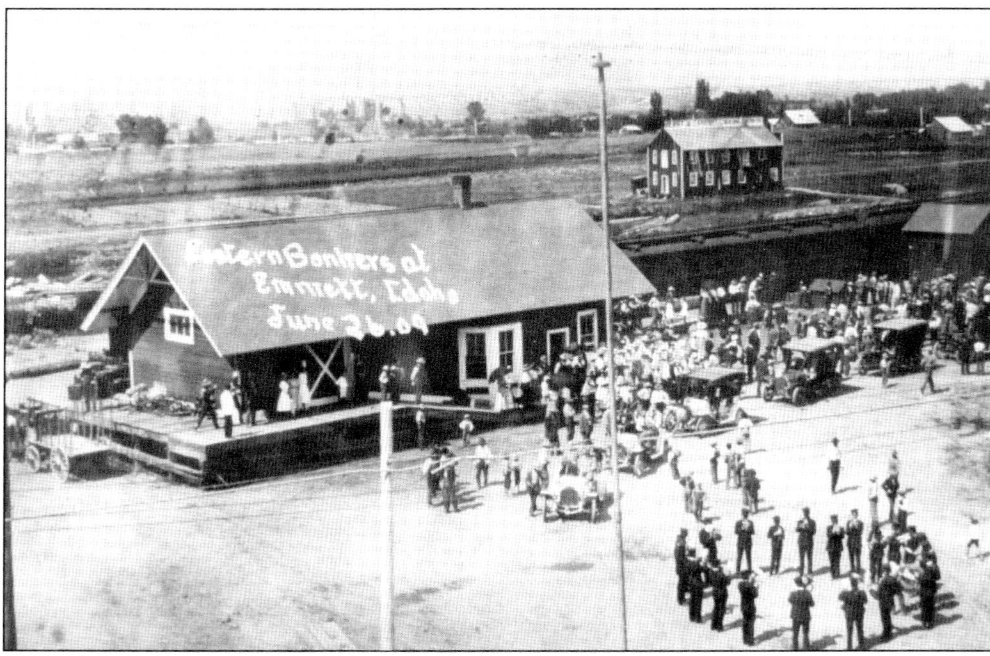

The whole nation was growing, and Emmett was no exception. The eastern bankers were looking for opportunities to invest their money. Because of the railroads, it was possible to travel across the country and look at possible places for investment. Bankers were welcomed to Emmett in 1909 for such a purpose.

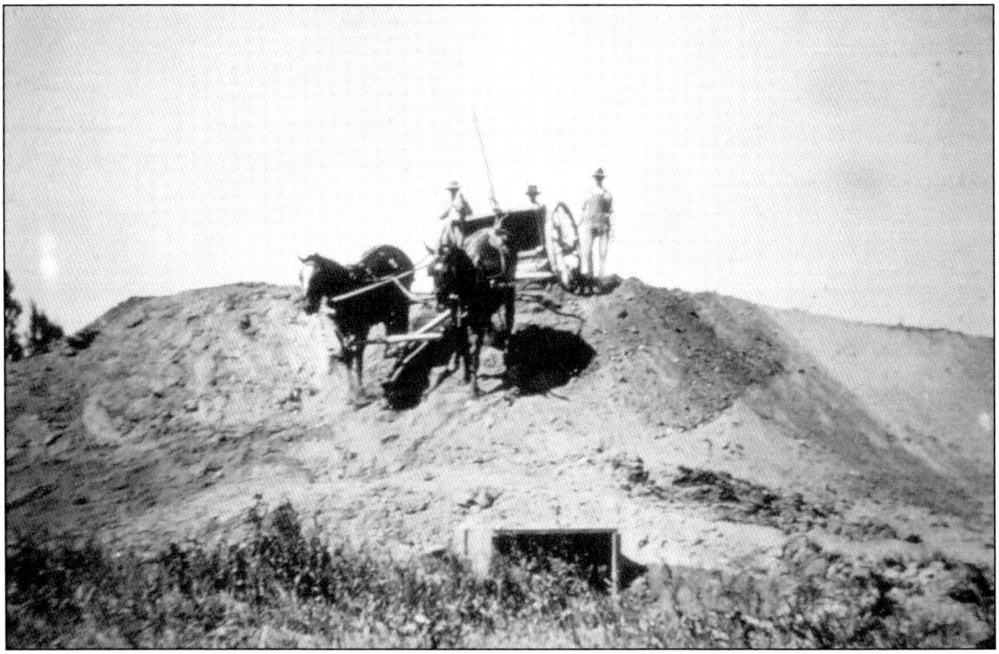

Camps were set up about four miles apart along the rail line where men and horses could board. Men were paid 50¢ an hour, and it took four months to build this section of the line. Here, a crew is building the roadbed with a fresno scraper so the tracks could be laid.

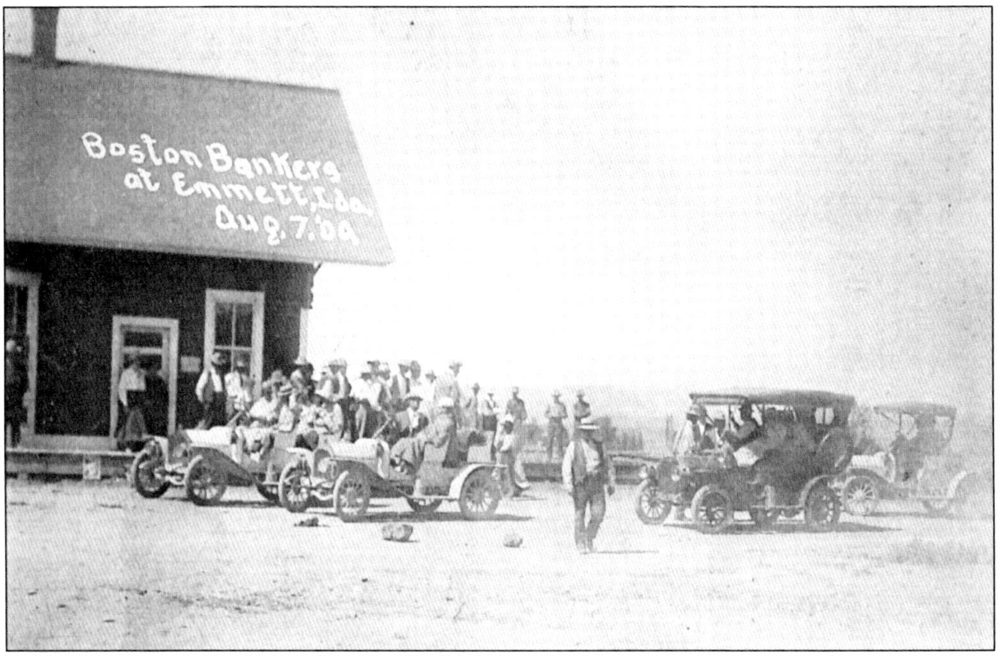

The Boston bankers came in August 1909 to investigate fruit orchards. The return on orchards was high and took only a few years to begin making money. The following is from a postcard: "While Emmett has not been extensively advertised, the opportunity for permanent settlers, either with or without means, is unprecedented. Fortunes have been accumulated in a few years by settlers who came here comparatively poor."

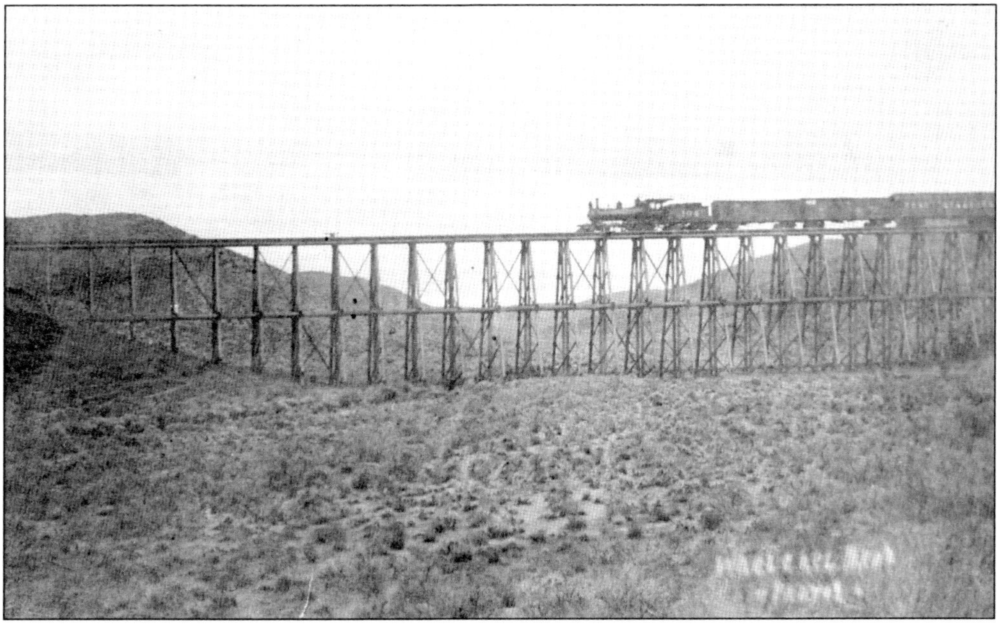

Trestles that were 50 and 70 feet high had to be built to cross the gullies that existed between Middleton and Emmett. A trestle had washed out, so the temporary track detoured around it. The train swayed so much that the passengers were afraid of wrecking. One passenger remarked that the ride was more dangerous because of the trestles than on any other place on the trip from Chicago.

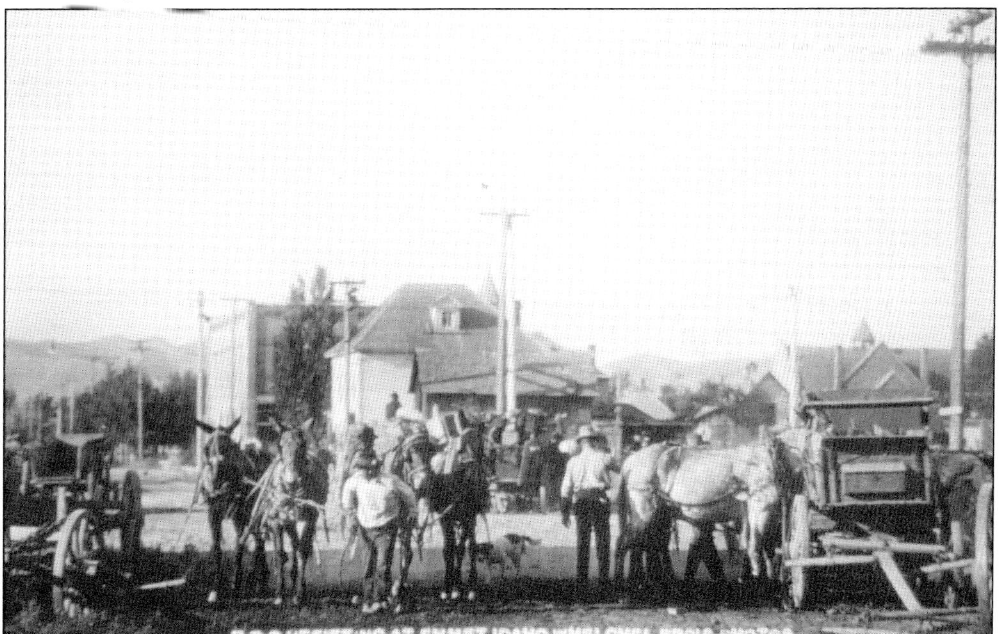

All of the building on the railroads was good for the economy. In 1913, the railroad was extended to McCall. Here, the railroad is being outfitted at Emmett. Trains were usually loaded with goods going both directions. They brought freight in—usually merchandise for stores—and livestock, lumber, and agricultural products were shipped out.

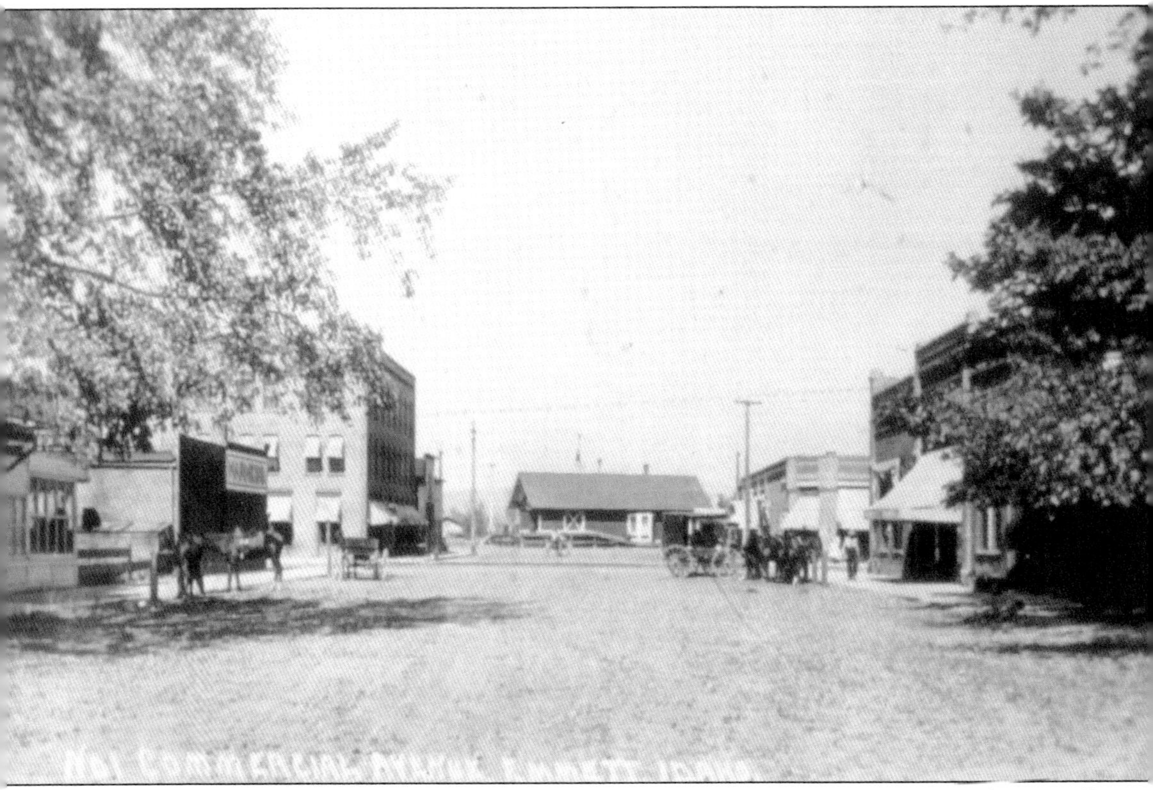

This was the main street of town as the train depot was the focus of most activities. The Russell Hotel was completed in 1904 to accommodate train travelers. The coming of the train encouraged settlers because people felt that Emmett was a boomtown. Many of them came in immigrant railroad cars, which also carried their stock, tools, and household goods. In one year, the receipts for the Idaho Northern tripled, and freight more than doubled. The tempo of the town increased, and the new town sprang to life. The railroad's extension to McCall added more people and products. Businessmen could see that Emmett, with its many resources, would be a supply town for the surrounding communities, and the railroad would play an important part in this development.

Six

HORTICULTURE

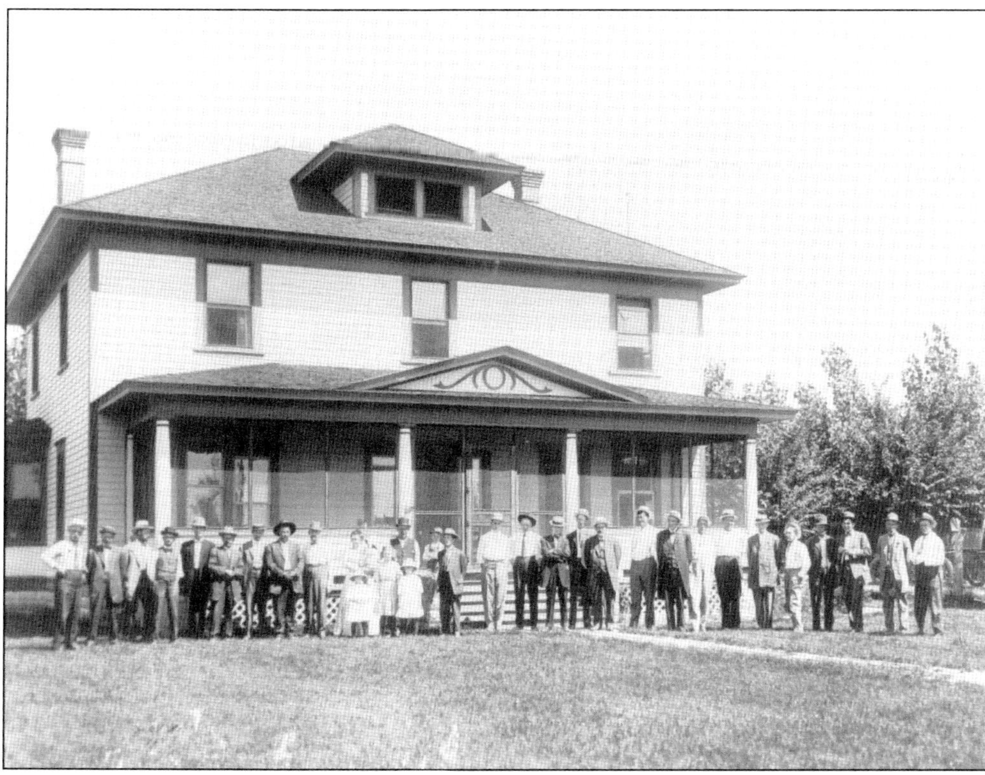

This opulent house was built by J.R. Field, who was an experienced, successful horticulturist. He produced cherries, apples, peaches, and prunes in his extensive orchards on the east slope, north of Cherry Lane. He is credited for beginning the first commercial sweet cherry orchard in 1908. His orchards were thought of as exemplary for other growers.

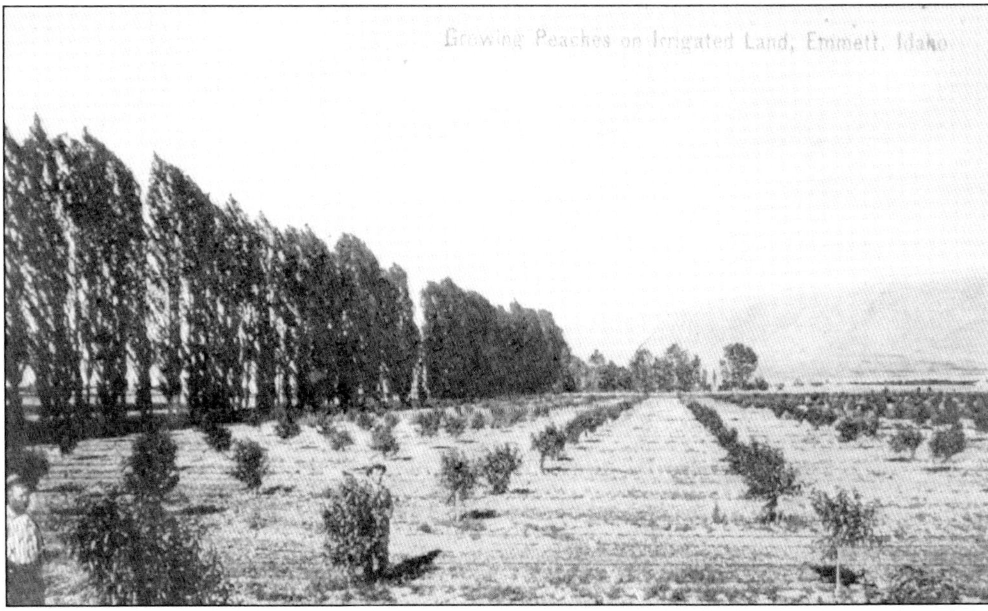

These postcards display both the peach orchard on the ranch of Boise Riggs (above) and the Model Fruit Farm belonging to H.F. Hopper (below). Both exemplify the prolific growth of trees and orchards in the late 1800s and early 1900s. Thanks to the sheltered valley's excellent air drainage and fertile soil composed of volcanic elements and decayed vegetation, fruit trees were capable of growing as much as five feet in 12 months. This resulted in profits for the ranchers. Joseph Degen, who planted one of the first orchards in the Emmett Valley, made profits of $1,600 after five years' growth from peach and apricot trees planted on seven acres. By the mid-1970s, one third of Emmett's economy was sustained by the fruit industry. (Both, photograph by Stevens Studio, published by the Idaho View Company.)

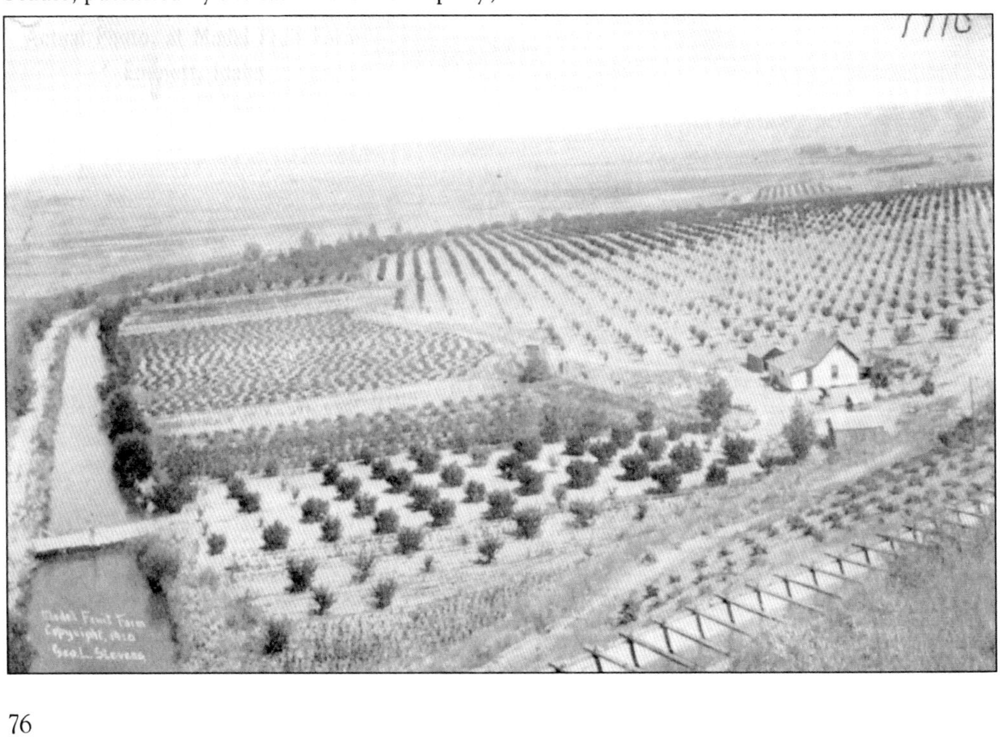

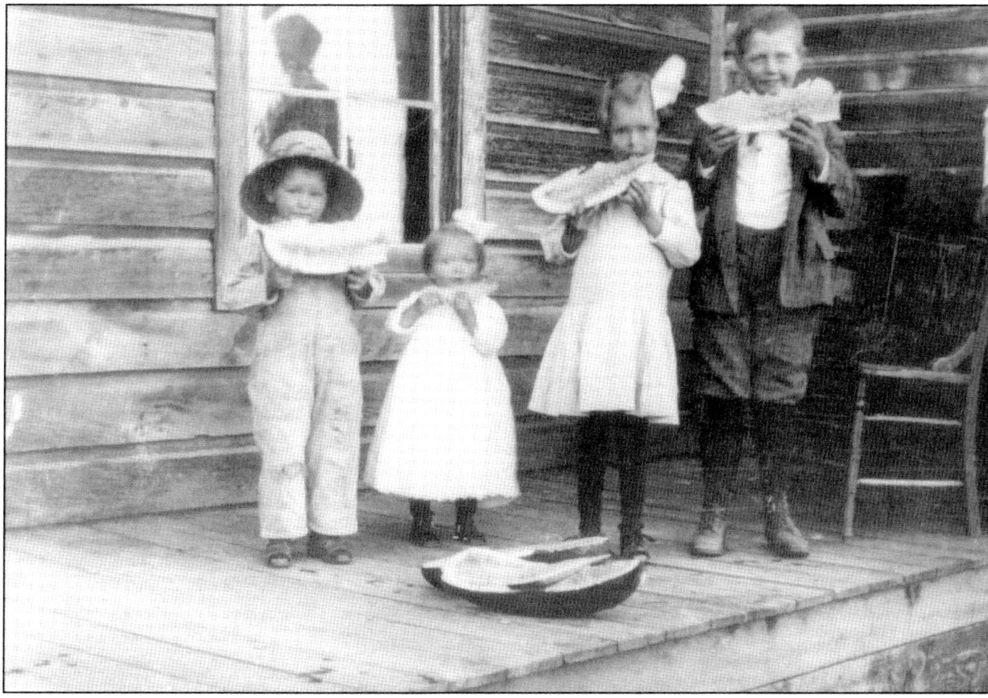

Here, the children of Robert McElfresh eat watermelon on Thanksgiving Day 1918. The watermelons were placed in the middles of haystacks to keep them cool and dry and extend their life. This worked as well as refrigeration, and there was no power bill to pay. It made a delightful treat for Thanksgiving.

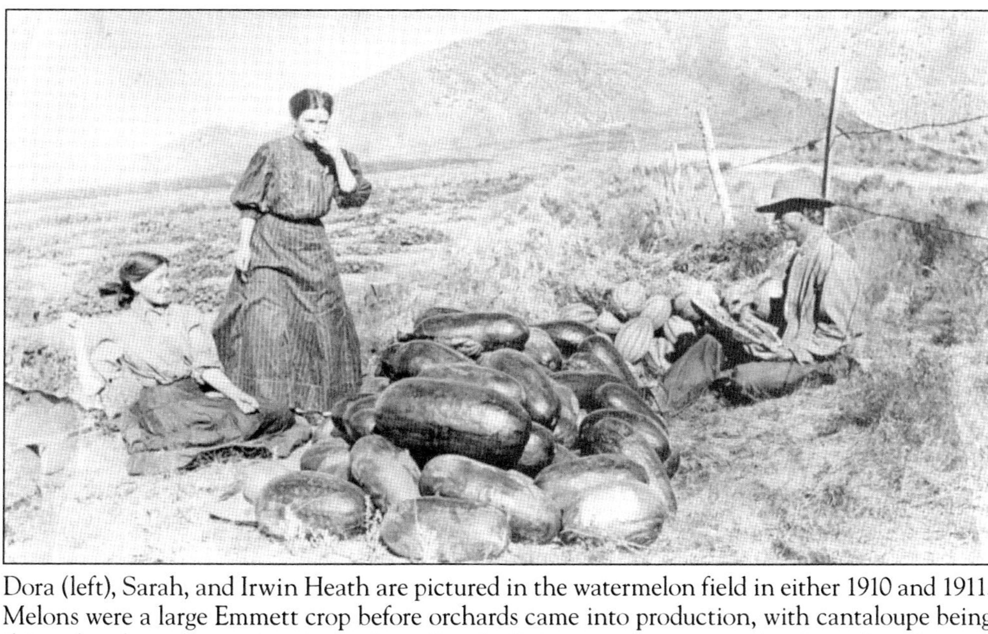

Dora (left), Sarah, and Irwin Heath are pictured in the watermelon field in either 1910 and 1911. Melons were a large Emmett crop before orchards came into production, with cantaloupe being shipped as far as Pennsylvania on the railroads. Boise was always a good cash market that was close. Melons were a good crop because they were easy to grow and shipped well.

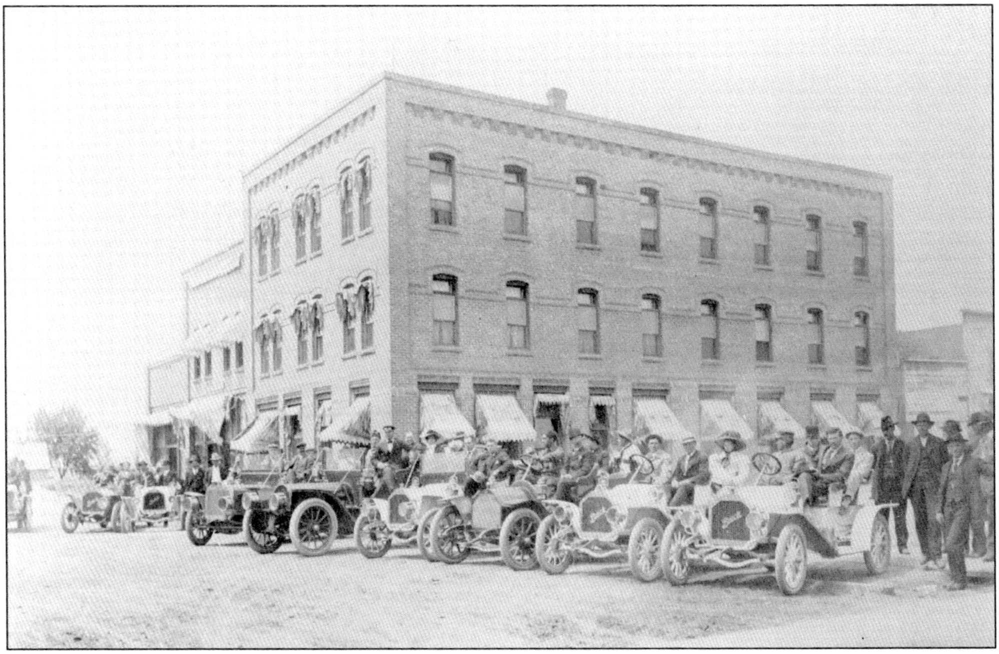

In front of the Russell Hotel, cars purchased with fruit profits line the street in downtown Emmett. A 1916 issue of Emmett's newspaper, the *Index*, states, "Business has improved greatly since the commercial orchards have come into production. There are no empty buildings in town. Every place that was vacant is now occupied."

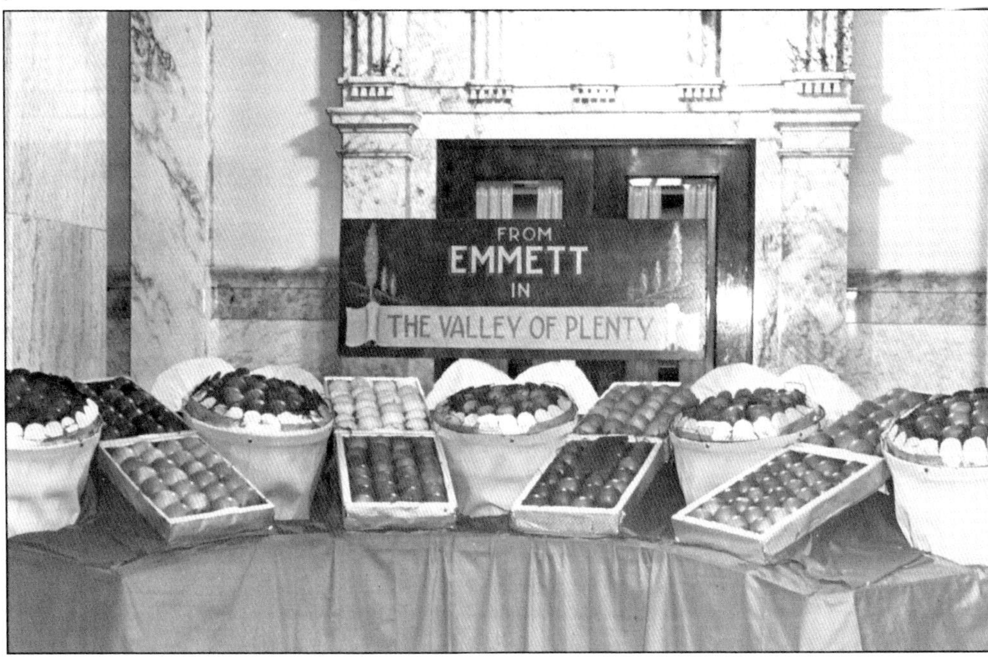

With fruit being shipped worldwide—prunes going to London, apples going to Australia and Asia, and much of the fruit going to the eastern United States—Gem County soon became well known for its produce. Frequently, at local fairs, residents had winning exhibits and premium fruit awards. Displayed here is an exhibit at the state capitol in Boise in 1950.

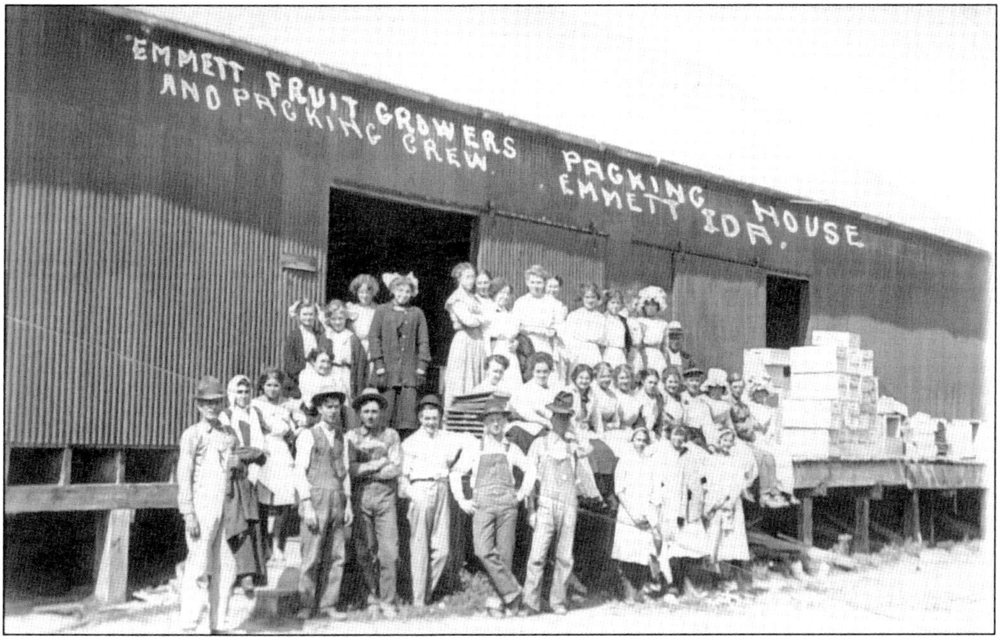

Once the fruit was in demand, packing and consolidating it became paramount. The first packing shed was built in the late 1800s by Ed Hayes to sort and pack his prunes. More sheds, such as the one pictured here in 1912, were established to compensate for the abundance of fruit. The river was used to transport the freight out of town until the railroad took its place.

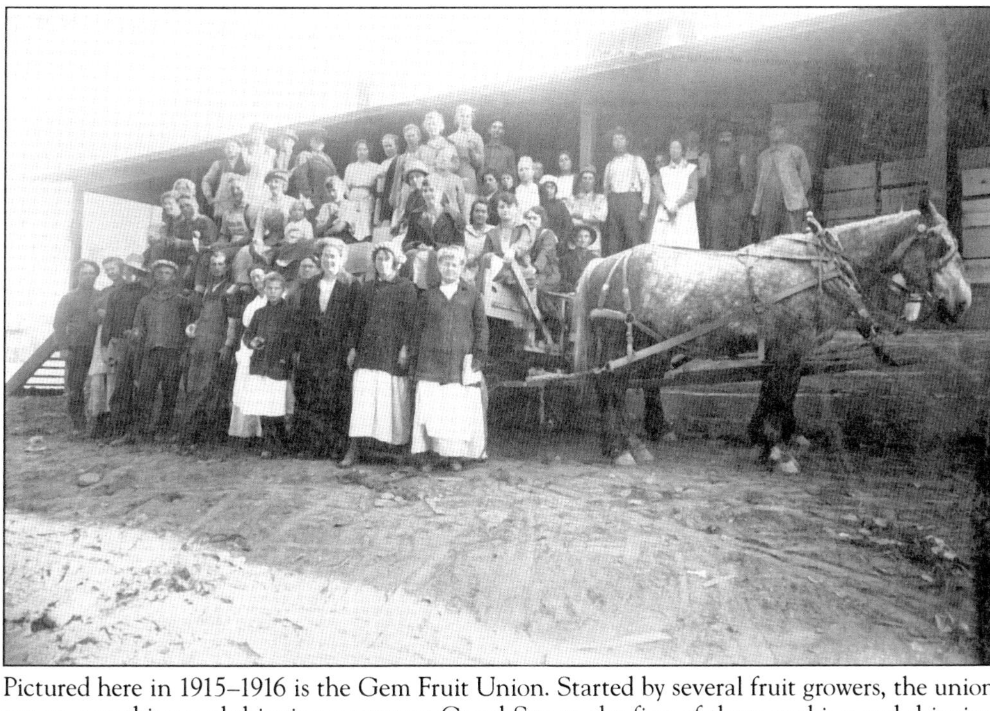

Pictured here in 1915–1916 is the Gem Fruit Union. Started by several fruit growers, the union put up a packing and shipping center on Canal Street, the first of three packing and shipping sheds to be located on that route. By the 1940s, Emmett was known as the foremost shipping point for sweet cherries in the state.

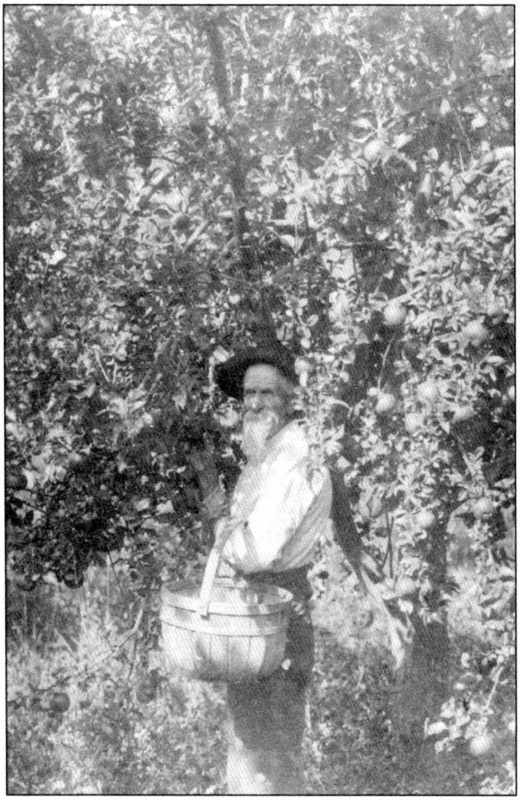

John F. Daily is seen here picking fruit from one of the many trees on his 100-acre ranch located on the corner of Fourth Street and Boise Avenue. He and his wife came from Missouri looking for peace and prosperity. Daily was known for his well-kept lawn, garden, and orchard.

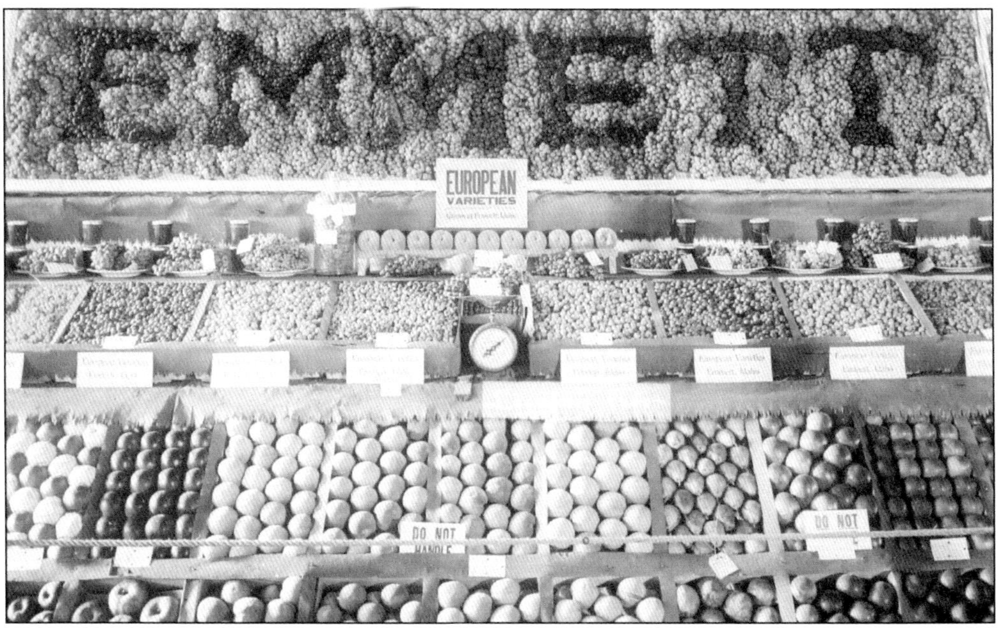

Emmett's dazzling display of fruit won a grand prize in 1910 at the Boise State Fair. The large orchards and packing plants helped to stimulate Emmett's economy and keep its businesses strong. Figures from 1976 county agent Earling Johannesen state that 80 percent of the income from the fruit business is spent in the Emmett area.

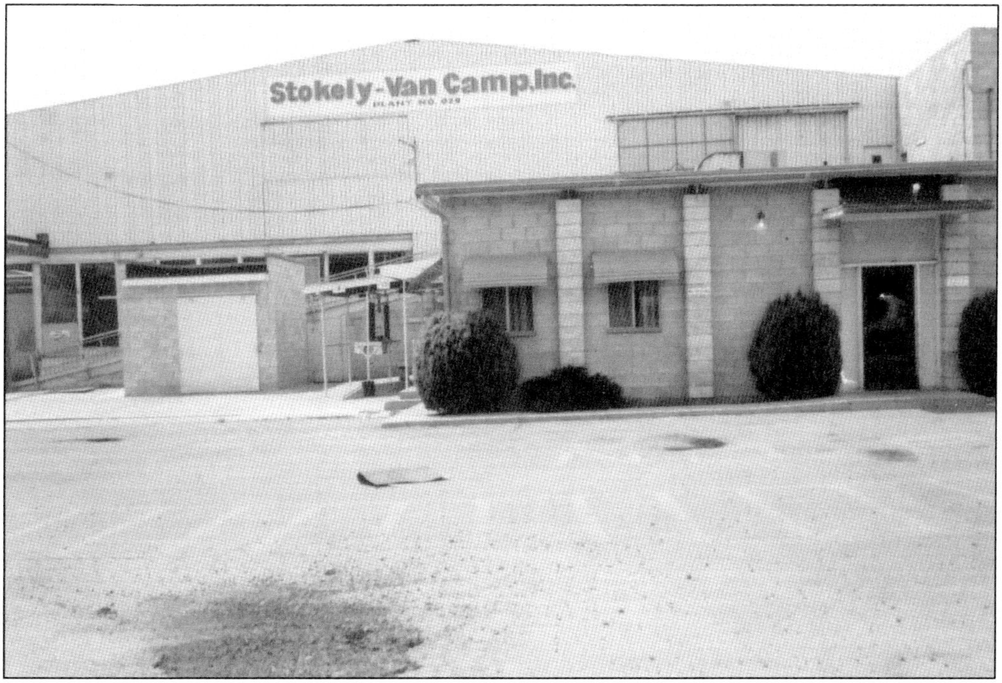

Gem Canning Company, established in 1946, produced the Indian Gem label, with products like creamed corn, sour cherries used in making maraschino cherries, apples, and juices. It was primarily seasonally operated and employed several hundred people. The plant was purchased by Stokely-Van Camp and, because of recession and a corn-flooded market, was closed in April 1980.

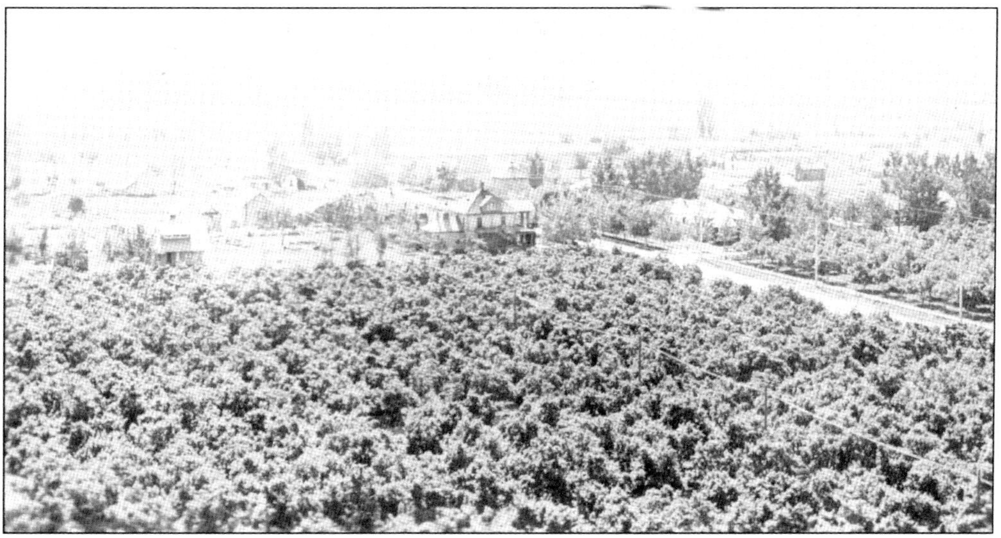

Where Emmett City Park and the courthouse are today stood Ed Hayes's prune orchard in 1894. Prunes were one of Emmett's largest fruit commodities. In September 1899, a shipment of prunes was transported down the Payette River. The barge was loaded with 1,000 crates of fruit and took 14 hours to reach its destination. This was the first shipment of fruit to be transported on the river. The railroads had not been built yet in the area; the Idaho Northern Railroad came to Emmett in 1902. Emmett, so renowned for this particular fruit, named its baseball team the Prune Pickers.

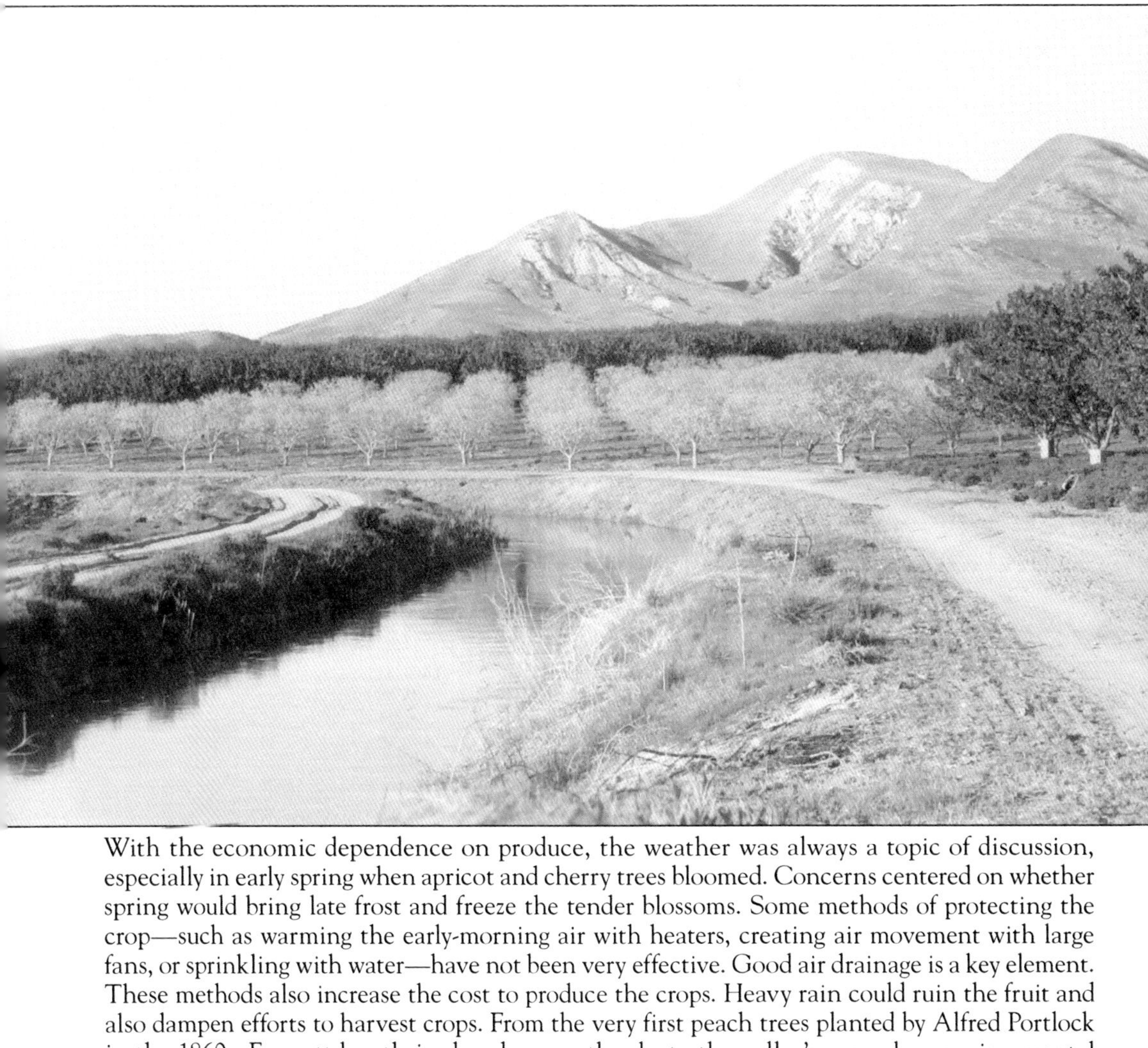

With the economic dependence on produce, the weather was always a topic of discussion, especially in early spring when apricot and cherry trees bloomed. Concerns centered on whether spring would bring late frost and freeze the tender blossoms. Some methods of protecting the crop—such as warming the early-morning air with heaters, creating air movement with large fans, or sprinkling with water—have not been very effective. Good air drainage is a key element. These methods also increase the cost to produce the crops. Heavy rain could ruin the fruit and also dampen efforts to harvest crops. From the very first peach trees planted by Alfred Portlock in the 1860s, Emmett has thrived and grown thanks to the valley's exemplary environmental conditions, which have provided the community with economic growth and sustainability. Shown here is a blossoming apricot orchard along the canal, with Squaw Butte in the distance. (Photograph by Jackson Photo Studios.)

Seven

Letha, Ola, Sweet, Montour, and Pearl

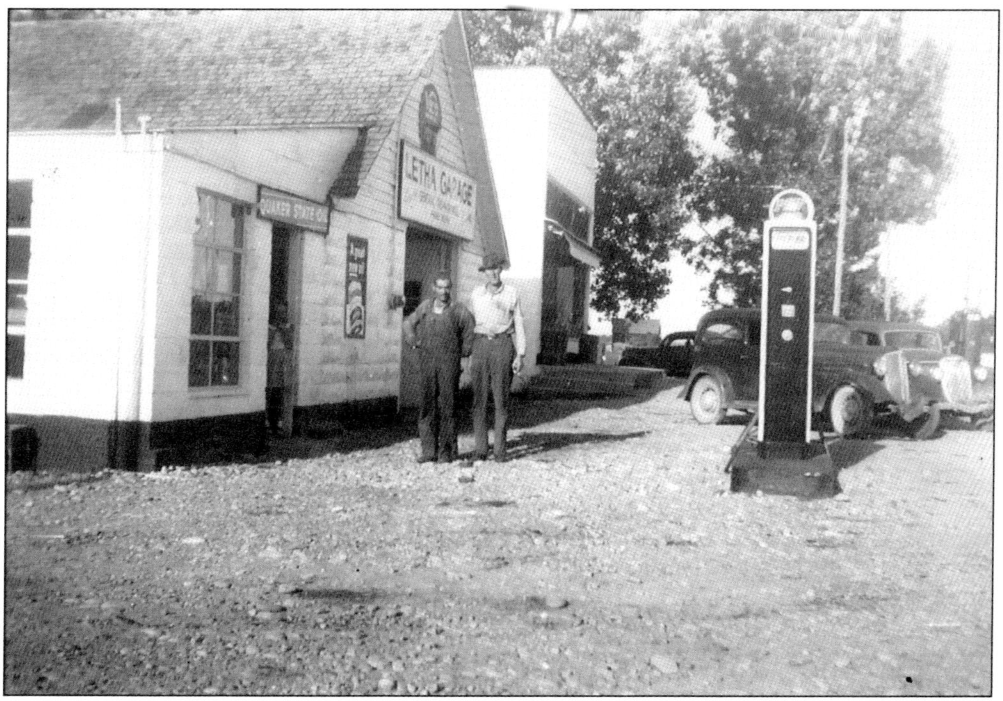

Pictured at the Letha Garage and Store in June 1947 are, from left to right, an unidentified girl, Dick Steiner, and Jiggs Ashley.

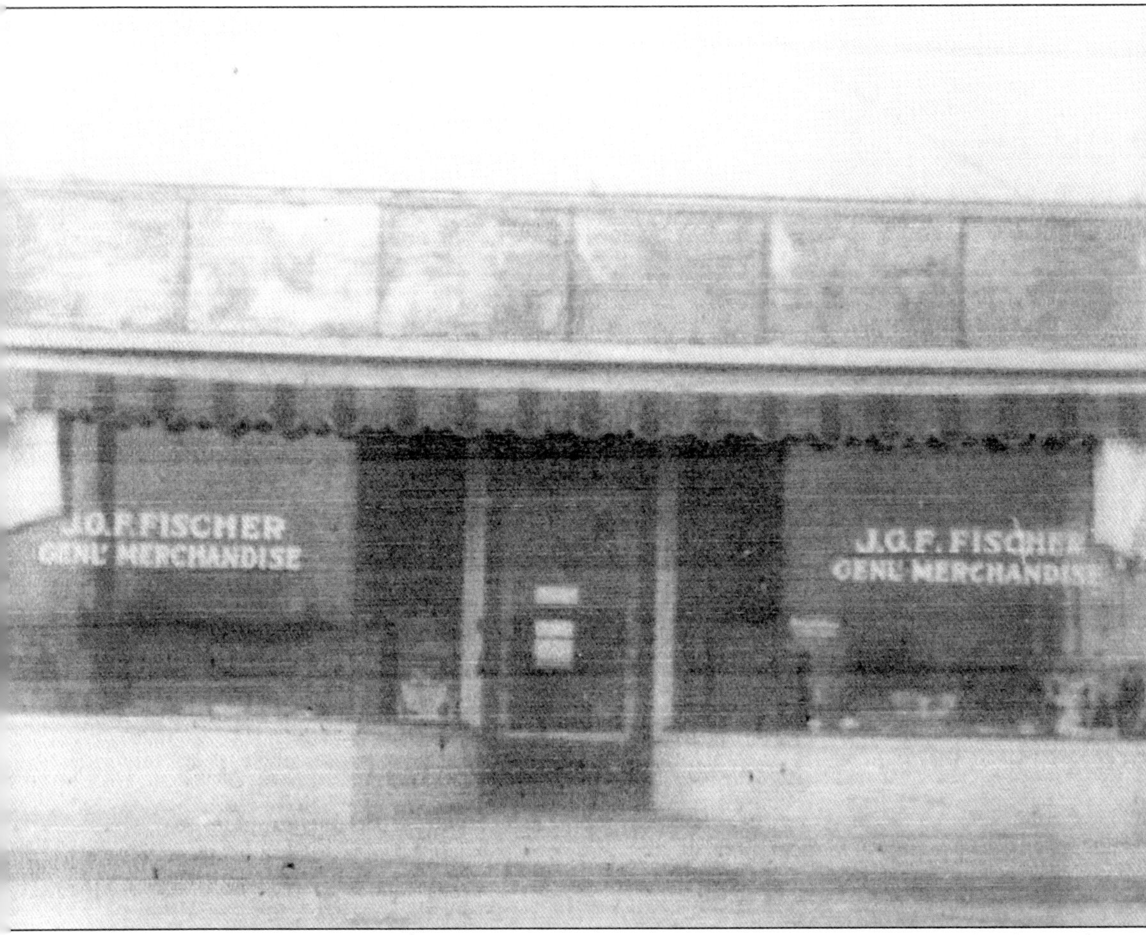

The Letha Store was built in 1929 by J.G.F. Fischer. There were two general stores, a lumberyard, an elementary school, a Baptist church, which was built in 1912, and a Church of Jesus Christ of Latter-day Saints, which was housed in a hall bought from Colonel Barnard. W.W. Wilton named the town after his daughter. He and Colonel Barnard had hoped that Letha would become a major rail center. They had the town platted and were ready to sell lots, but their dreams never materialized. It is a very rural area of farms and sheep, cattle, and horse pastures. Located nine miles west of Emmett, Letha is serviced by the other community but does have its own modern fire station. The river near Letha is a popular fishing spot, and there is good duck hunting nearby.

This area was homesteaded and settled early because of the traffic to Oregon Territory. The first school was the Anderson School, which was established in 1888. This one-room brick building served as the school for many years before Letha built a new facility in 1953, which served the community for 50 years. Today, the students are bused to Shadow Butte School, which was built in 2001 on the bench.

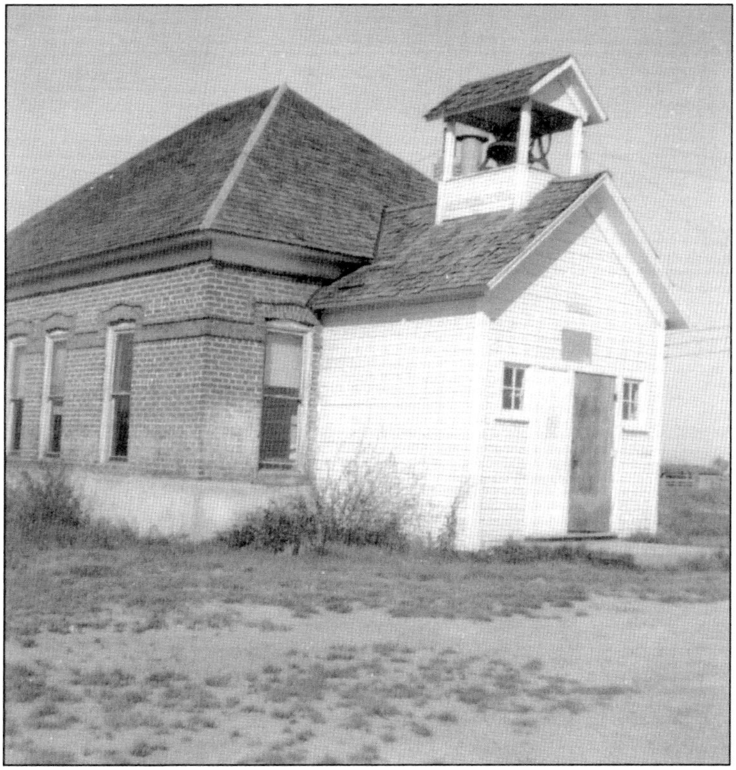

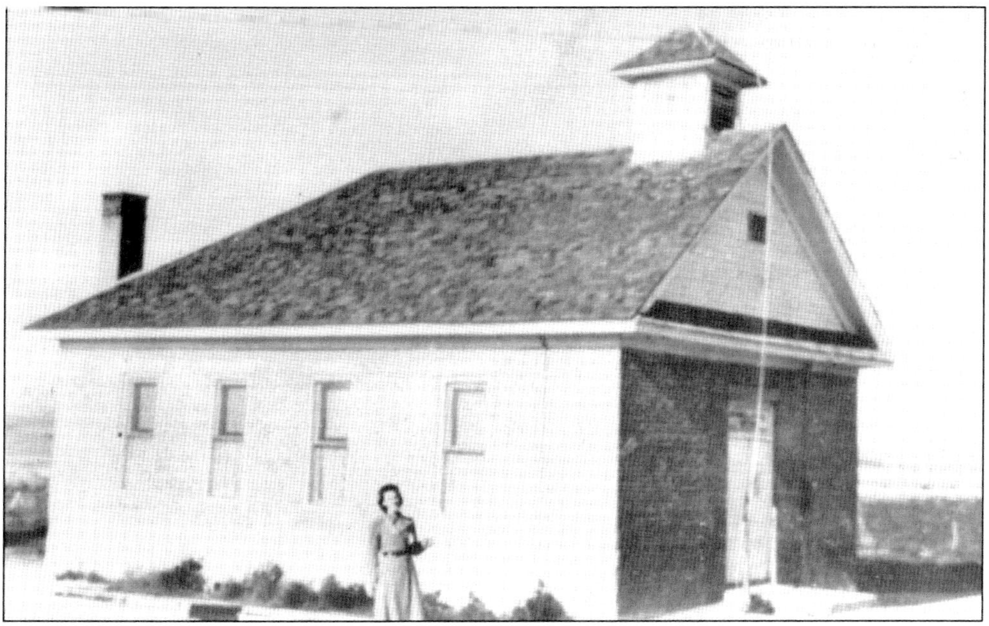

Bramwell was located three miles south of present-day Letha and was homesteaded between 1900 and 1924, after the railroad had been built between Nampa and Emmett; a railroad station, a school, and a cemetery gave it permanency. It was named after Franklin S. Bramwell, who was stake president of the Union Stake of the Church of Jesus Christ of Latter-day Saints at LeGrande, Oregon. Shown is Phyllis Hudson, a teacher in 1940. All that remains today is the cemetery.

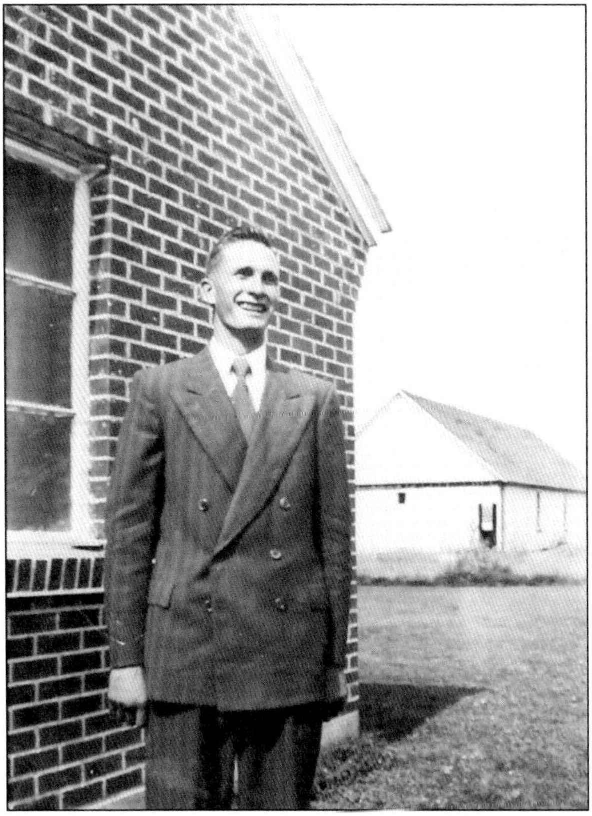

The Church of Jesus Christ of Latter-day Saints built a nice brick church in 1950 in Letha. This building has been remodeled recently, and two congregations currently meet there. Shown is Richard Jensen, a member in 1951. The former meetinghouse, originally a recreation hall built by Colonel Barnard, can be seen in the background. (Courtesy of Wenona Jensen.)

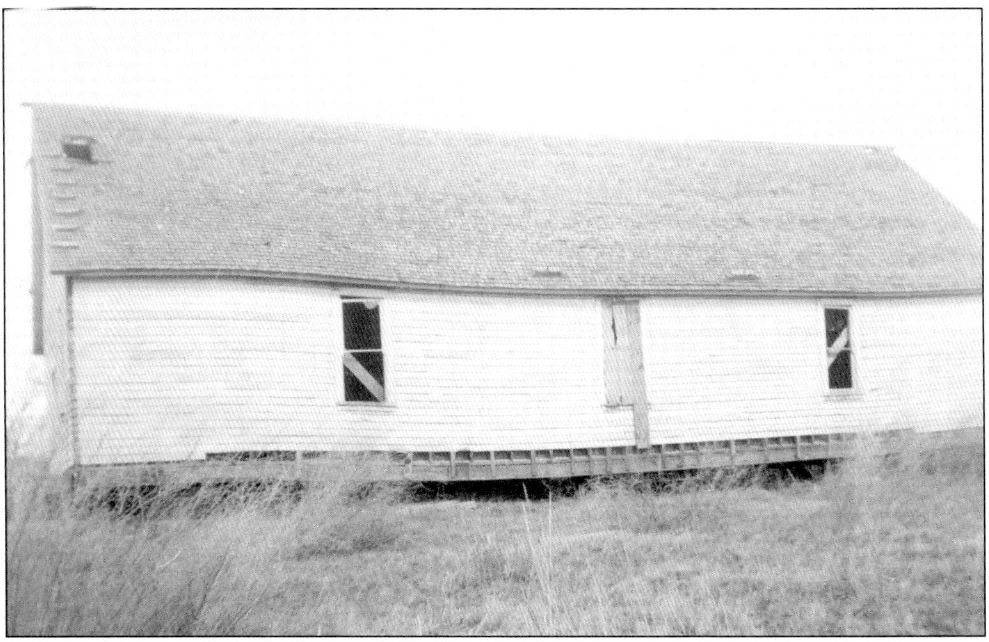

The Church of Jesus Christ of Latter-day Saints sold its former building to the Central Mesa Grange. It was moved to Mesa Road on the Emmett Bench, where it is still used today to promote the economic and political well-being of the community and of agriculture.

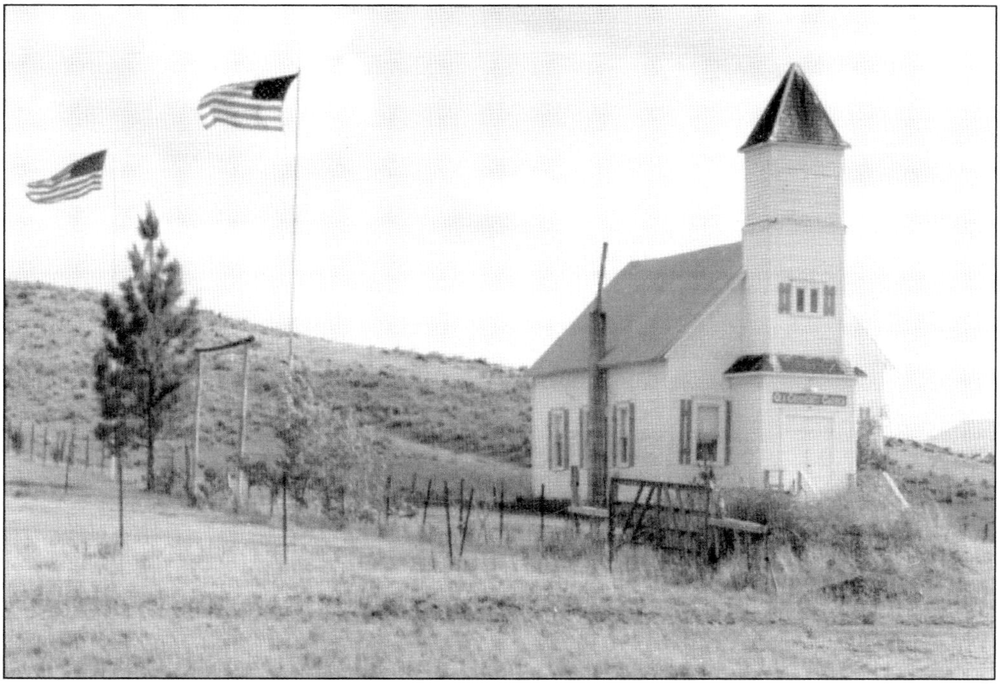

James Ballantyne brought his family with five small children in 1872 to live on Upper Squaw Creek. The family was familiar with struggle, privation, and sacrifice. Ballantyne wanted a church, so he donated the land and had this structure built in Ola in 1907. Church services, Sunday school, weddings, memorials, and performances by the schoolchildren are held here. The siding is currently being replaced by grants from the Idaho Community Foundation.

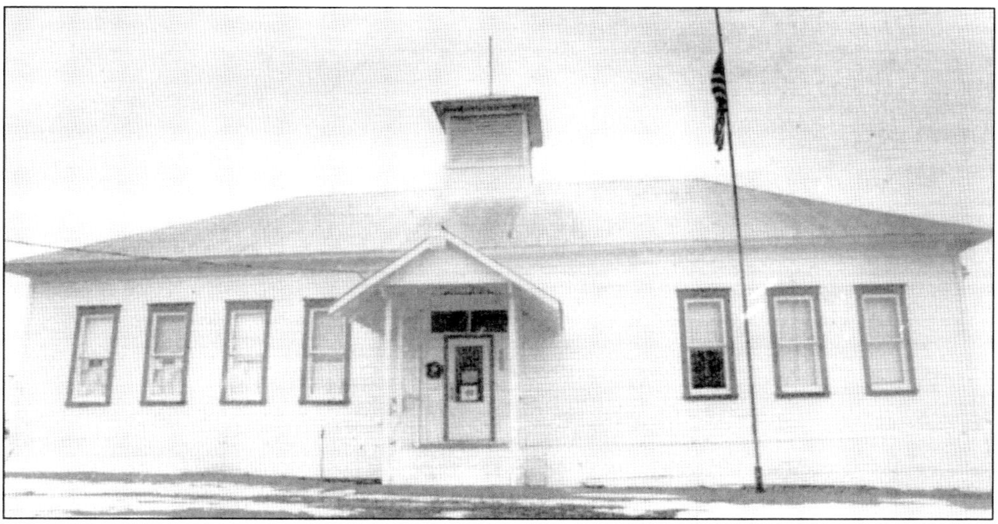

The Ola School was built by pioneers in 1910. Now, 104 years later, it is still in operation, with Amy Davis as teacher. Parents still want a good education for their children and are matching funds with the Libri Foundation, a nationwide nonprofit organization that donates new, quality, hardcover books to rural public libraries. The Ola District Library and the Ola Ladies Club donated $350 in January 2014.

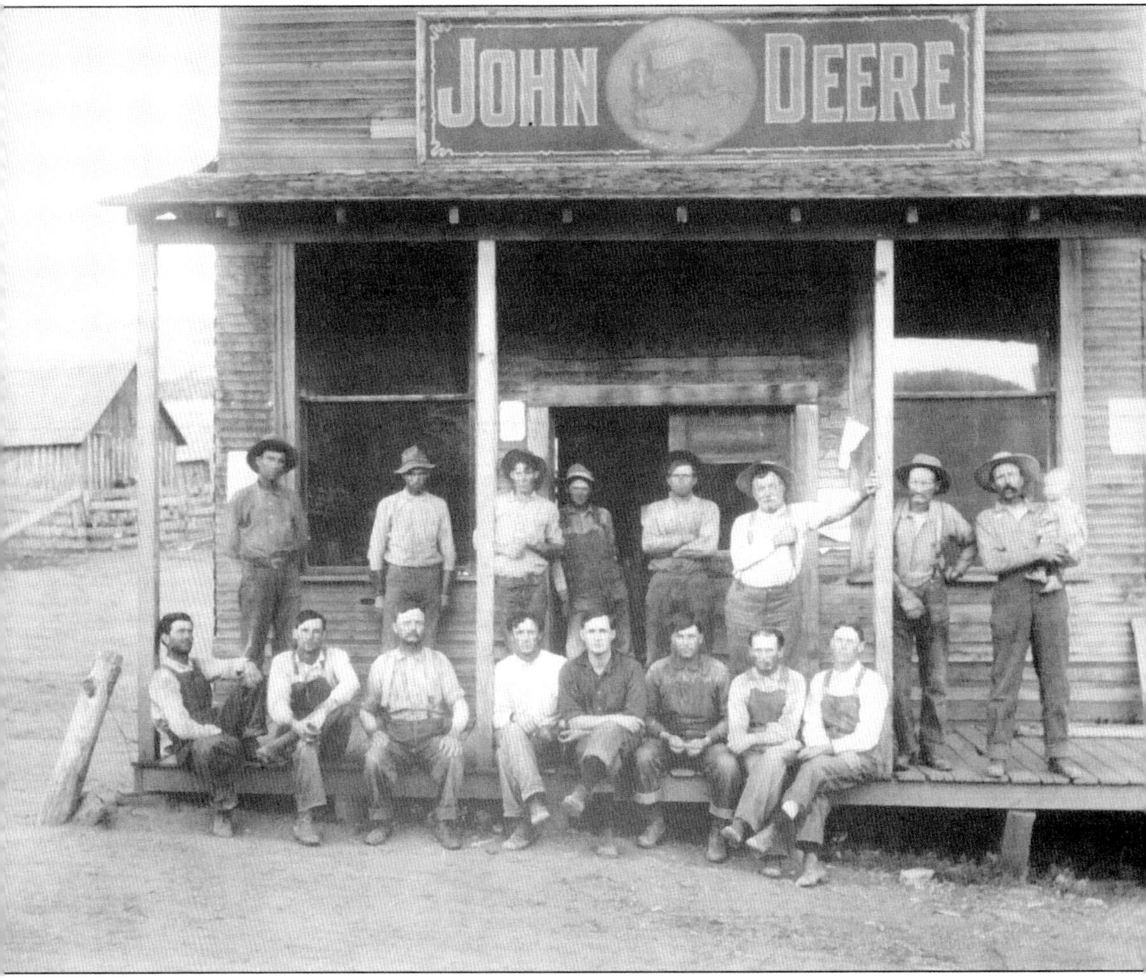

Sherman Glenn homesteaded 160 acres two miles west of Ola on his 21st birthday and proved up seven years later. In November 1902, he founded the Sherman Glenn Store at Ola and became postmaster for the first time. Matt Zapp, assessor at the courthouse in Idaho City, offered Glenn an appointment as deputy assessor in 1903. Glenn sold the store to John Holbrook and moved to Idaho City. When Zapp's two-year term was up, Glenn ran on the Republican ticket, got the job, and appointed Zapp as his deputy. He and his wife bought back the store October 1, 1908, and he served as postmaster at Ola until 1915. This 1915 image shows, from left to right, (first row) Lon Phillips, Al Symers, J.W. Cronk, Tom Whitlock, John Linebarger, Roy Shawver, Jim Cooper, and Allen Cronk; (second row) Sam Davenport, Frank Bowman, O.F. Blessinger, Roy Werton, Jim Hughes, Jim Loyd, Charley Webb, George Webb, and Asa Glenn.

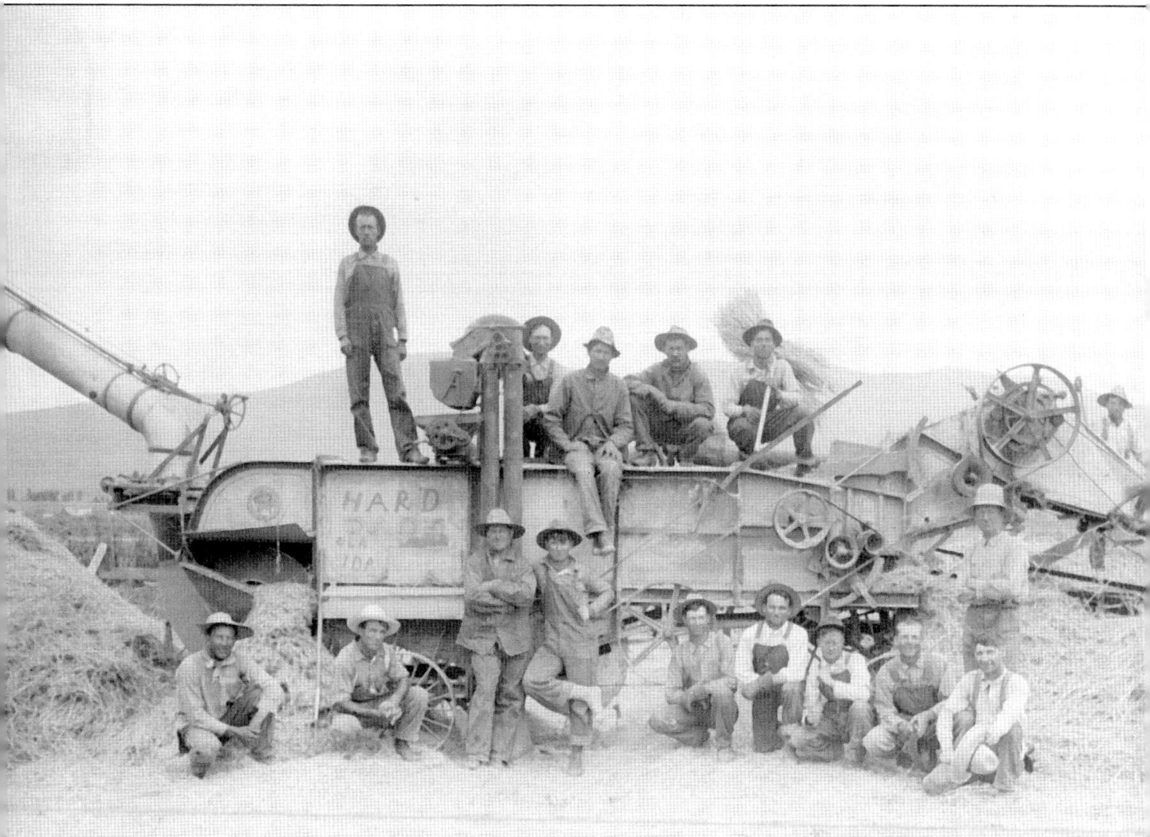

Mr. and Mrs. Lafayette Knowlton and their family settled in the Thunder Mountain boomtown of Sweet in 1905. Nell, their daughter, was working for Bill Talley's mother in one of the town's four hotels when Bill first noticed her. Bill reminisced, "I was managing the store then and was working pretty hard and was gone four or five days at a time freighting supplies from Boise by team, but we managed to find time for courting." Nell Knowlton married Bill. He mused," All of Sweet was like one big happy family. Each helped his neighbors with their work." Pictured is a work party comprised of the neighbors threshing grain in Sweet. The men are, from left to right, (on top of the thresher) Ed Lively, unidentified, Al Church, Wes Woody, Harve Douglas, and C.F. Campbell; (on the ground) Bill Yergerson, Fred Orr, Joe Amos, Durard Montgomery, unidentified, Emmett Woody, Rodney Jensen, Moral Johnson, Kelly Elliot, and Jim Knowlton.

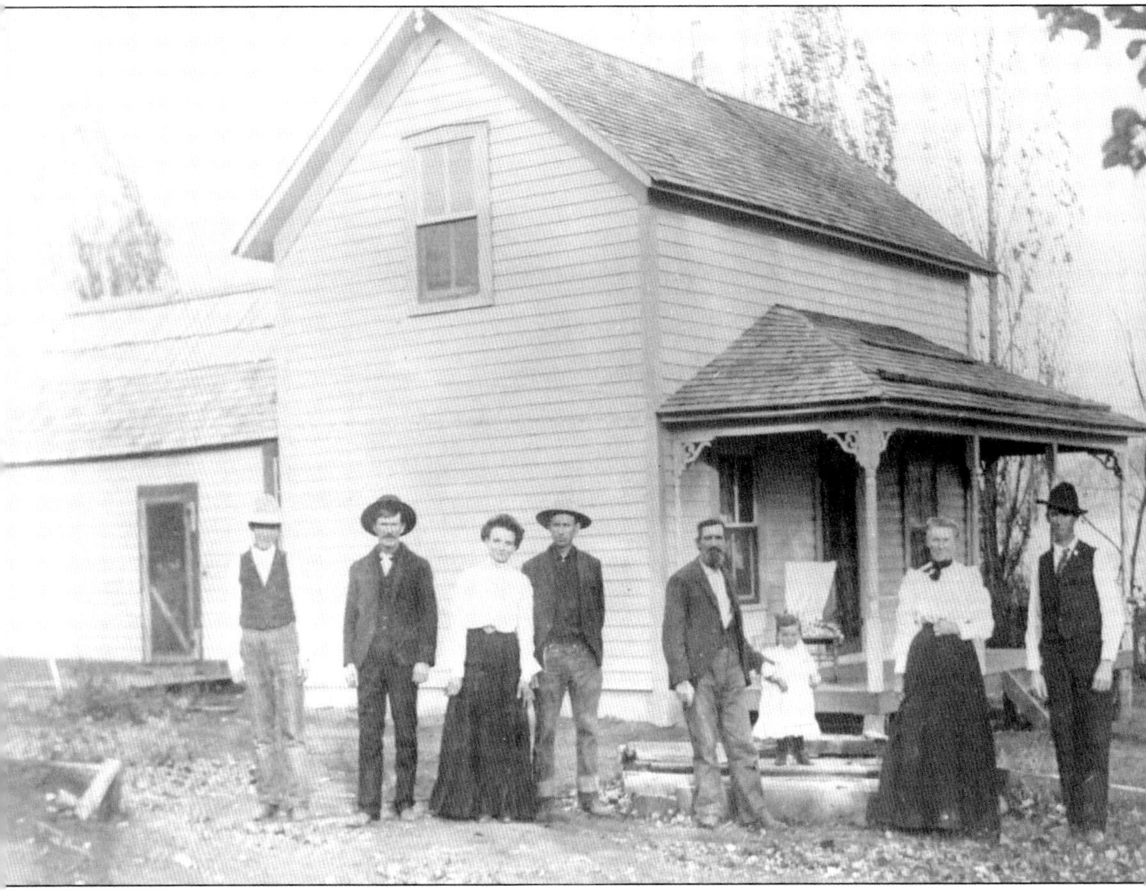

Joseph DeMasters was born January 27, 1849, in Condon, Lafayette County, Missouri. He brought his family to Idaho in 1877, located in the Boise Basin, and became involved in freighting between Kelton and the basin. Later, he moved to Oregon, but soon afterward moved back to Idaho and took up a homestead near Ola in 1888. He developed a splendid ranch and lived there until 1912, when he and his wife moved to Emmett. Seven sons were born to this family: Jesse in 1876 (in Oregon), William in 1878, Irb in 1881 (in Ola), Milton in 1884, Ben in 1886, and Claude in 1891. This photograph of the DeMasters family was taken about 1906 at their homestead ranch at Ola, Idaho. Pictured, from left to right, are Claude H., Irb and his wife, Clara, Jesse M., father Joseph H., Irb's son Frank, mother Mary S., and Ben.

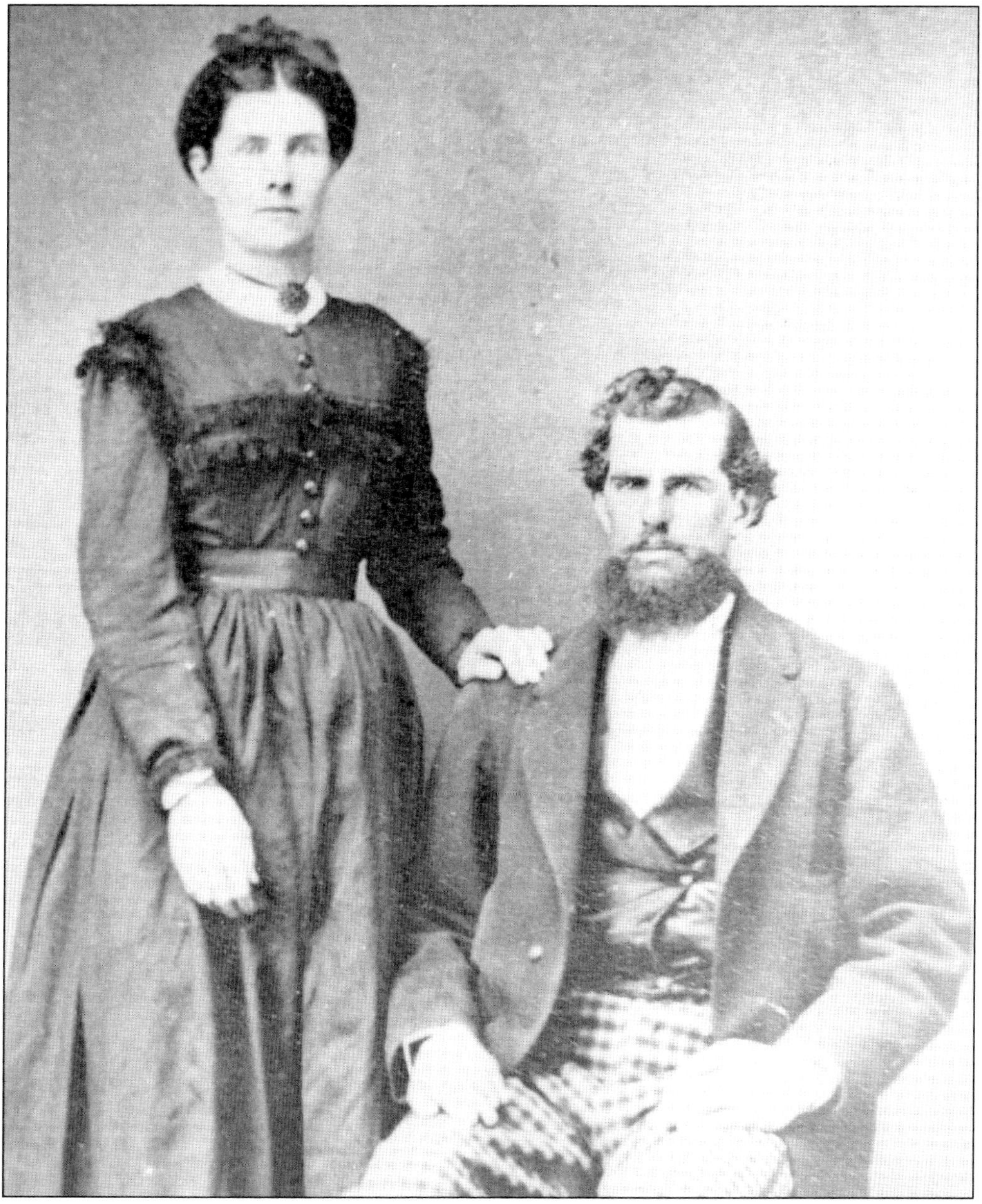

Carroll Baird homesteaded one half mile west of present-day Ola on Squaw Creek. The cabin was built where the Indian Trail crossed the creek. The trail was used by miners taking the shortcut to Oregon or the Boise Basin. Ola was established as a post office July 22, 1882, by Baird, who began homesteading and pioneering with his family when he was 10 years old and was thrilled with this homestead on Squaw Creek. Stella Baird was used to pioneering too, as her family had gone to Oregon, but considered this a lonely place as there was no other woman within 20 miles. She said, "I longed for companionship of one of my own sex." She would often be alone day after day and night after night with her small children, imagining the Indians coming to attack her. Finally, the people erected a 25-by-25-foot log fort nearby. Baird encouraged the Ballantynes and their large family to settle in the area, and gradually, other families came, and the community of Ola grew.

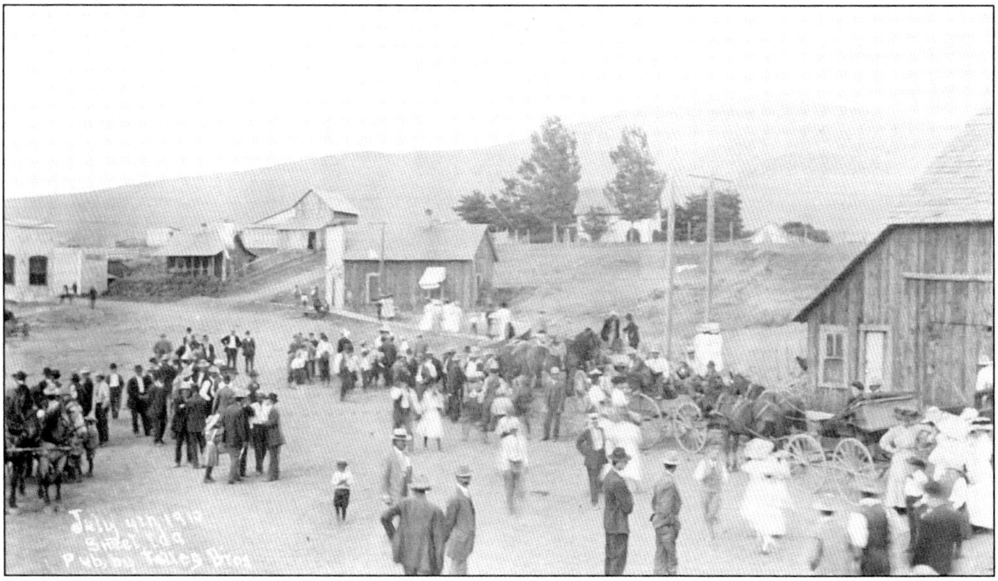

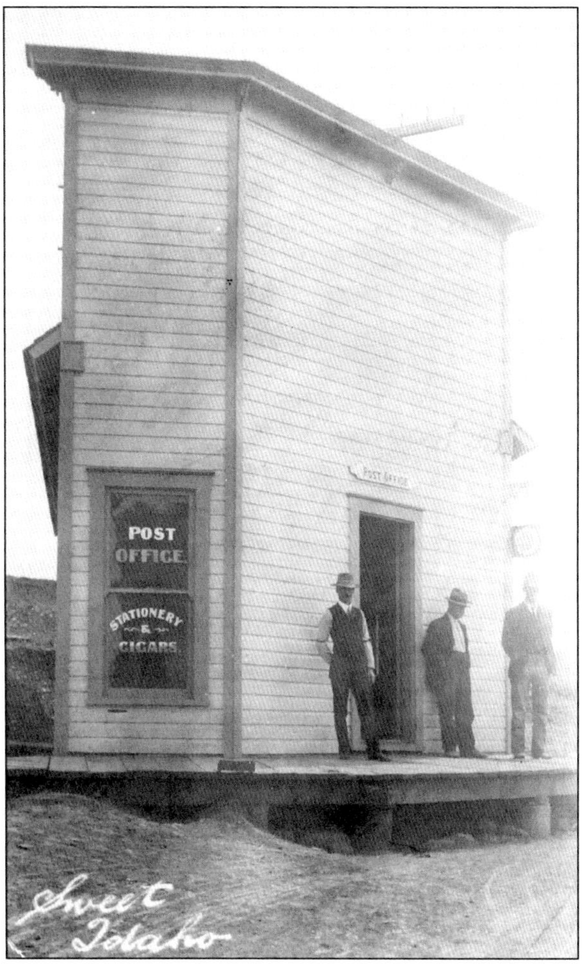

Freedom was eagerly celebrated on July 4, 1910. The Sweet community was so patriotic that it erected a large flagpole that could be seen for miles. When Old Glory flew, everyone knew it. In a severe windstorm in 1907, the flagpole came crashing down, killing W.I. "Ed" Lamb, a local saloonkeeper.

Ezekiel Sweet arrived in 1877 and settled near the east side of the foothills. Although his home was a mile from the main road, he applied for a post office and requested the name Squaw Creek. The name was rejected because it was too long, but he was such an active, dynamic person with charisma that he was eventually granted the contract even though it was not convenient for the people. When he reapplied, he kept it short and requested Sweet.

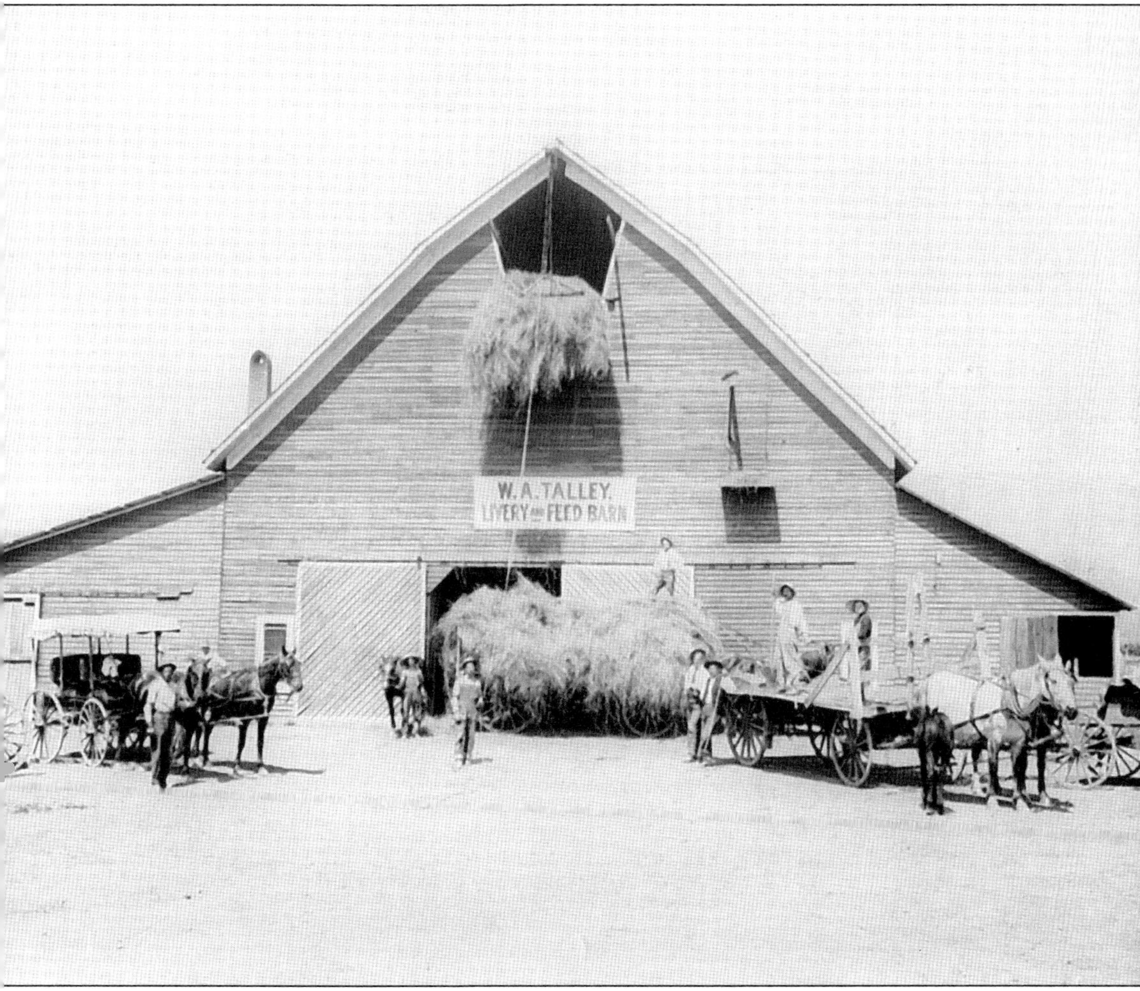

The Talley family probably had a greater hand in the early development of Sweet than any other of the sturdy pioneers who settled there. The Talleys started their business in April 1905, with William A. "Bill" and his brother Gilbert as members of the business. Bill lived at his Sweet home for 82 years, 22 years of which he operated a general merchandise store while his father ran the livery. William A. Talley was born in Smith County, Kansas, the youngest son of Wesley A. and Emma White Talley. When he was two years old, they followed Wesley's brother John Talley to the Sweet Valley. They came by rail to Caldwell, when track was still being laid there, crossed the Payette near Emmett, went up over the big butte, and came down into the grassy flatlands along Squaw Creek. When Gem County was created in 1915, Bill served a term on the first board of commissioners by appointment from Governor Alexander to serve the unexpired term of Sam Connaughton and his position as chief anesthetist to Drs. Clark and Cummings when they performed surgery.

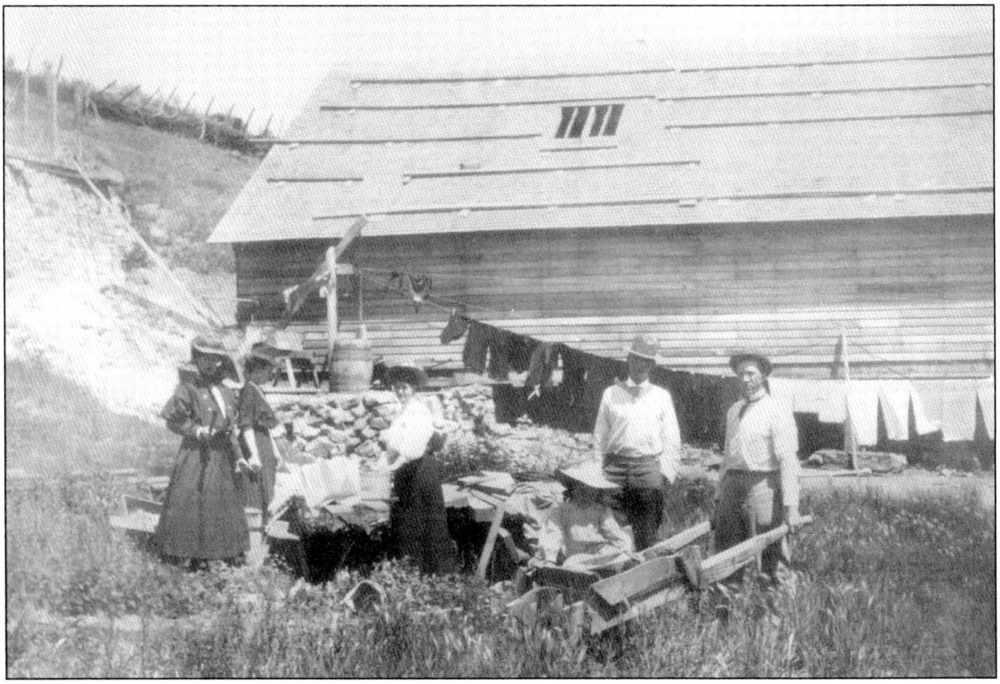

The warm springs has blessed many people. The Indians used it to clean fish. George Croats used it to grow fruits and vegetables. Brian Neilson built several cisterns for cooling. Laundry was done here. Roy Stone built the hotel. Pictured at Roystone in 1909 are, from left to right, Angie Larkin, a Mrs. Seeds, Rilia Peery, Fred Larkin, and Frank Brown at Roystone in 1909. Current owners are the Johns family.

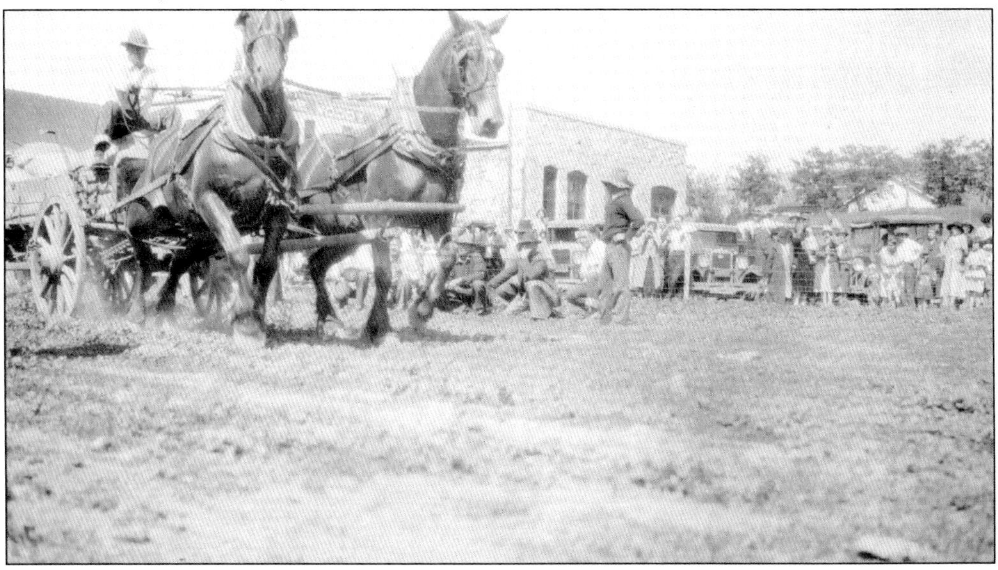

Horses were vital to the development and settling of the West. Charles Biggers is seen participating in a horse-pulling contest on July 4, 1932, in Sweet. Settlers would challenge each other to see which team could pull the most weight. Since July 4 was a day of celebration, this was a good time to hold the competitions. The hard part in a competition like this was to make sure all the variables were equal. (Courtesy of Kennie Lynn Klingback.)

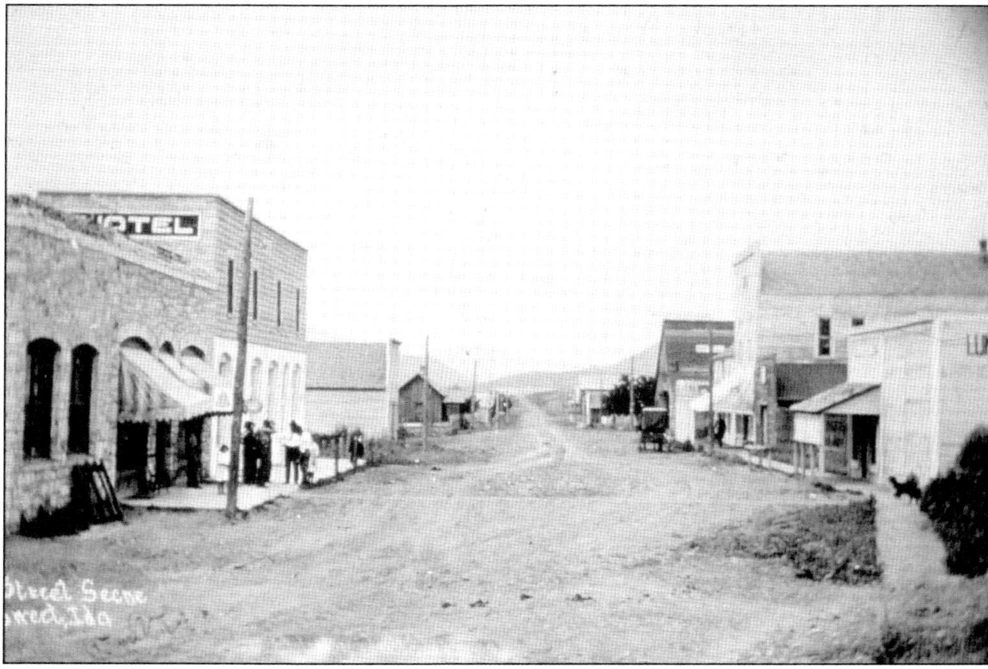

Trade and commerce thrived on this heavily traveled route in Sweet to the mining districts to the north and east. The Woody Hotel was built in 1899 from lava rock and lumber. There were three other hotels at this time. When a fire ravaged the town in 1924, the second story of the Woody suffered major damage and was removed. The remaining structure was reroofed with a slant roof.

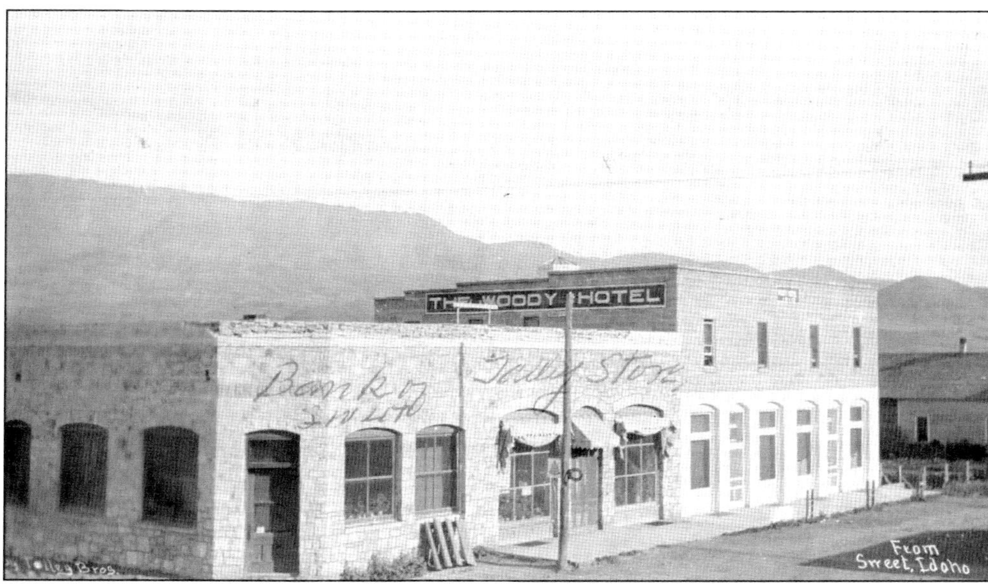

The Bank of Sweet was a welcome business to the growing town of Sweet, Idaho, in 1907. The name was later changed to the Farmers & Stockgrowers Bank. By 1920, it was moved to Montour, which seemed to have the most potential because of the location of the railroad there, but closed by 1934 because of unforeseen circumstances caused by the Depression.

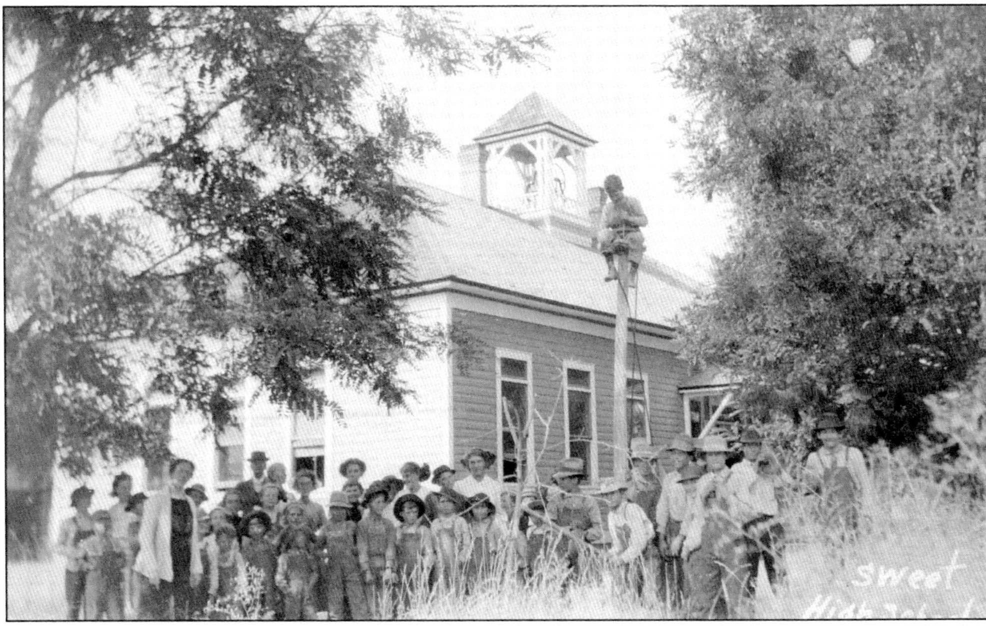

Schools were needed for the rising generation. The first school was built in 1905 using lumber supplied by the Pugh mill at Dry Buck. A Mr. Smith was the first teacher. It was a struggle because of distance, weather, and the lack of transportation, but school was held three months of the year. The settlers knew how important it was to be able to read and write.

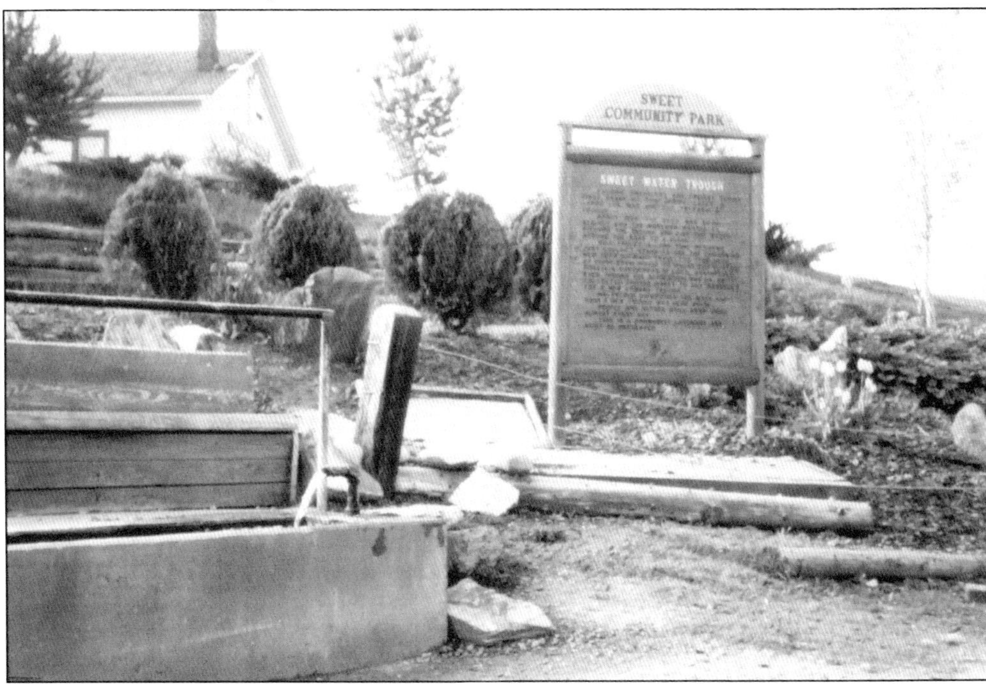

Sweet may be the only city with a licensed and active water right to a spring. Hand-drawn maps from the 1850s list the area near present-day Sweet as "Sweet Water," a notation that reflected the abundance of springs in the valley. The original Sweet water trough utilized a hollowed log, but it was later replaced by one made of concrete. The pure, clear water is still in demand.

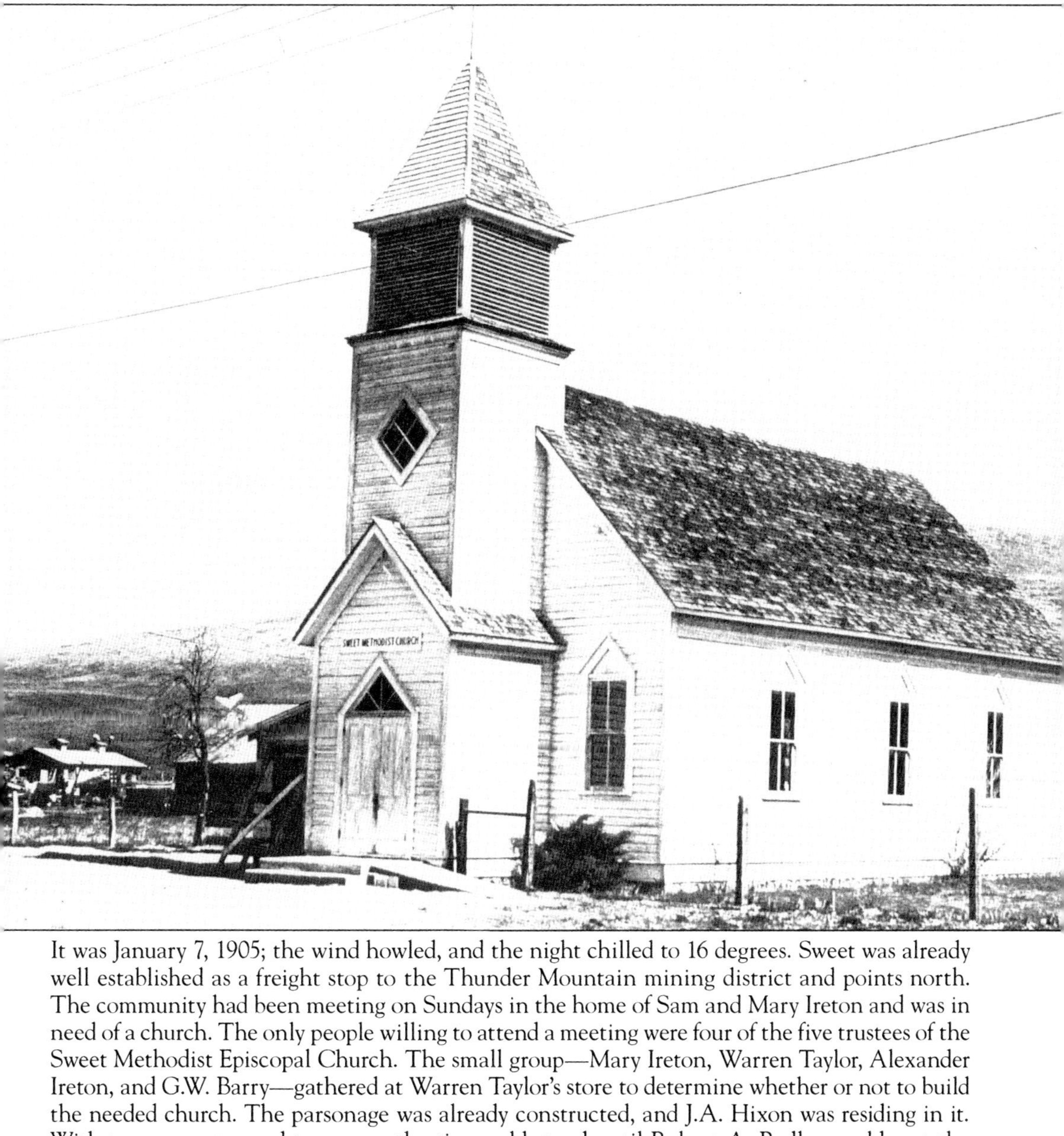

It was January 7, 1905; the wind howled, and the night chilled to 16 degrees. Sweet was already well established as a freight stop to the Thunder Mountain mining district and points north. The community had been meeting on Sundays in the home of Sam and Mary Ireton and was in need of a church. The only people willing to attend a meeting were four of the five trustees of the Sweet Methodist Episcopal Church. The small group—Mary Ireton, Warren Taylor, Alexander Ireton, and G.W. Barry—gathered at Warren Taylor's store to determine whether or not to build the needed church. The parsonage was already constructed, and J.A. Hixon was residing in it. With two yea votes and two nays, the tie would stand until Robert A. Badley could cast the deciding vote.

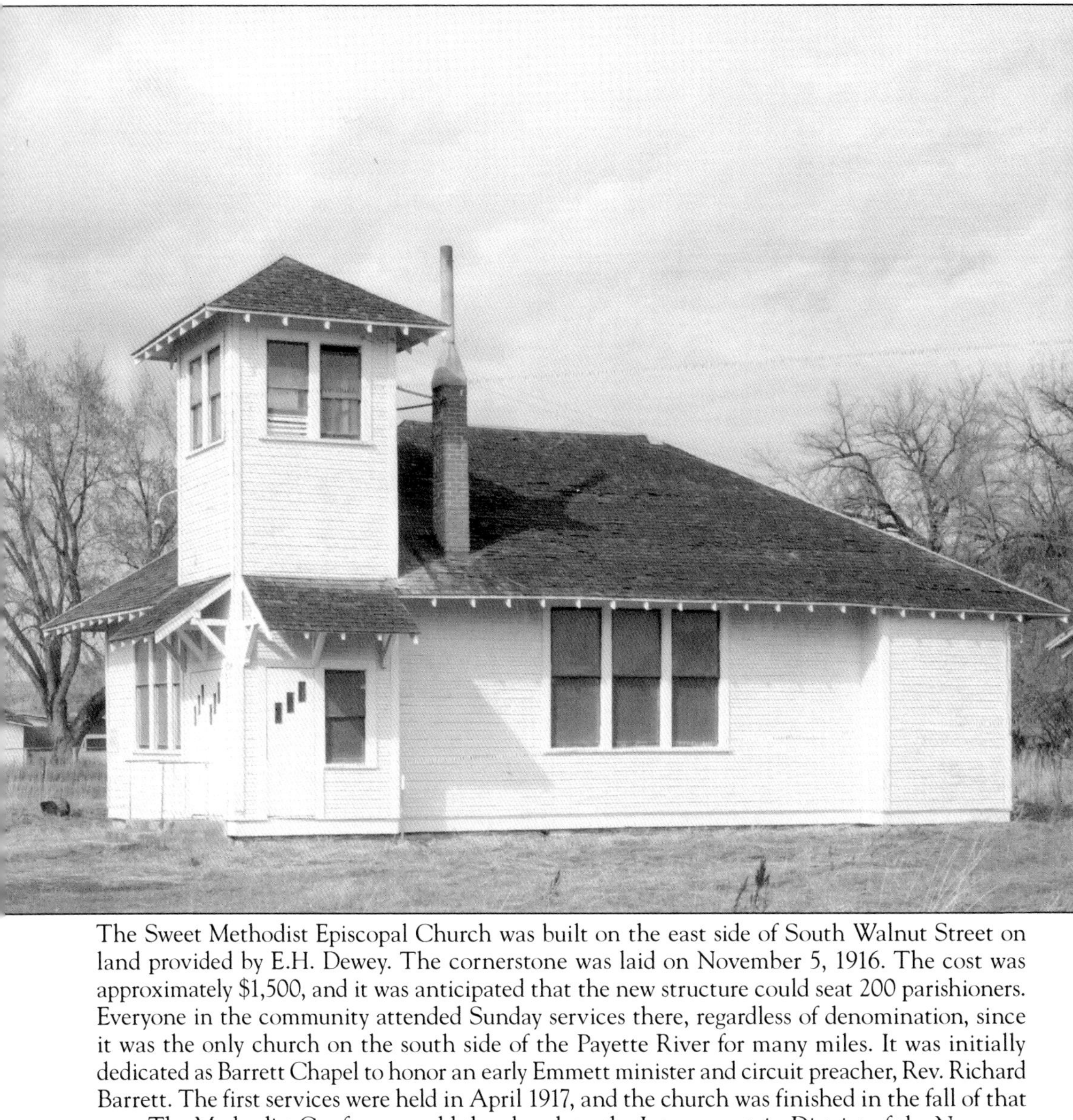

The Sweet Methodist Episcopal Church was built on the east side of South Walnut Street on land provided by E.H. Dewey. The cornerstone was laid on November 5, 1916. The cost was approximately $1,500, and it was anticipated that the new structure could seat 200 parishioners. Everyone in the community attended Sunday services there, regardless of denomination, since it was the only church on the south side of the Payette River for many miles. It was initially dedicated as Barrett Chapel to honor an early Emmett minister and circuit preacher, Rev. Richard Barrett. The first services were held in April 1917, and the church was finished in the fall of that year. The Methodist Conference sold the church to the Intermountain District of the Nazarene Church. The communities of Sweet and Montour were separated by a river, so there were many duplications in services, even though they were only three miles apart.

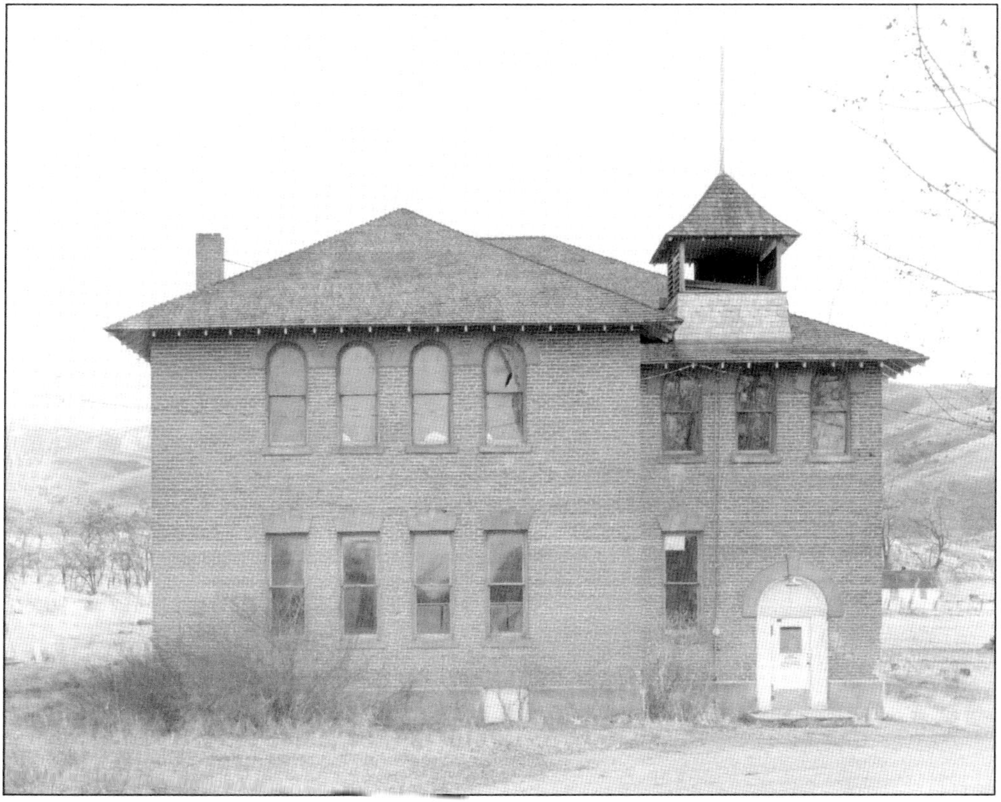

When E.H. Dewey platted the townsite of Montour in 1911, he made provision for the school. It was located at the southeast corner of Broadway and Park Street. Constructed in 1913, it was funded by a $6,700 bond issue. High school students were added in 1924, eliminating the need for them to spend the school year away from family at the Weiser Institute.

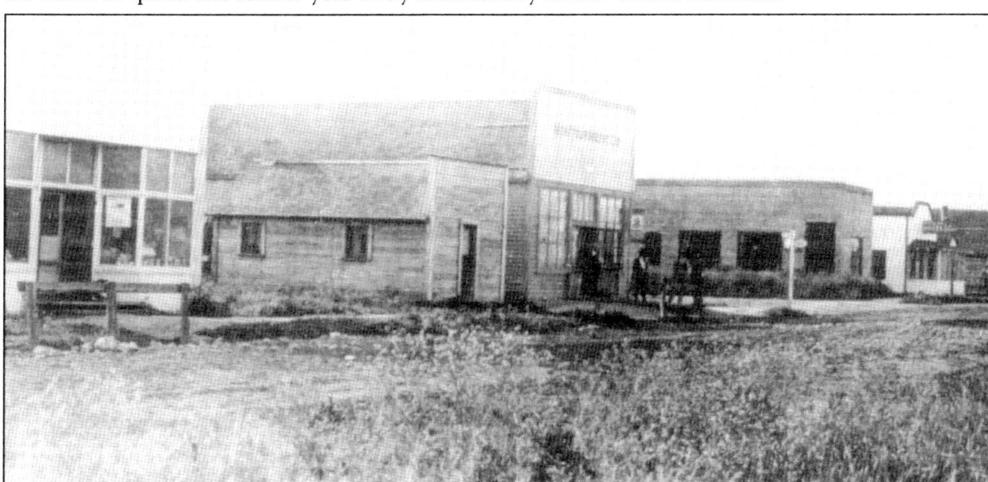

Frank E. Volkmer purchased a commercial lot in 1914 and opened the Montour Mercantile. In 1920, the Montour Mercantile, Brown Trading Company, and Butte Hardware of Sweet merged and became the Butte Trading Company, with Harry Sweet as president and general manager. By 1945, the firm was out of business, and the creditors were assigned the title.

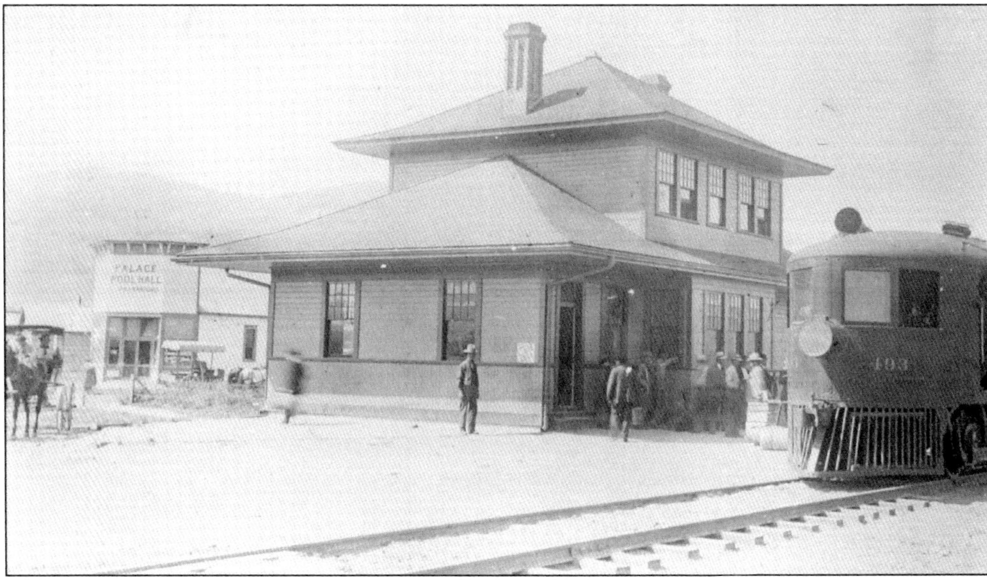

Eager to develop a rail route to the lucrative Thunder Mountain Mining District, Colonel Dewey began lofty plans in 1902 for the Idaho Northern Railroad to extend from Emmett to McCall. Mid-July brought the first train carrying railroad officials. The depot was constructed in time to serve regular passengers by September 1912. It was a railhead for thousands of cattle, horses, hogs, sheep, and turkeys.

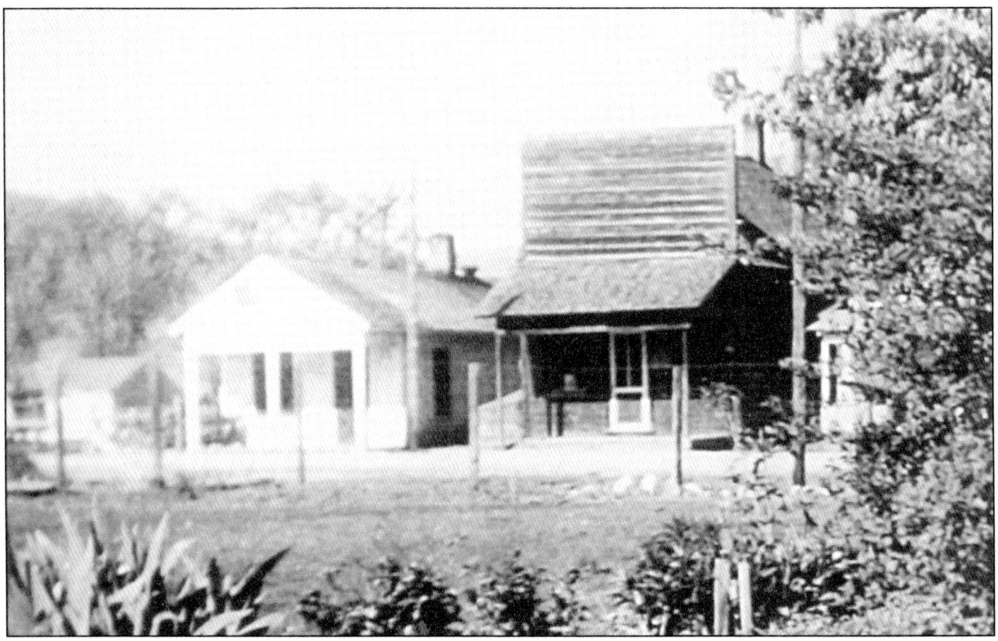

The original post office began in 1871 in a corner of the Marsh-Ireton home. Later, a simple white structure was built to serve as the post office, and Esther Palmer filled the role of postmistress from 1920 to 1958. Her long service and dedication to the community in part led to her defiance of the relocation order in 1978 from the Bureau of Reclamation, which bought out other local homeowners in an effort to fix flooding caused by Black Canyon Dam in Montour. Palmer refused to sell and continued to live here all her life.

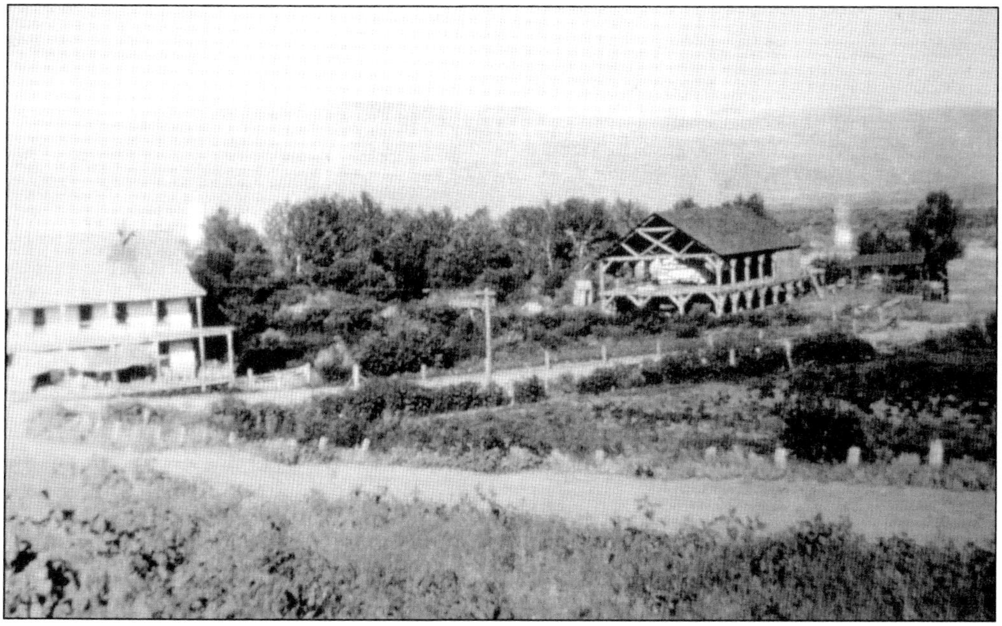

Built in 1896, the Kenna Plowman sawmill maximized the natural features of the Payette River. At a point where the river channel widens and drops, Plowman was able to construct a holding pond for the logs and a housing station for the electricity-generating turbine. As he was very enterprising, he also built a hotel. After his death, the mill was closed in 1907 and sold in 1910.

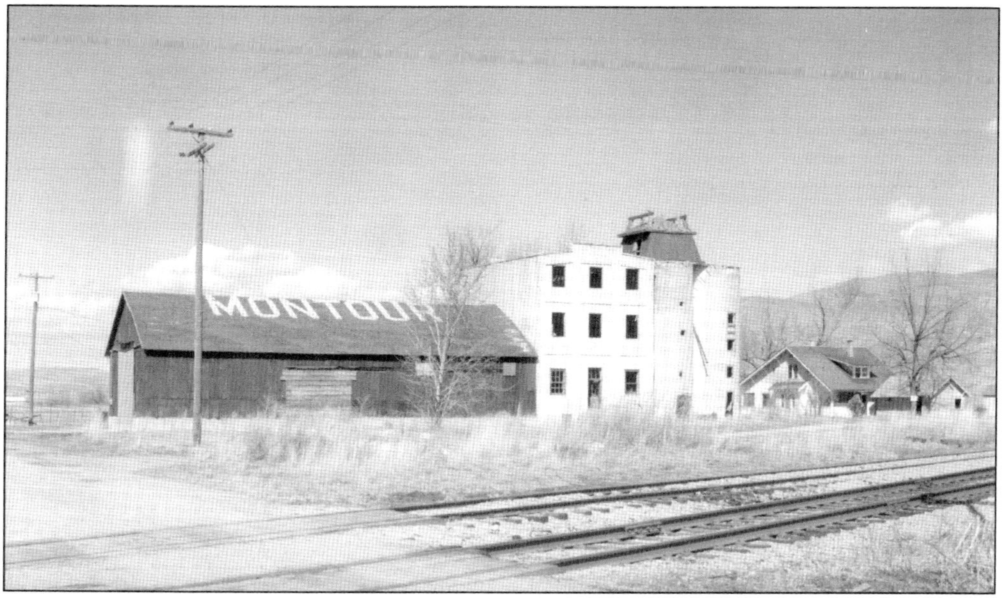

Harvey Pugh pursued a teaching career, and in the off-season, he worked for Bill Parish at the sawmill in Dry Buck. Late in June 1900, a fire destroyed the mill, and Pugh negotiated the purchase of the equipment. There was a great deal of growth around 1912. E.H. Dewey wanted the railroad to reach the Thunder Mountain goldfields. People were moving into Montour, so there was a lot of demand for lumber, which Pugh was willing to supply from his new mill in Dry Buck.With the expansion of 1912, he built the lumberyard and supplied the valley. After the sale of the sawmill in 1915, Pugh added the elevator and flour mill and built his new home.

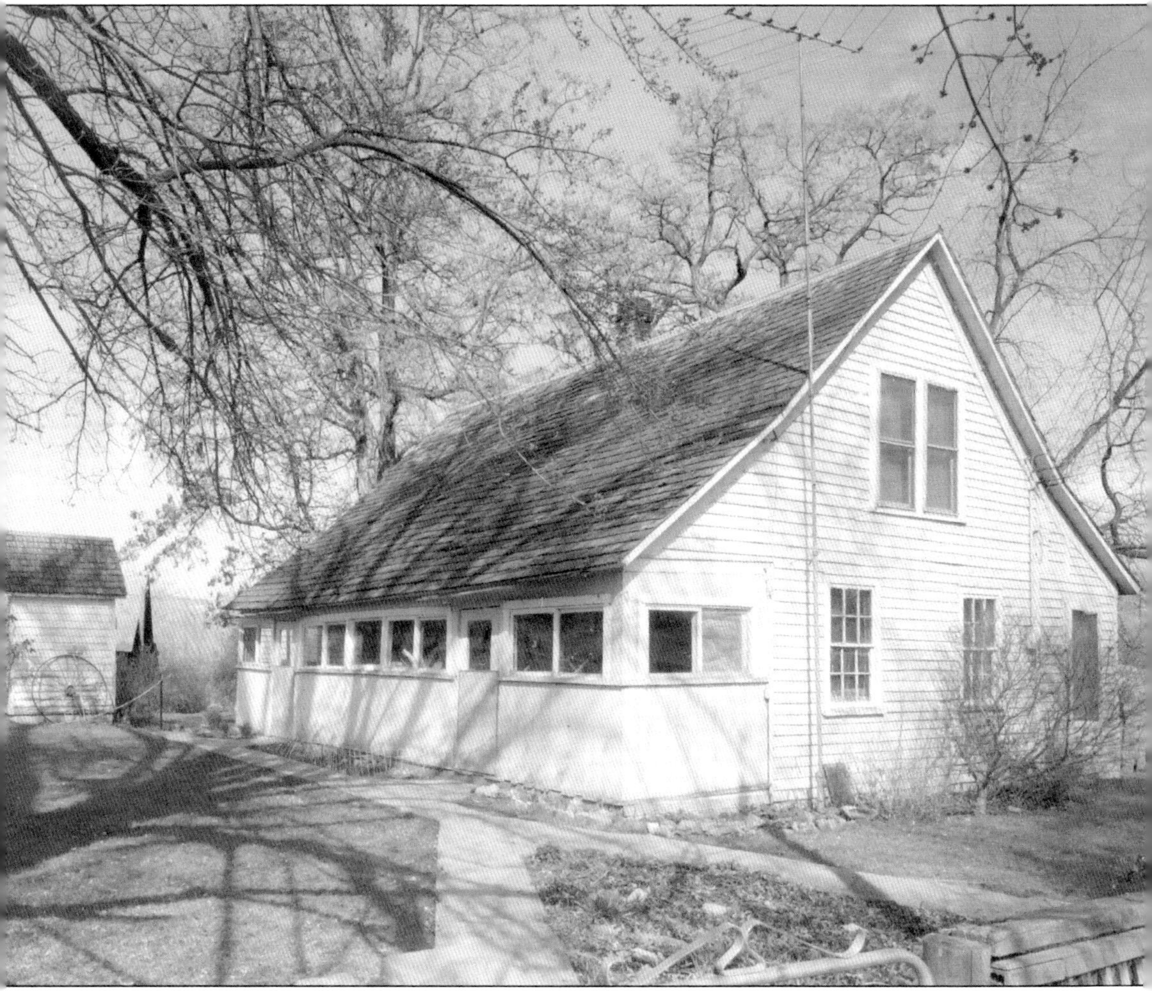

In 1862, gold was discovered in the Boise Basin. The western route to the basin included a treacherous hill that led to the lush valley known then as Squaw Creek. The Buoner and Reeves stage stop was established to allow men and beasts to rest after the difficult descent. By the 1870s, John Ireton had arrived from Clermont County, Ohio, and become a partner with William Mitchell and Edson Marsh. After Ireton married Marsh's half sister Josie in 1878, the duo of Marsh and Ireton bought out Mitchell, and the ranch began in earnest. By the time this picture was taken, Edson Marsh and the John Ireton family had left the valley. The ranch was sold in 1902 to Dr. Platt from Philadelphia. Within five years, he failed to make it profitable, and the ranch was returned to the Iretons. E.H. Dewey bought it in 1910 on behalf of the Idaho Northern Railroad and the future townsite of Montour. F.A. and Lucile McConnell bought the home and remaining land and eventually sold it to their son Alva in 1967.

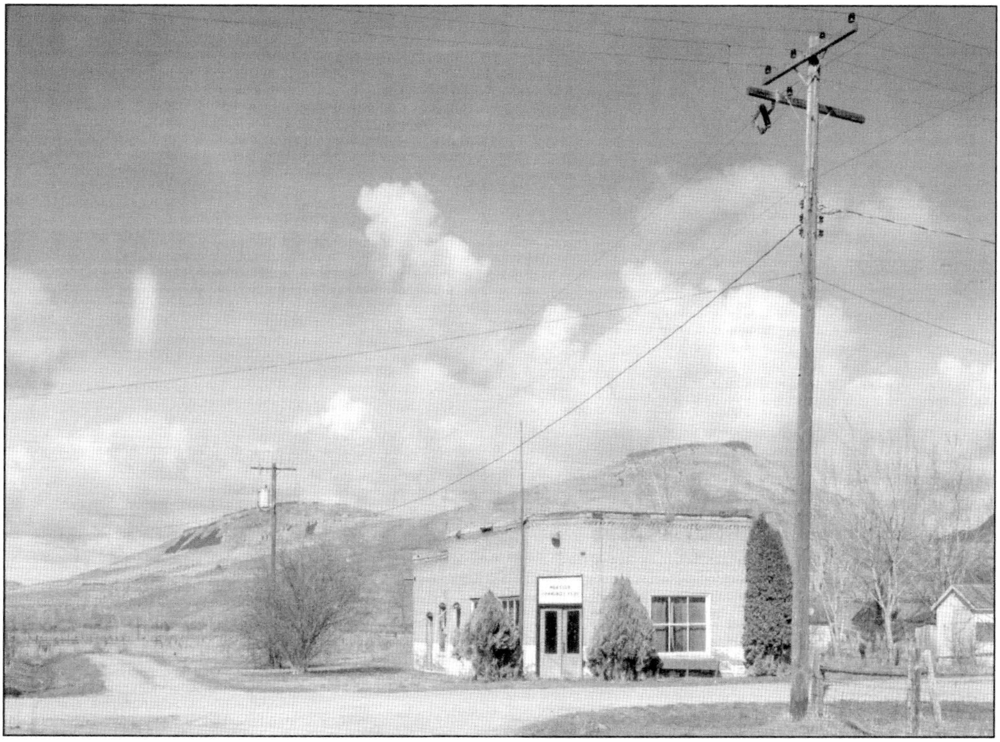

The former Bank of Sweet was acquired, reorganized, renamed, and relocated to Montour as the Farmers & Stockgrowers Bank of Montour under F.I. Newhouse in 1920. The bank was voluntarily liquidated in 1933, and in 1934, the deed went to C.D. Newhouse. The building transferred to H.A. Pugh in 1937, and to the Montour Ladies Aid Society in 1945.

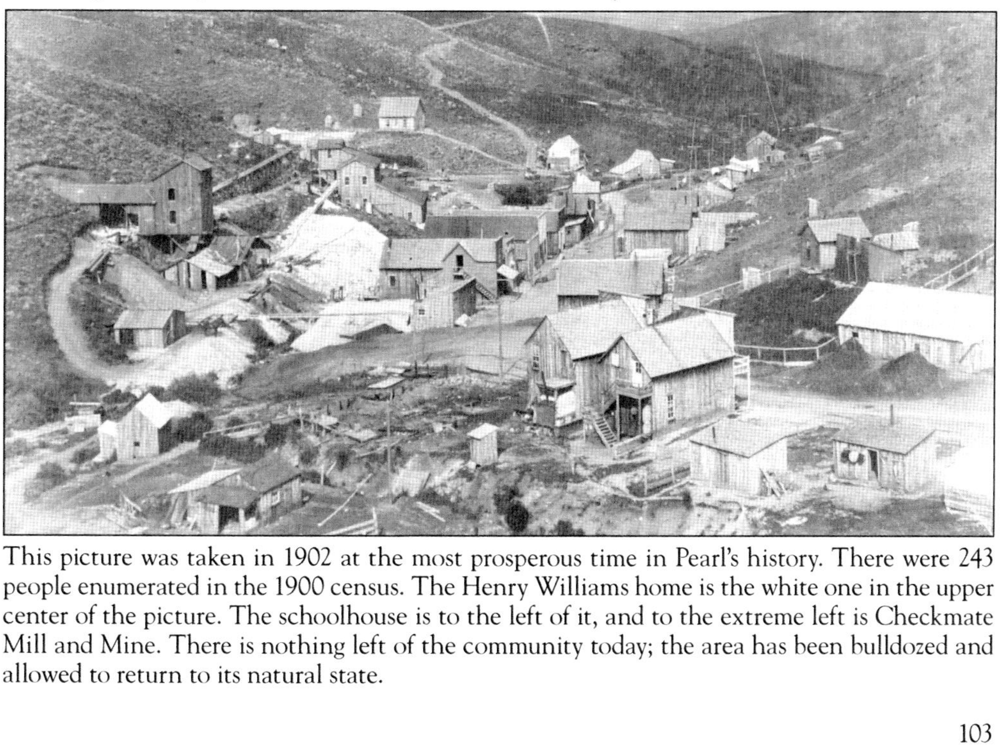

This picture was taken in 1902 at the most prosperous time in Pearl's history. There were 243 people enumerated in the 1900 census. The Henry Williams home is the white one in the upper center of the picture. The schoolhouse is to the left of it, and to the extreme left is Checkmate Mill and Mine. There is nothing left of the community today; the area has been bulldozed and allowed to return to its natural state.

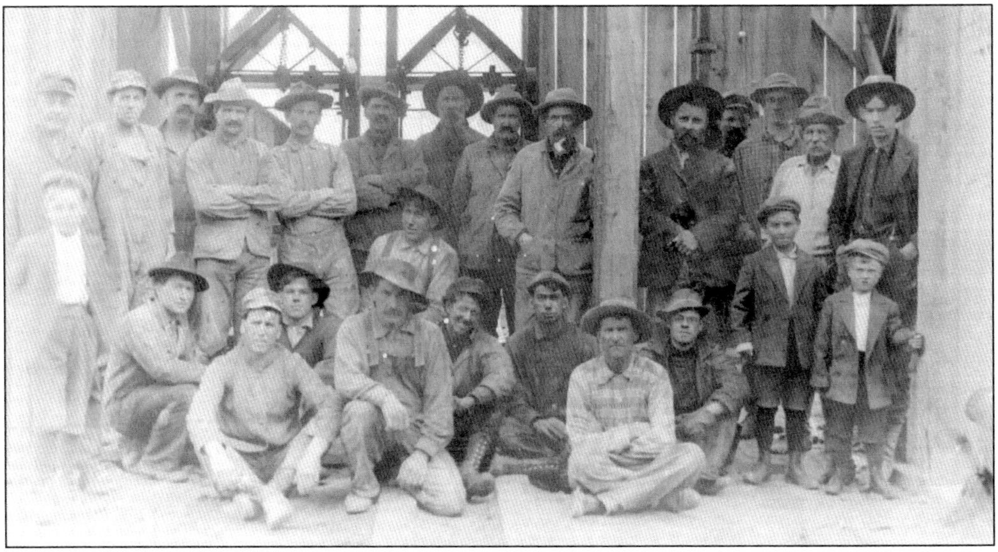

This is the Checkmate Mill and Mine crew. It was 1895 before even the crude methods of quartz operations were undertaken. Concentrators were then introduced into several of the mills of the district with the most satisfactory results. The camp then had a few steady producers and had shipped more ore and bullion than any mines in southern Idaho. With the completion of the Idaho Northern Railway to Emmett, it became the distribution point for the Pearl District. Merle Wells, in his book *Gold Camps and Silver Cities*, notes, "The mines became productive in 1894 yielding $30,000, followed by $80,000 in 1896."

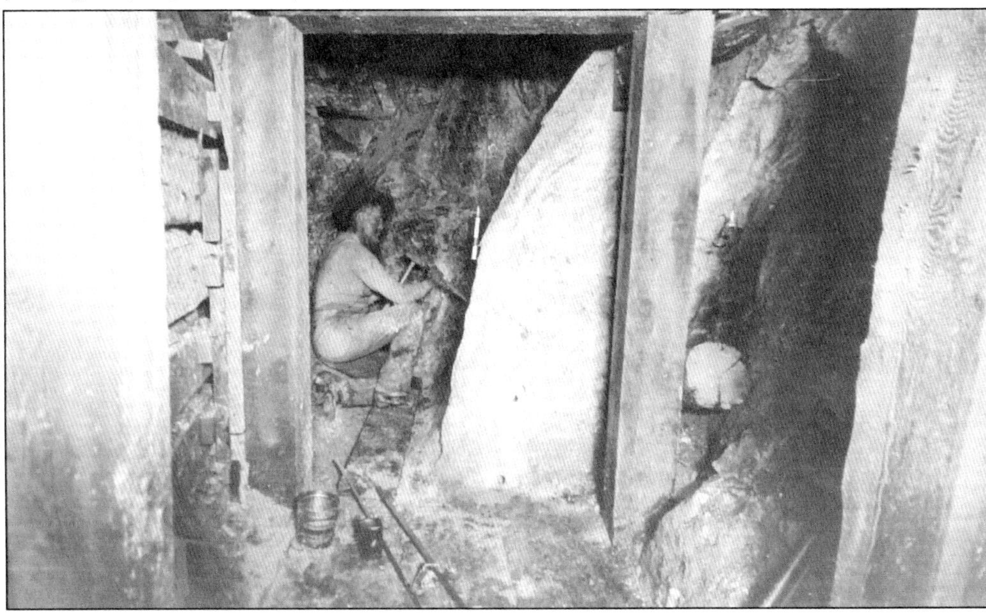

"Big Don" MacAskill works in the mineshaft to extract ore. Don was born in Nova Scotia and married there. He and his wife, Emma, moved several times and came west and settled in the boomtown of Eureka, Nevada. Eureka's ore gave out, however, and people moved on. In about 1902, Don and Emma moved to Pearl, Idaho, after having lived in Eureka for about 25 years. They remained in Pearl until Don's death in 1915. At that time, Emma moved to Star. Both are buried in the Pearl Cemetery.

Eight

Timber

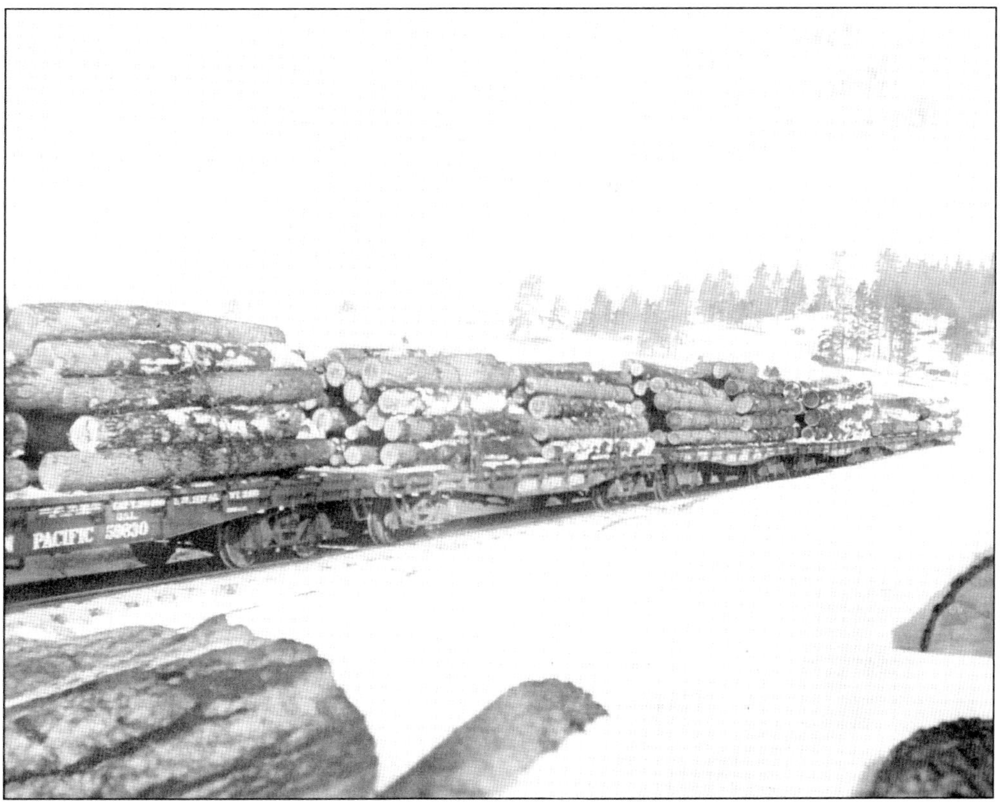

The completion of the railroad was a big boon to the logging industry. No longer were there log drives, which were dangerous. Logs could get lost or hung up on sandbars or sustain damage if they were sent down the river. With the use of trains, all of the logs got to the mill and were turned into lumber.

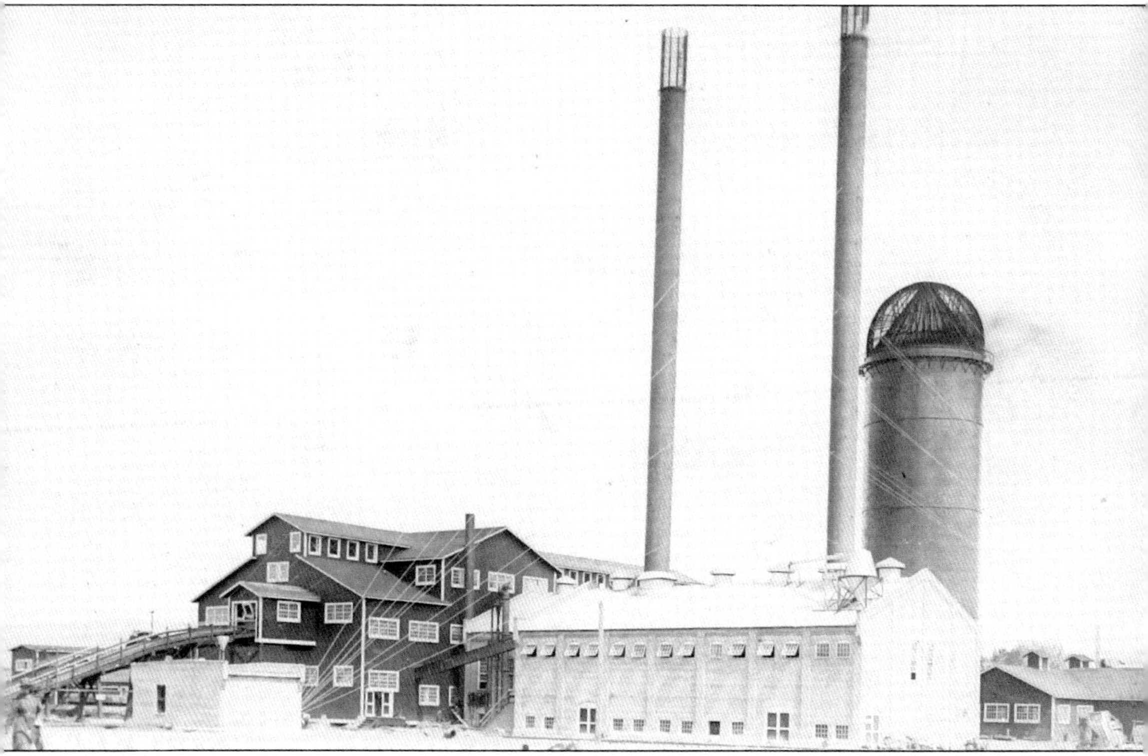

The sawmill was the mainstay of the economy in Emmett for 94 years. An estimated 1,500 workers were employed at the height of its operation. Boise Cascade operated a sawmill, plywood plant, cogeneration power plant, and a beam-manufacturing facility in addition to running sawmills at McCall, Cascade, Horseshoe Bend, and Council. One by one, the mills were closed as they failed to make a profit, and in 1982, even the sawmill at Emmett was shut down. The plywood plants and the cogeneration plant operated until 2001. The beam plant was able to operate another 10 years. That facility was moved to a more modern plant in Homedale in 2011. Closure of the Emmett facility was due to the lack of economic viability, decreased demand for housing, and the decreased supply of timber due to policy changes by the national forests.

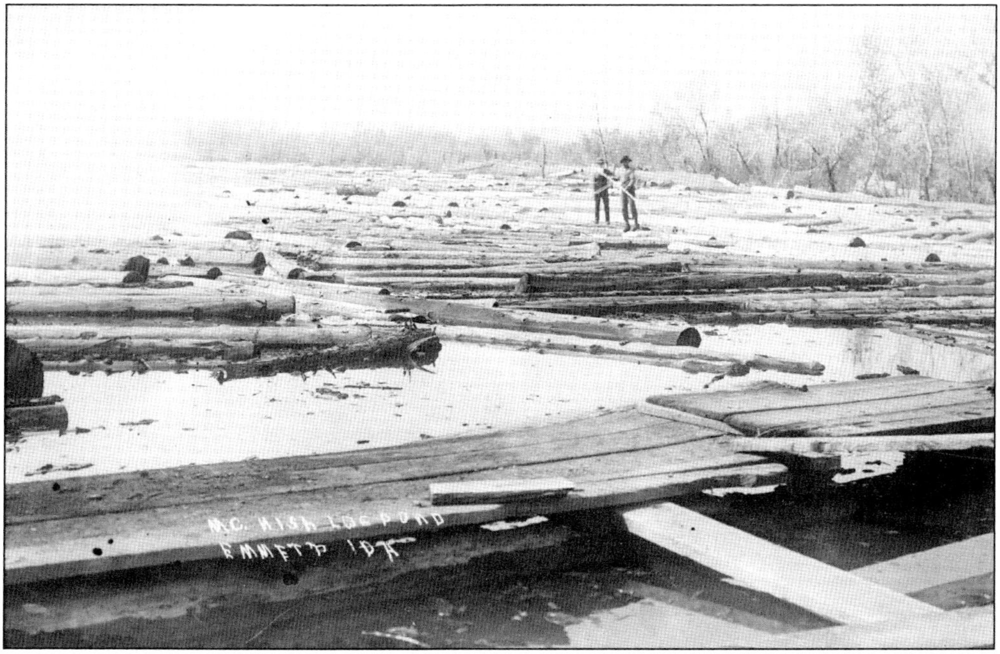

McNish and Allen owned a sawmill, which had been built by Basye-Walker in 1883. In 1909, the mill had an annual output of six million board feet. In 1917, the Boise Payette Lumber Company purchased this mill and built a bigger one. This was a time of expansion and growth as lumber was in great demand. (Courtesy of the Idaho Historical Society, No. 73-199.12.)

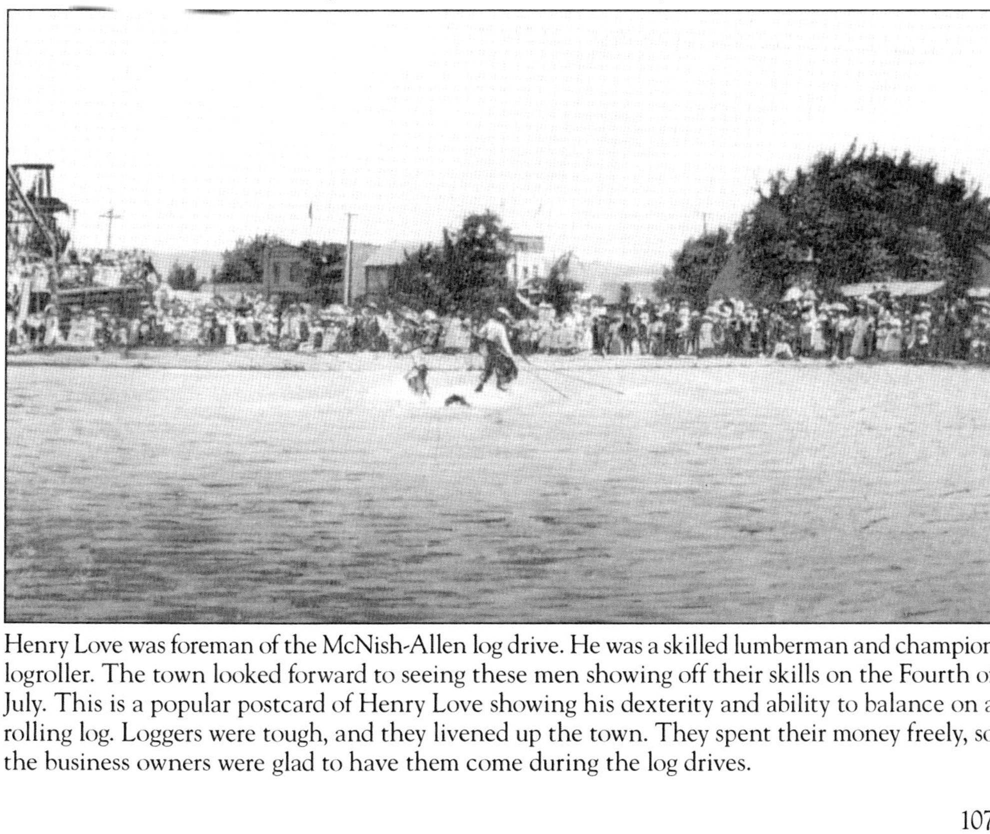

Henry Love was foreman of the McNish-Allen log drive. He was a skilled lumberman and champion logroller. The town looked forward to seeing these men showing off their skills on the Fourth of July. This is a popular postcard of Henry Love showing his dexterity and ability to balance on a rolling log. Loggers were tough, and they livened up the town. They spent their money freely, so the business owners were glad to have them come during the log drives.

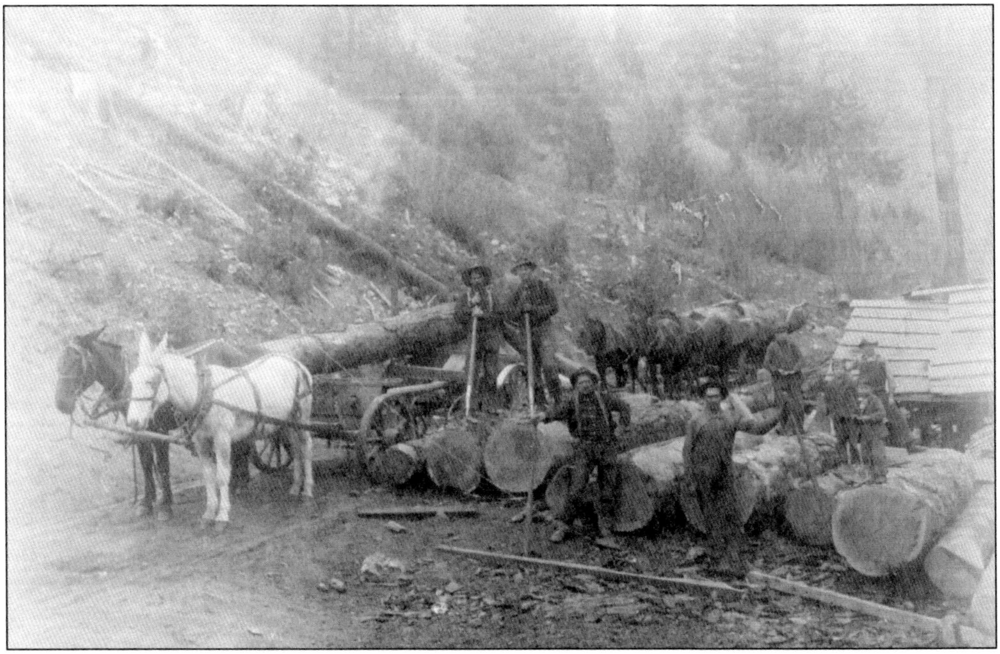

Horses and mules were used in logging. An article that appears in the March 8, 1906, *Index* states "that four million feet were cut last year. Very little was sent out of town. Probably the largest out-of-town order was from the Lincoln Mine at Pearl . . . Every particle of slabs, strips and chunks used for fuel has been cleaned up, an unusual occurrence at this time of year."

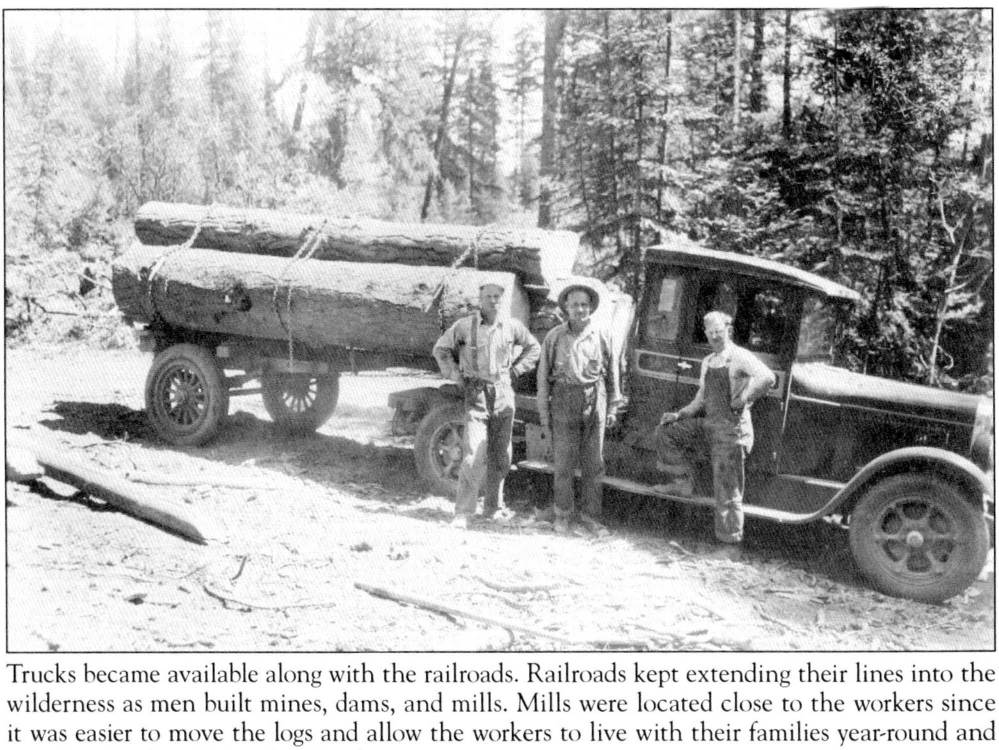

Trucks became available along with the railroads. Railroads kept extending their lines into the wilderness as men built mines, dams, and mills. Mills were located close to the workers since it was easier to move the logs and allow the workers to live with their families year-round and provide schools and churches for them.

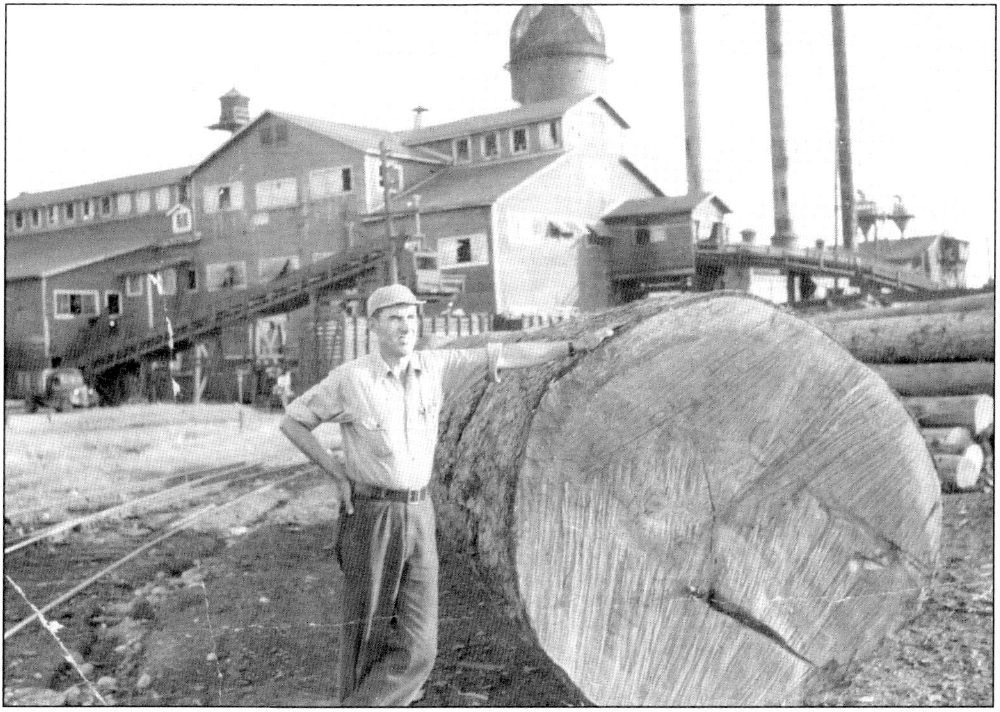

The Boise Cascade lumber mill at Emmett is shown in the background of this August 1949 image. In the foreground is Martin Zabula standing beside the largest log ever to be sawed at the mill. This mill had been operating for 32 years before it met this challenge. (Courtesy of Art Gratton.)

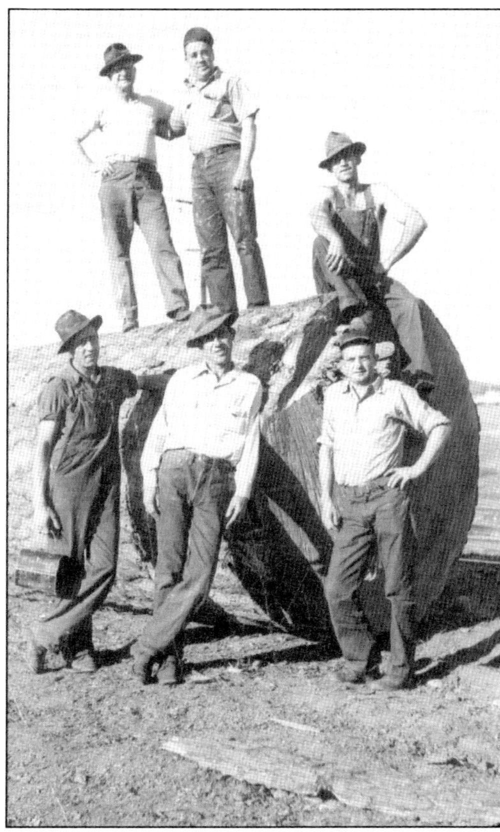

This giant yellow pine sent through the mill in August 1949 was the largest log ever sawed there. It yielded 3,000 board feet of lumber. It had to have a portion cut off so that it would fit into the saw. Standing on top are Art Gratton (left) and Joe Zabula, and sitting is Frank "Pop" Corn. Standing below, from left to right, are the Jones brothers and Hessie Goins. (Courtesy of Art Gratton.)

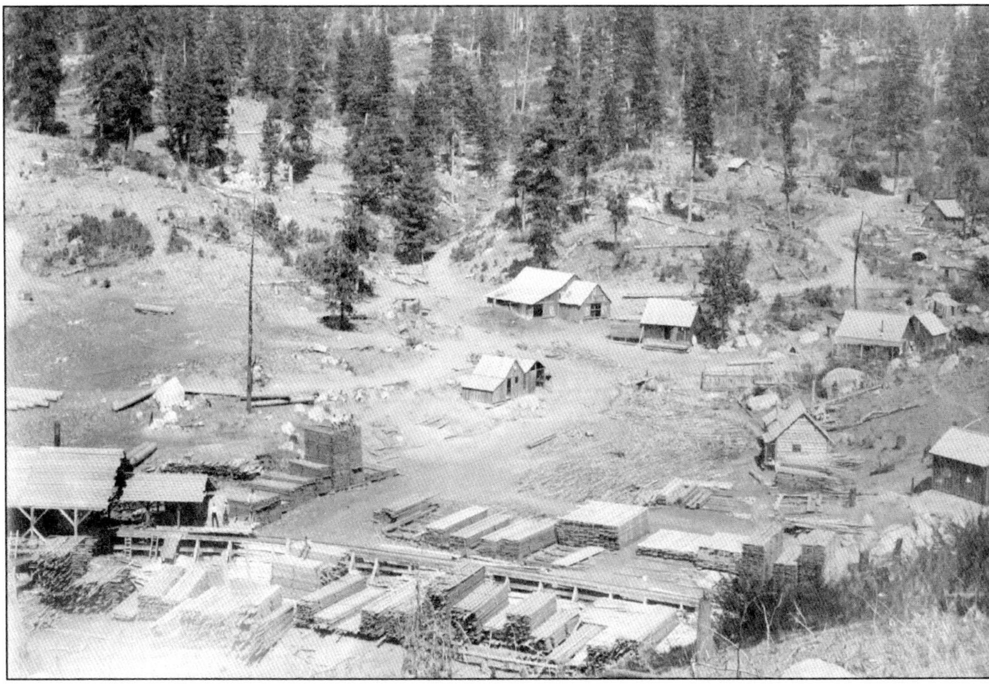

It was relatively easy to start a mill. The state did not regulate the timber supply as it does today. There were at least four mills near Dry Buck: Joe Youngbar's mill, Knox and Parrish Mill (that was purchased by Pugh), Scrivner's Mill, and the Reed and Stanley Mill.

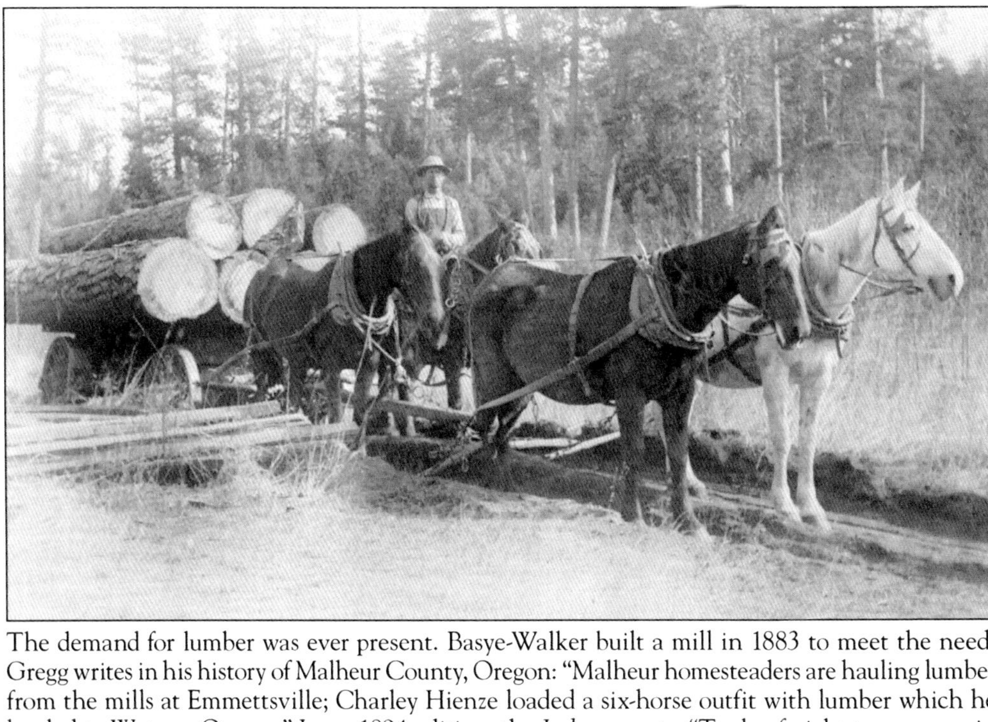

The demand for lumber was ever present. Basye-Walker built a mill in 1883 to meet the need. Gregg writes in his history of Malheur County, Oregon: "Malheur homesteaders are hauling lumber from the mills at Emmettsville; Charley Hienze loaded a six-horse outfit with lumber which he hauled to Watson, Oregon." In an 1894 edition, the *Index* reports, "Twelve freight teams were in town on the same day."

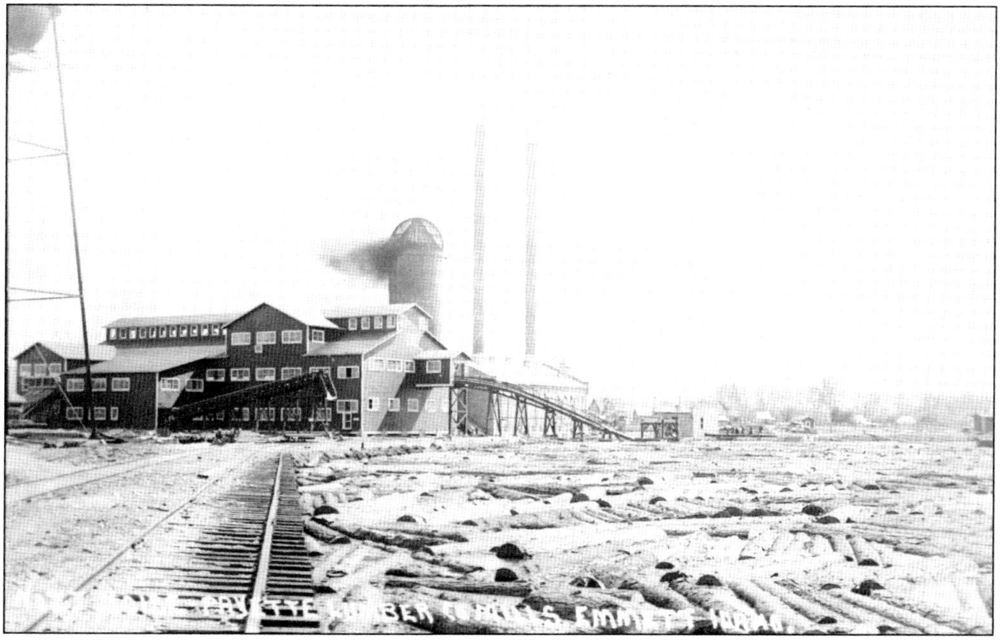

Boise Payette Lumber Company purchased the McNish-Allen Mill and replaced it with this big facility, designed by Fred Horskotty of Portland, in 1917. It employed 300 loggers, and it took the same number of men to run the mill. If anyone was in need of a job, he could most always find one at the sawmill.

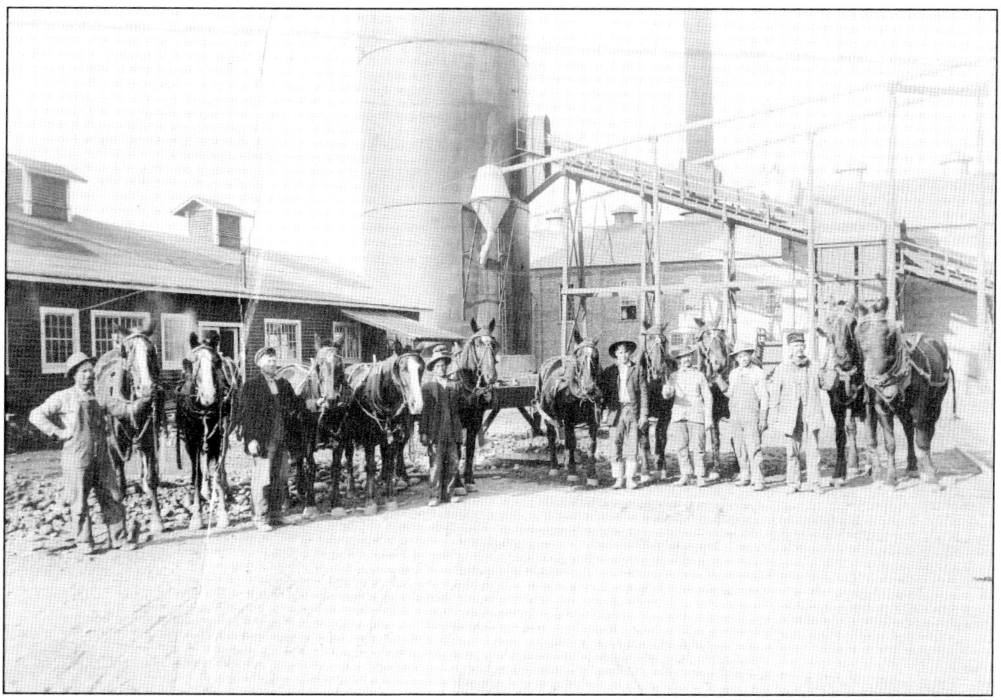

In 1919, teams pulled lumber from the saws to the pilers. When the lumber cured, it was hauled to the planer. Pictured, from left to right, are Earl Yaton, Charley Goodsell, a Mr. Cox, Walter Knouse, Otto Marchant, and two unidentified men.

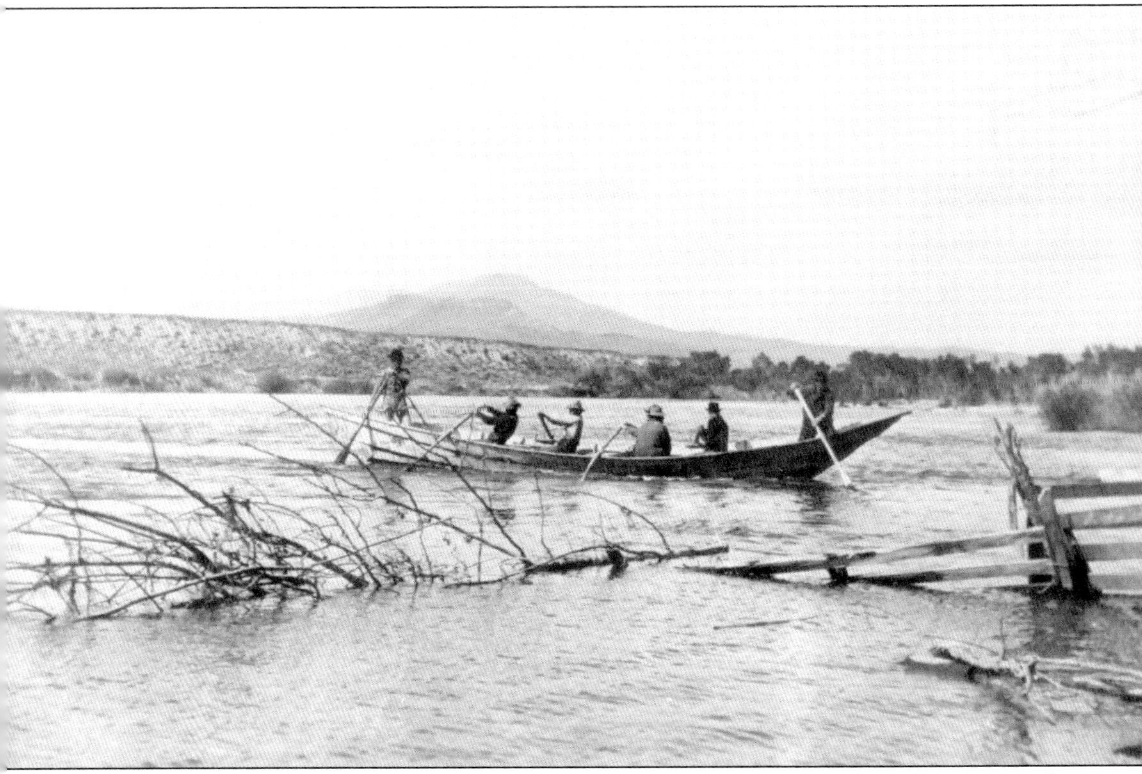

Special boats called bateaux that were pointed on each end were used on the log drives. These sturdy, flat-bottom boats were used to transport men and equipment to wherever the action was the hottest, as well as to provide a working platform once they got there. The men used peavey hooks to loosen the jams and get the logs moving again. Jam boat crews consisted of three assignments. The oarsman would row to the jam, and the bowman hooked his pike pole into the nearest log and pulled the boat alongside. Then, the oarsman would jump out and hold the boat as the bowman and the sternman exited to attack the pile of logs with their peaveys. The jam often broke suddenly, so at the first sign of loosening, the men would run for the boat, jump in, and try to quickly row away from danger. This log drive occurred on the Payette River, and this boat is positioned about where the river bridge is located, given that Squaw Butte can be seen in the background. (Courtesy of Idaho Historical Society, No. 66-26.19.)

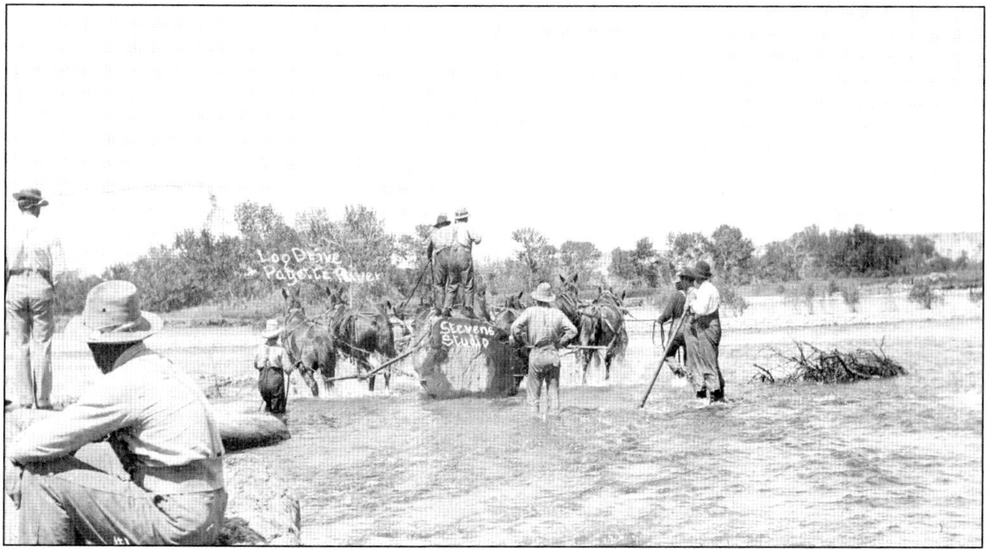

This is one of the last log drives that occurred on the Payette River. Loggers worked most of the winter cutting the logs so that they would be ready for the river in May or June, when the water was high. The flushgate below Smith's Ferry would be opened, and logs would come streaming down the river, getting hung up on sandbars and islands. Men would have to get them moving again with peavey hooks and stout draft horses; it was dangerous work. In 1905, seven men drowned as they threaded logs through an area called "Hell's Half Acre" on the South Fork of the Payette River. By 1918, the log drives were discontinued, and the railroad was used to transport logs to the mill. A steady supply of logs was then available all year long, and the work did not need to be seasonal.

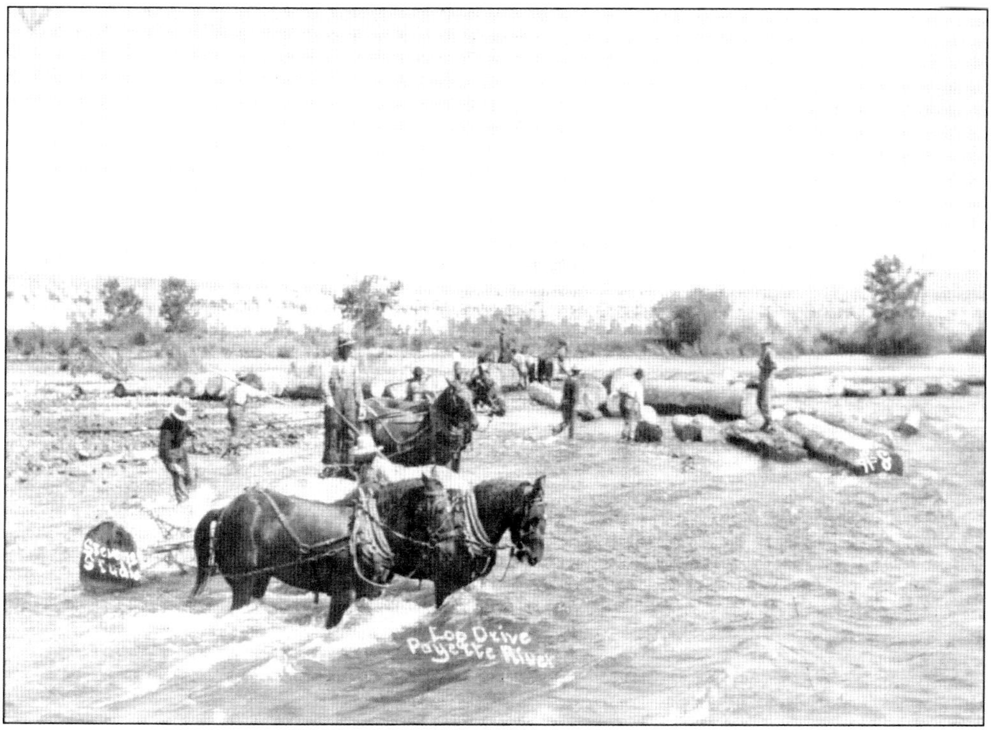

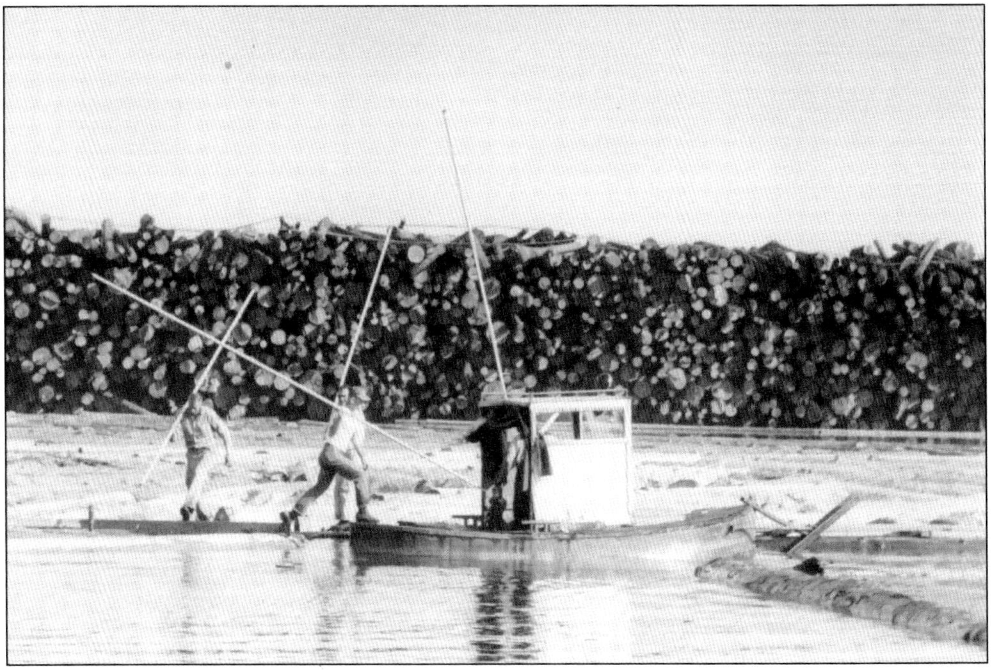

Working with logs took a great deal of skill. These men are feeding logs into the slip for delivery into the mill. Log ponds were built because of the ease of moving logs in the water. They also provided a ready source of water in case of fire, and the water washed off the dirt and grime that dulled the saws and kept the logs moist so they would not splinter when sawed.

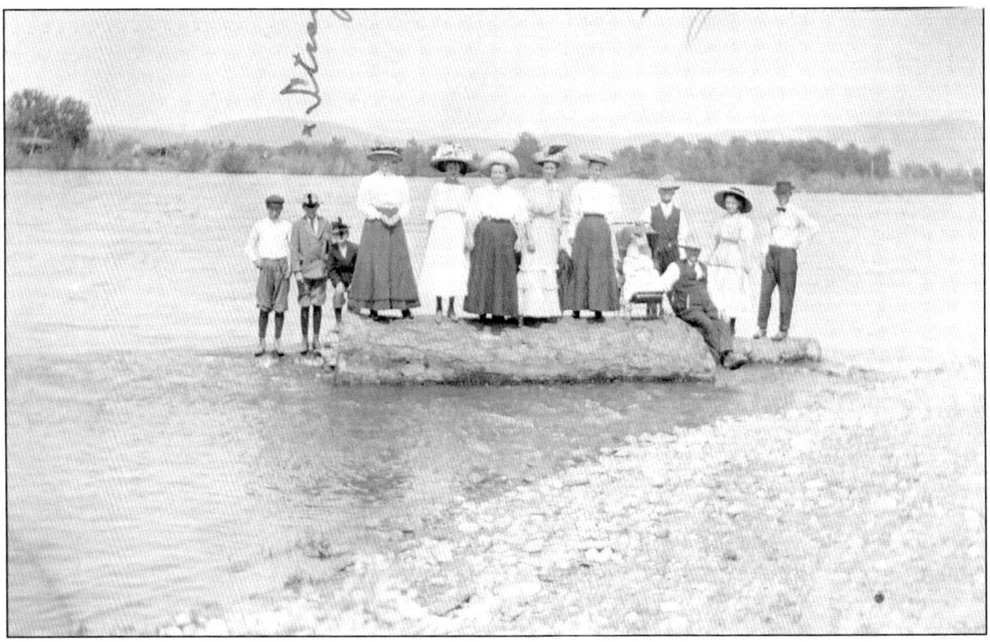

A left-behind log was an ideal place for a picture of this group that was looking for a unique photograph and an entertaining evening. The river was a place where something was almost always happening. Perhaps this was a hot summer day, and the water cooled members of the group off as they waded.

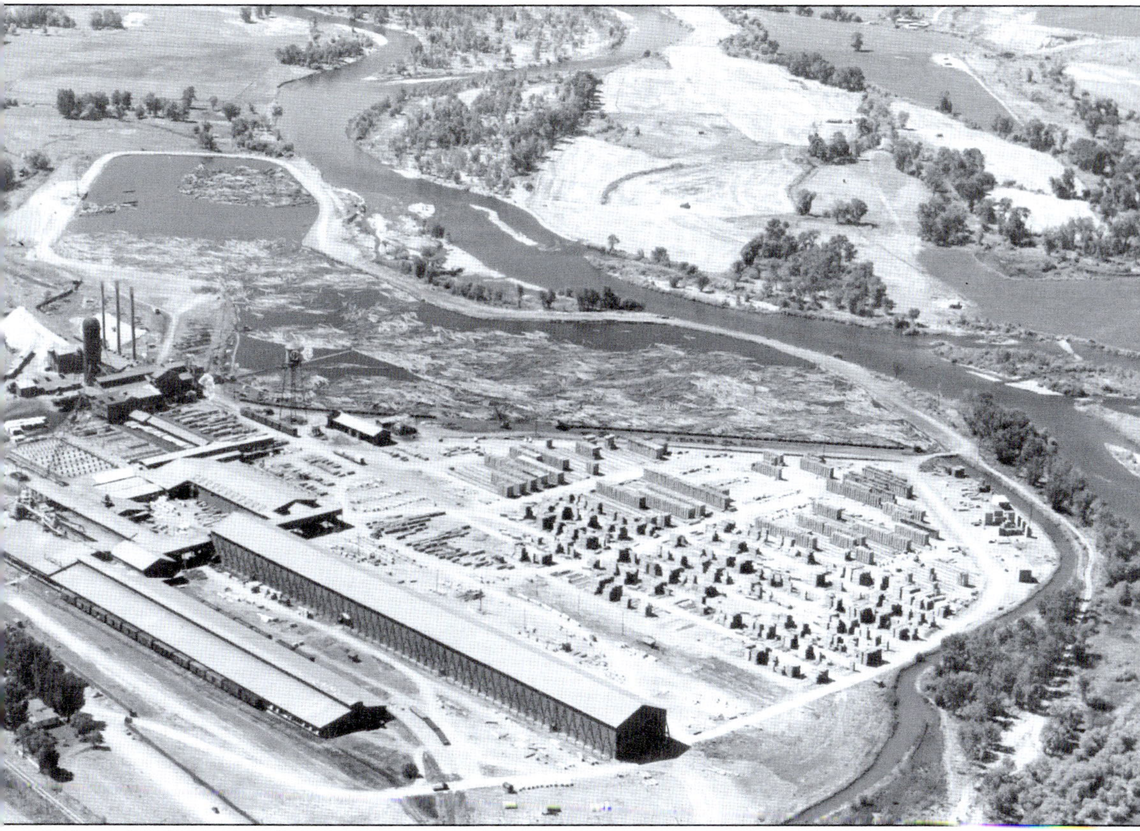

There has been a mill on this site since 1872. There has been a great demand for lumber and Emmett has had the resources to furnish it. Boise Payette Lumber purchased the McNish-Allen Mill and erected a new big facility in 1917 and has maintained control of the facility through the years. It has been the mainstay of the community because it was the largest employer in town. It was a blow to the community when the mill closed in 2001. Adrian Godfrey's poem "Emmett Mill Closes" expresses the people's feelings when the mill closed: "Just another lumber mill shut down In another little western town. Several hundred got their final pay. Several hundred jobs just went away. / 'No big deal' in our economy. The whole darn state is booming; don't you see. But lots of us were feeling sick inside, The day that noisy, vibrant giant died. / In that great throbbing Titan of a plant, Of all the town's endeavors dominant, Through four-score years and forests' worth of wood, Four generations earned their livelihood. / The massive pines were cut and smoothed and dried, Then loaded, shipped by trainloads, nationwide To build a million houses, churches, shops, And on and on—a list that never stops. / Now it's a lifeless thing, no more a mill— / Its screaming saws, its whining planers still. But many of us will recall with pride our days with this great giant, ere it died. / Just another lumber mill shut down in another little western town. Several hundred got their final pay and dropped a tear or two—and went away."

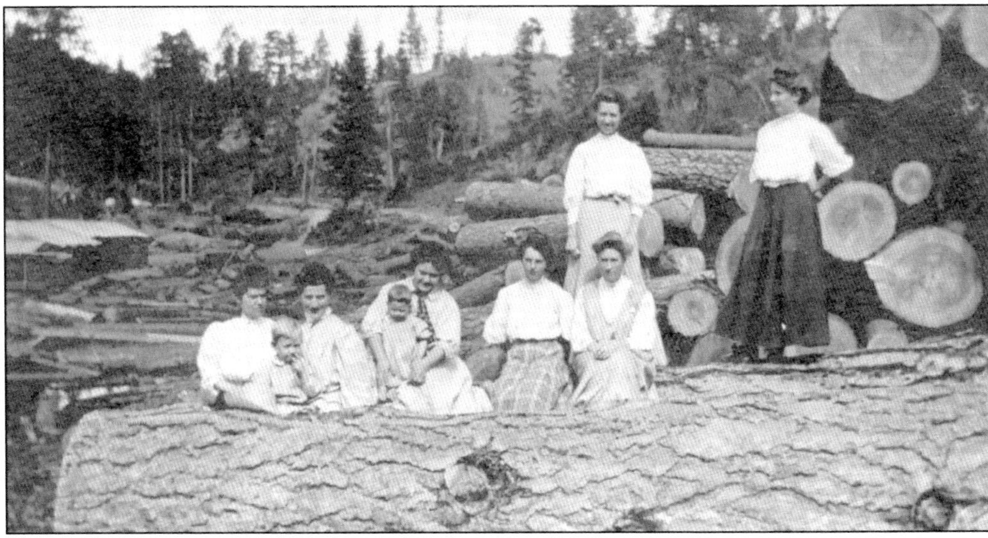

In the early years, mills were built near the logs because of the difficulties in transporting lumber. These ladies and two children spent a pleasant afternoon on an outing among the old-growth timber. This postcard was mailed in 1908 and was signed "Mrs. Pugh and Mrs. Medford." The Pughs owned a mill at Dry Buck.

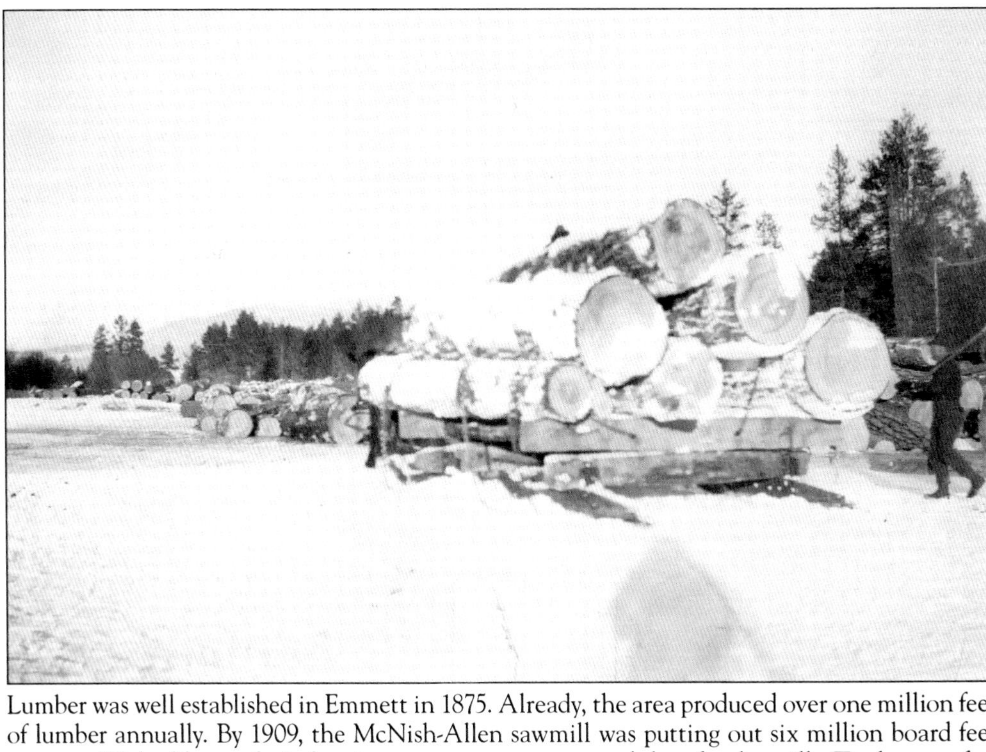

Lumber was well established in Emmett in 1875. Already, the area produced over one million feet of lumber annually. By 1909, the McNish-Allen sawmill was putting out six million board feet per year. With old-growth timber, it was easy to secure enough logs for the mills. Timber was fast becoming the mainstay of the economy.

Nine

WATER

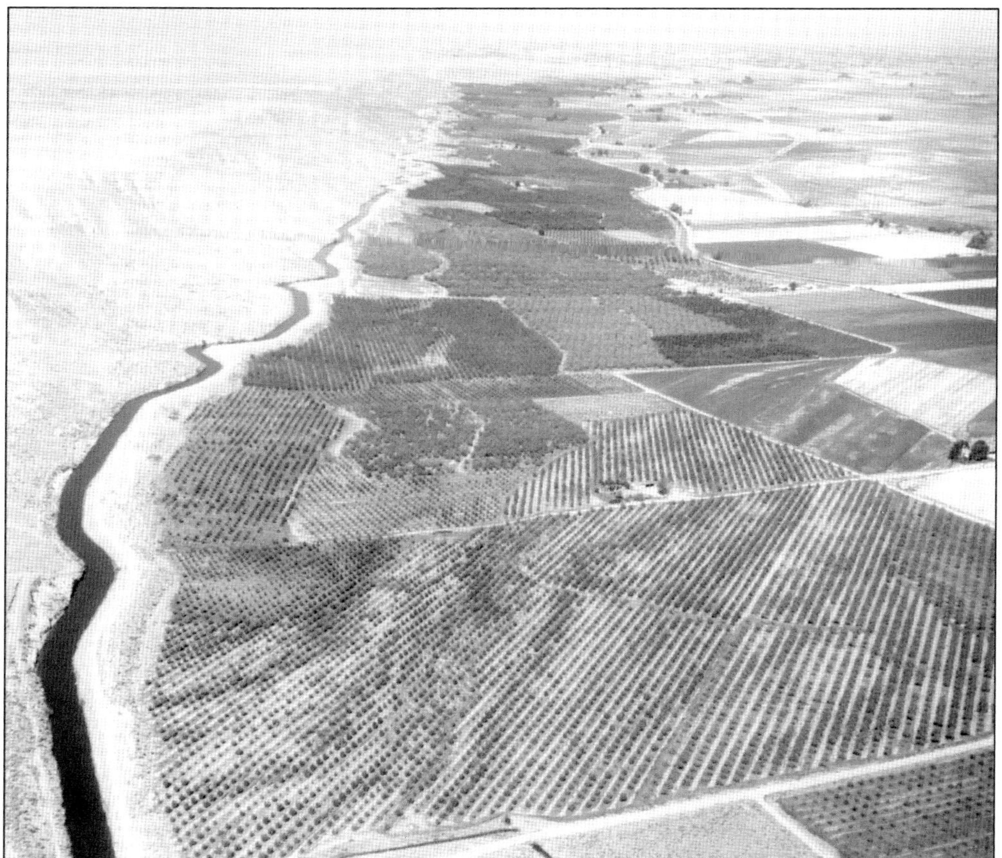

Water was vital to the early settlers of this valley. Though their dreams were filled with struggles and triumphs, residents had one goal in mind: to provide water to the Emmett Valley. They had visions of farms, orchards, and homes. The dreams did come to life, and their visions became a lush, green valley known as the "Valley of Plenty."

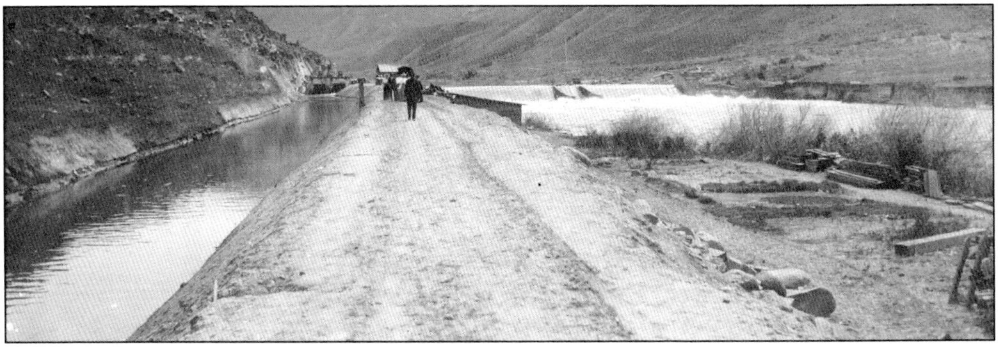

Dreams of building a dam on the Payette River for irrigation started as early as 1894. The cost of a main canal of 32 miles from the point of the diversion dam, canals, tunnels, and laterals was estimated at $300,000. The dam was located at the Gem–Boise County line, and work was to done by contractors Farrison and Kessell.

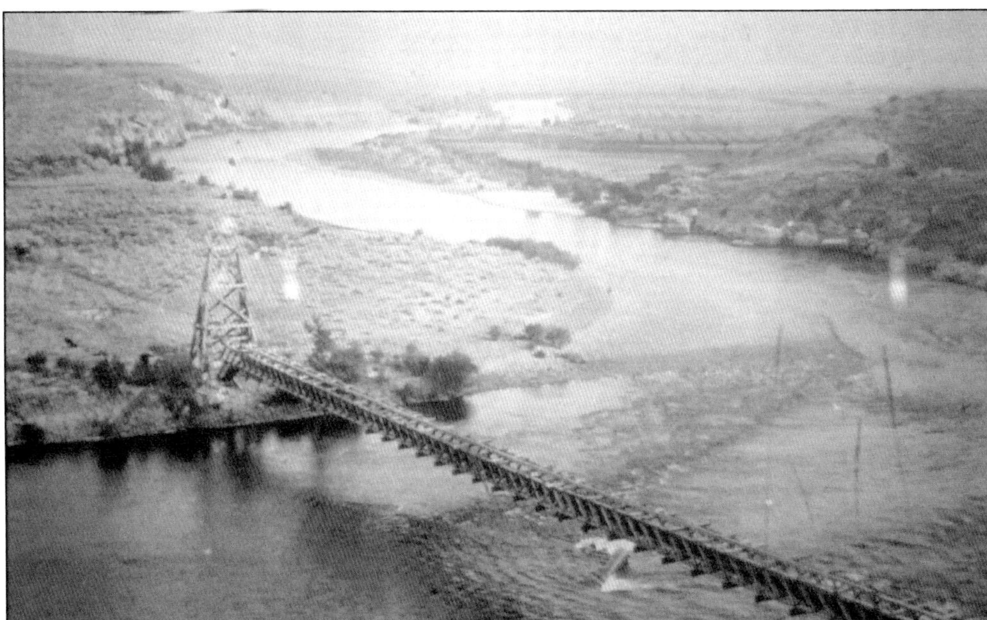

Anxious landowners on the bench area and the south side of the valley would pay $32 per acre for water rights. Irrigation water was delivered to the land on the south side of the river by a siphon.

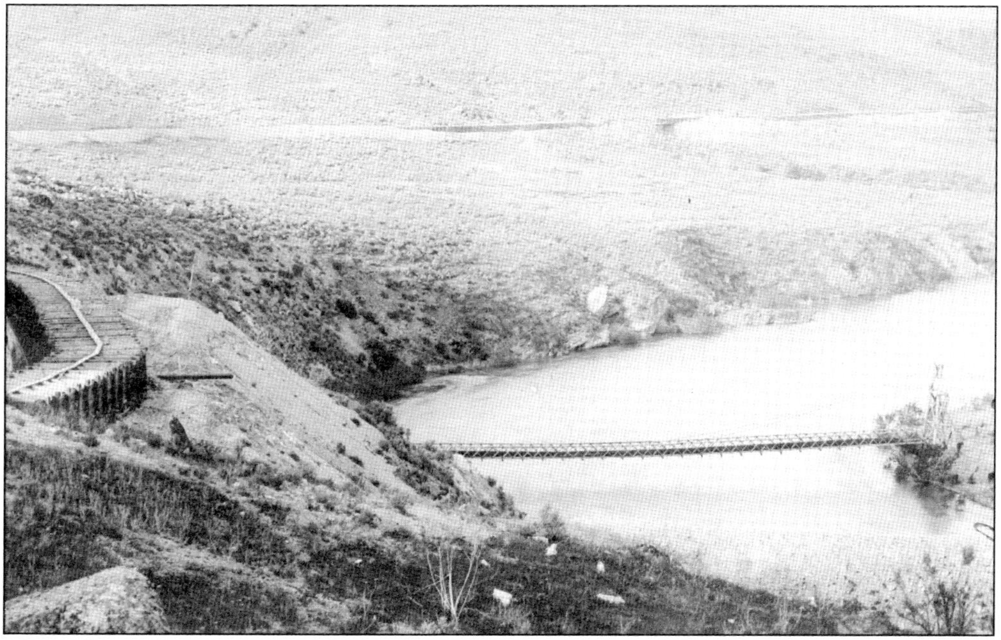

The siphon was suspended by cables connected to a support tower on the south side of the Payette River. It was prone to breaks and leaks, and repairs were costly to the district. By 1913, the condition of the siphon was deteriorating quickly. Between 15 and 20 concrete collars were constructed to give temporary relief from the serious leaks.

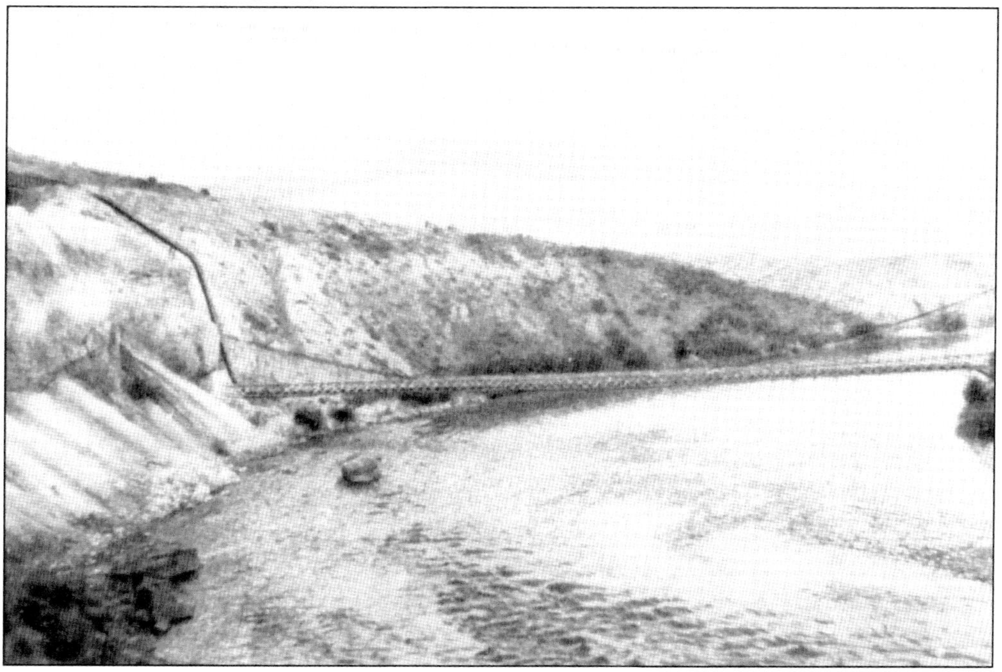

The siphon was made out of steel pipes that were laid down the hillside from the main canal and carried across the river. In 1913, Zenas M. Vaughn, a civil and hydraulic engineer, inspected the siphon and concluded that it was unsafe and in very bad condition. He suggested to the board that a new structure be built as soon as possible to replace it.

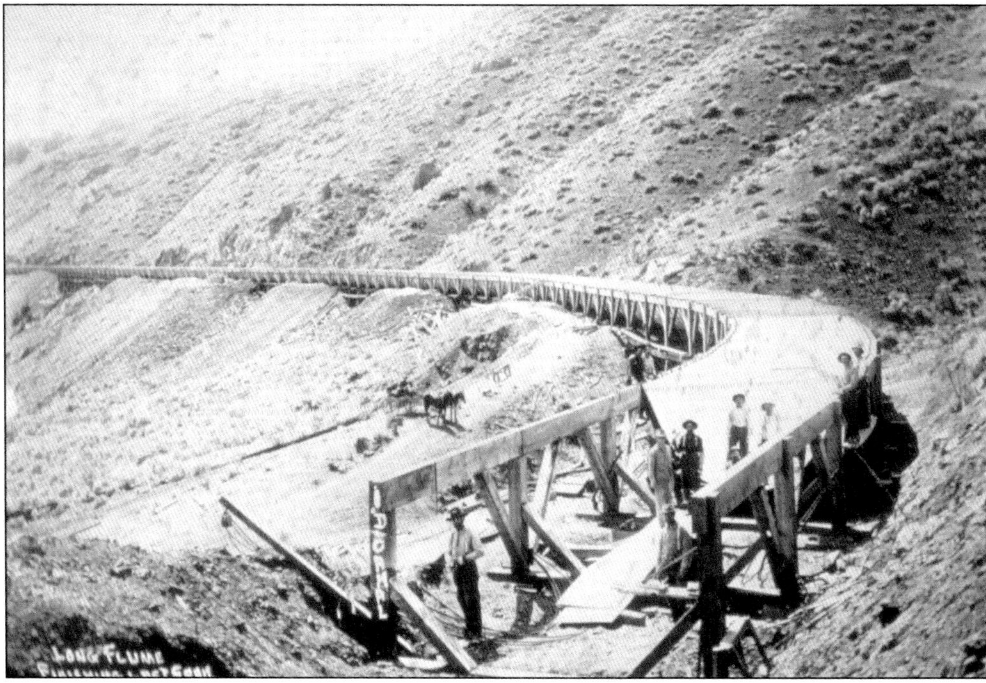

The canal system was a total engineering wonder, winding around the hillsides and flumes across gullies and lowlands, following the canyon to within four miles of Emmett. There were 19 flumes and 3 tunnels. Six miles from the dam's headgate, the canal tunneled through solid rock and continued its journey, clinging to the canyon walls to a point just below the present-day Black Canyon Dam.

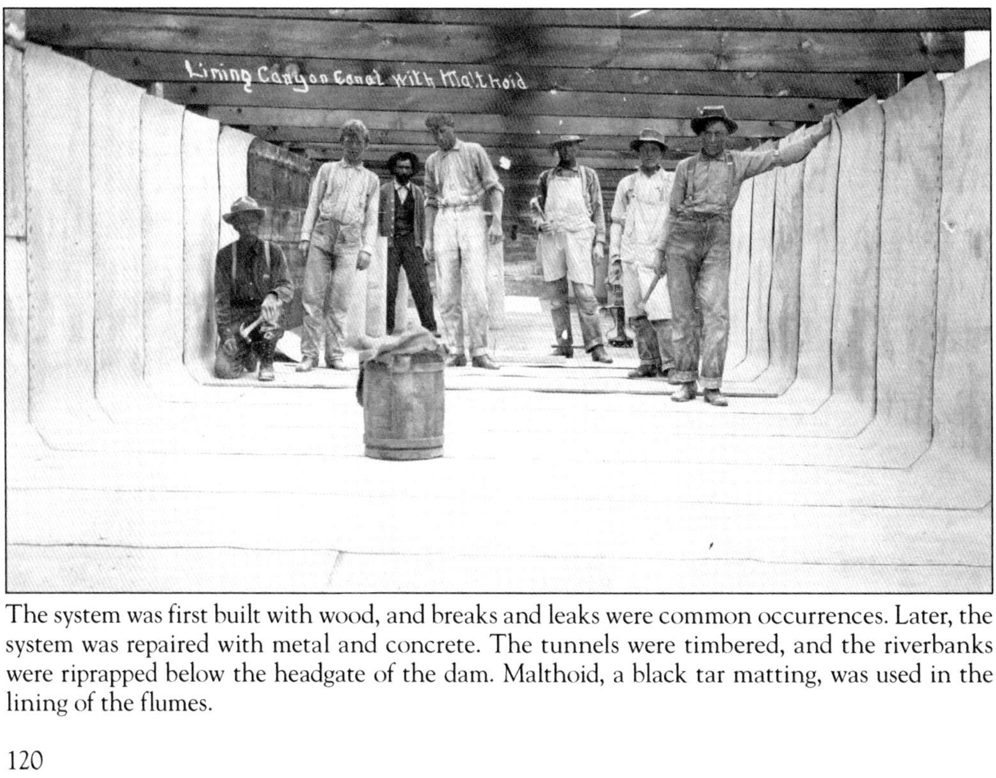

The system was first built with wood, and breaks and leaks were common occurrences. Later, the system was repaired with metal and concrete. The tunnels were timbered, and the riverbanks were riprapped below the headgate of the dam. Malthoid, a black tar matting, was used in the lining of the flumes.

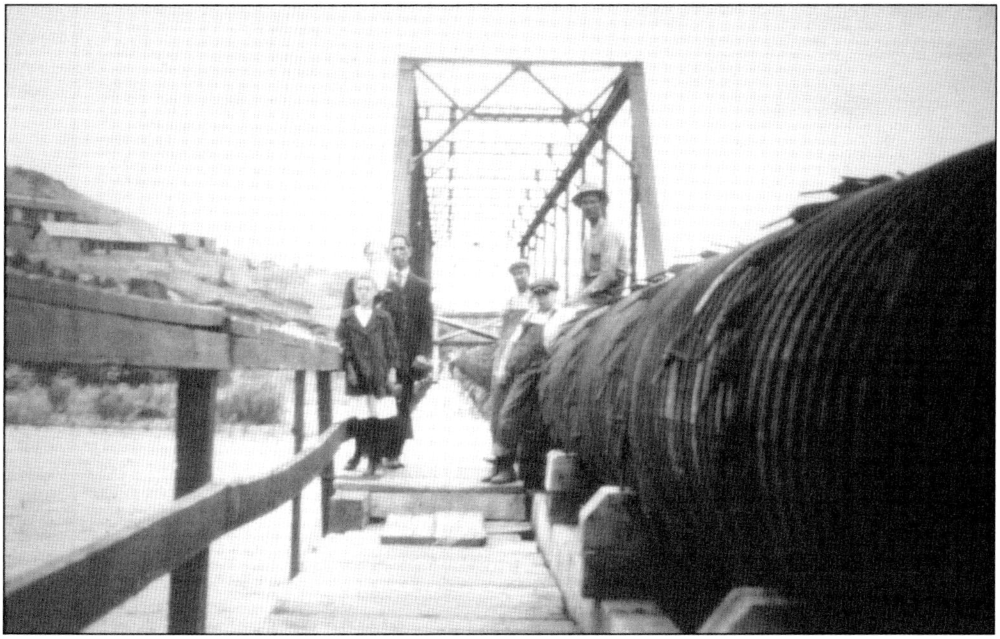

The new siphon was planned for a location about an eighth of a mile from where the old siphon was in place. The new design would include a steel bridge to support the 40-inch-diameter wooden stave pipe of the siphon across the river. Improvements were also made to the siphon's headgate located at the Cherry Gulch Flume, with a twin semicircular galvanized steel pipe replacing the wooden flume.

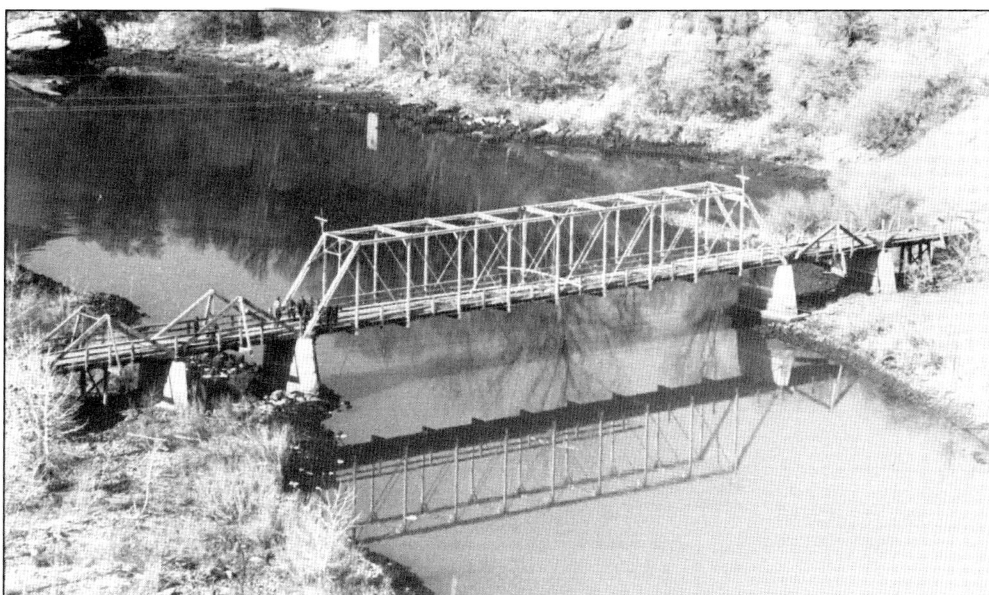

The siphon was removed when the Black Canyon Dam was built. The narrow, one-lane steel bridge was used by the public until the completion of the Plaza Bridge in 1959. Quit Claim deeds were made to the Bureau of Reclamation in 1961. In 1983, the US Army Corps of Engineers held a training exercise for the demolition of the bridge. The bridge was demolished because of liability and maintenance expenses.

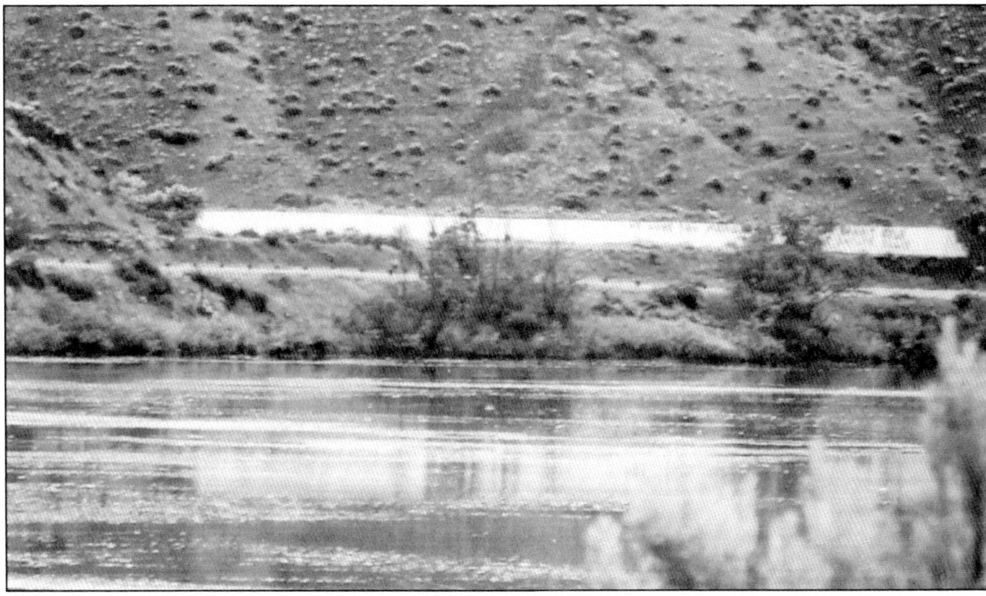

This image shows remnants of the old concrete canal and the base of a flume that delivered irrigation water from the first diversion dam. Trials and difficulties plagued the Canyon Canal Company. In September 1909, engineers made a thorough examination of the system to determine what would be necessary to put it in first-class condition. Flumes were unsafe—too small and placed on improper grades. Tunnels were also too small, and the canal was inadequate to supply the water needed. Interest in building a new dam began. The Reclamation Service showed great interest for a diversion point on the Payette River for a canal on the south side of the river to allow development of an additional 56,000 acres of irrigated lands under the Black Canyon Irrigation District as part of the Boise Project. (Both, courtesy of Carla R. Standley.)

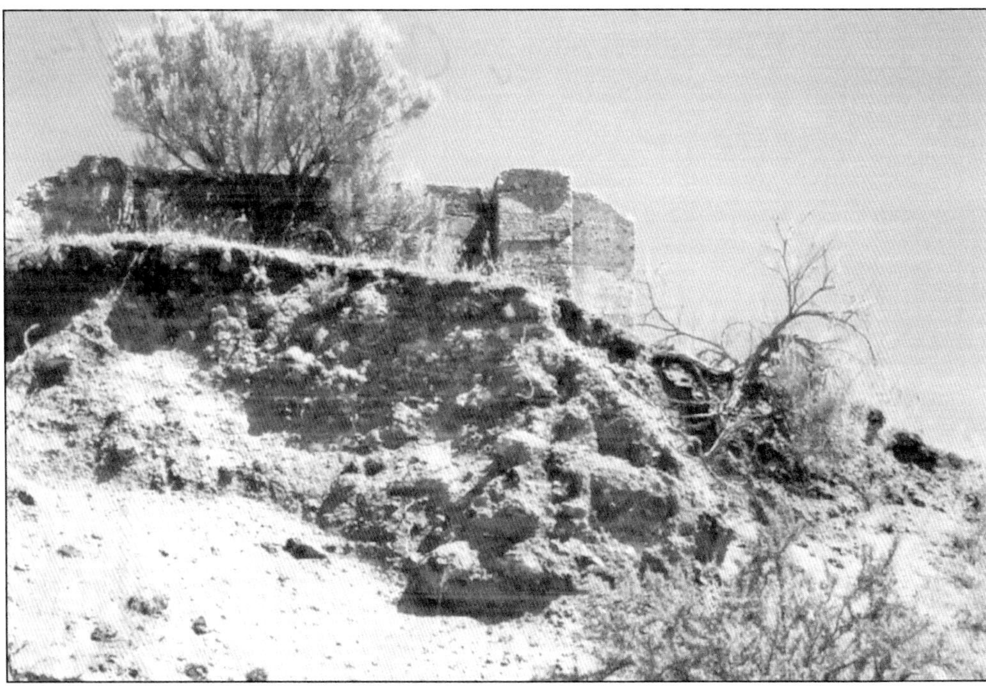

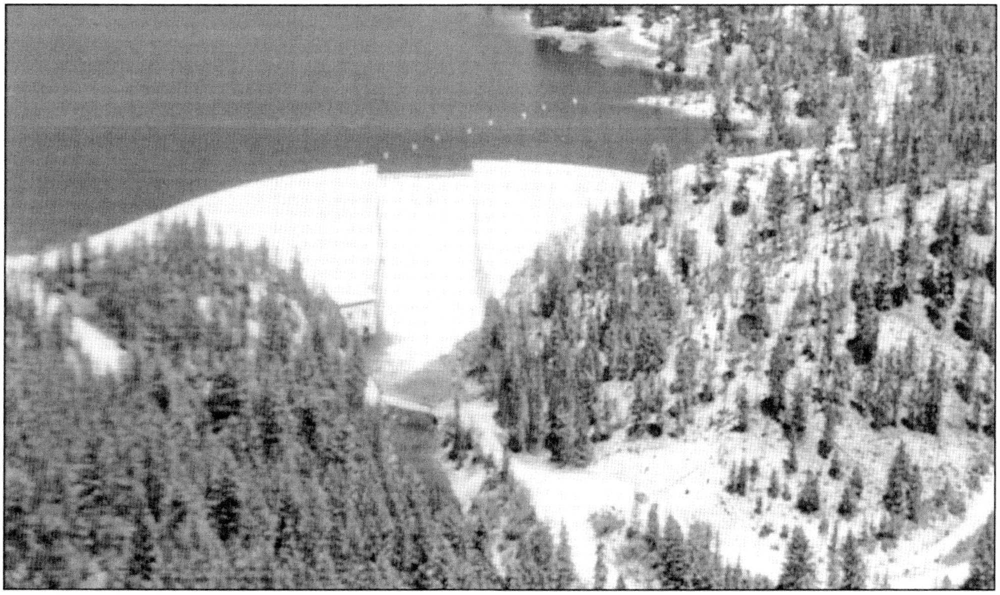

Completed in 1931, Deadwood Dam and Reservoir holds the majority of the storage water for Emmett Irrigation District, with 48,877 acre-feet of water entitlement. The Deadwood Dam was an intermediate step of reclaiming lands in the development of the Payette Division of the Boise Project under the Bureau of Reclamation. It assures a reliable and consistent supply of water for power production and irrigation at Black Canyon Dam. (Courtesy of US Bureau of Reclamation.)

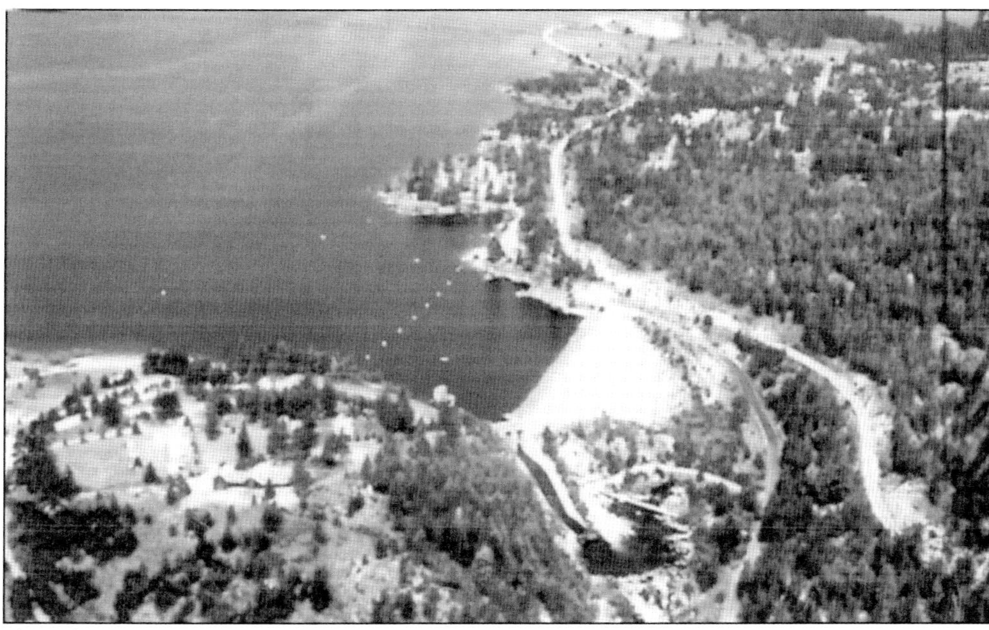

Plans for construction of Cascade Dam began in 1941, but because of World War II, they were withdrawn. Work did not begin until 1946, and it was completed in 1948. Cascade Reservoir is the largest of the five Boise Project reservoirs built by the Bureau of Reclamation. The others are Arrowrock, completed in 1915; Black Canyon, 1924; Deadwood, 1931; and Anderson Ranch, 1950. (Courtesy of United States Bureau of Reclamation.)

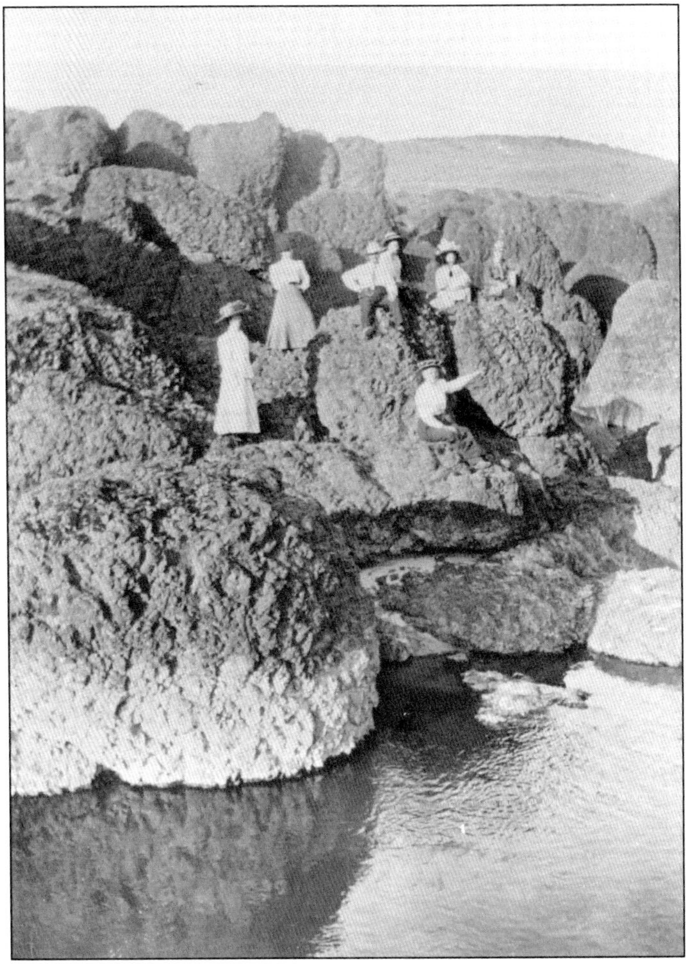

The Black Canyon Dam was built on a natural site in the deep, narrow, black basaltic rock of the Black Rock Canyon, located about seven miles northeast of Emmett. It is from this canyon that the dam received its name. Work began in 1922, with engineer Walter Ward at the helm. Pouring of cement began the following year, and completion was in 1924.

The Black Canyon Dam had two purposes. The main purpose was to reclaim 56,000 acres in the Black Canyon Irrigation District. The other was to give relief to the Emmett Irrigation District by providing a dam and pumping site that would eliminate the 16 miles of canal on the north side of the Payette River.

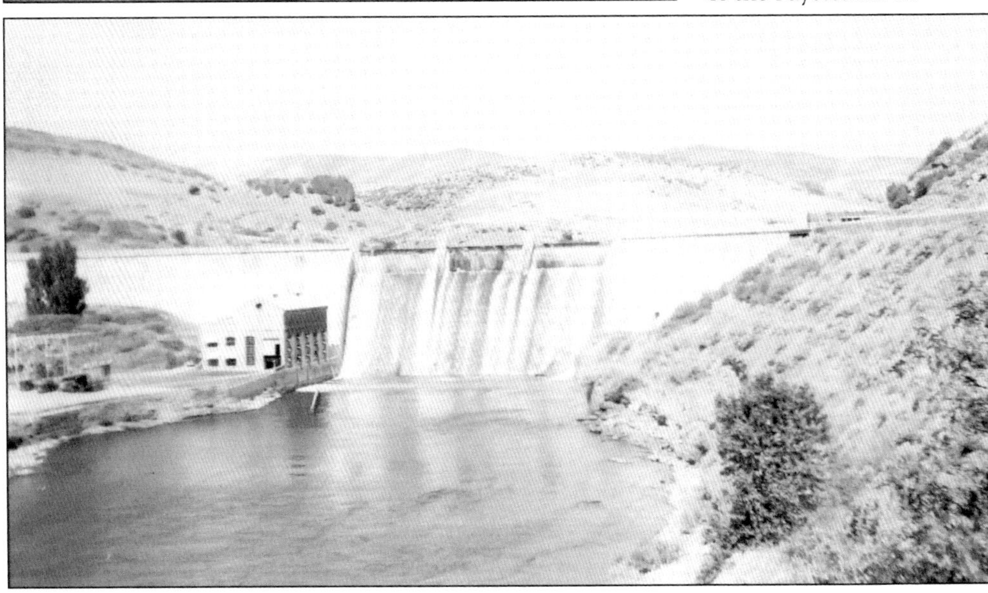

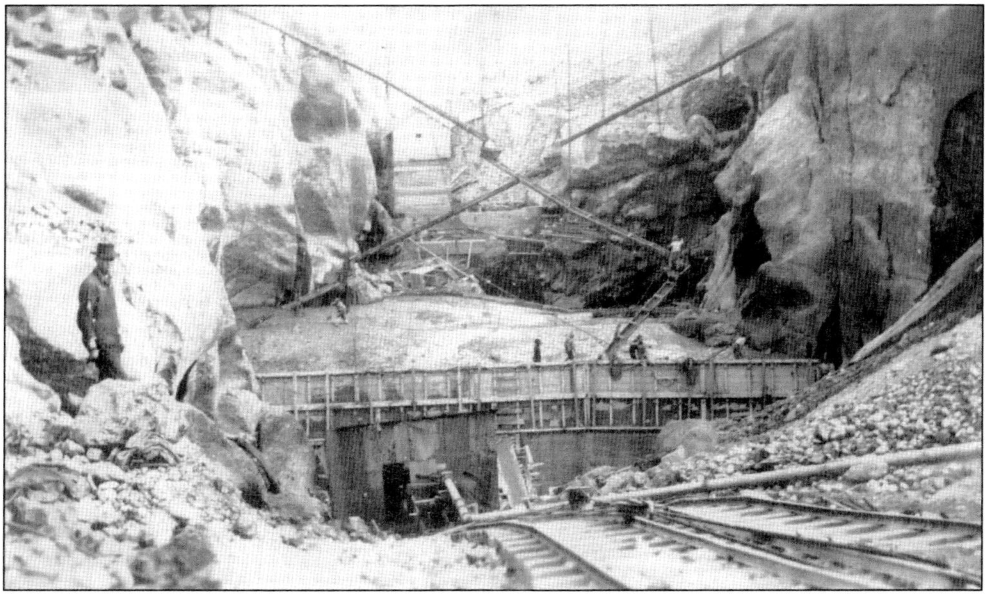

Two headgates were installed on the south side of the river section of the dam. The siphon on the bridge was abandoned, and a new one was constructed from the headgates at the dam to the head of the existing canal. Later, after the completion of the Black Canyon Canal, water would be carried through the canal directly from the headgate.

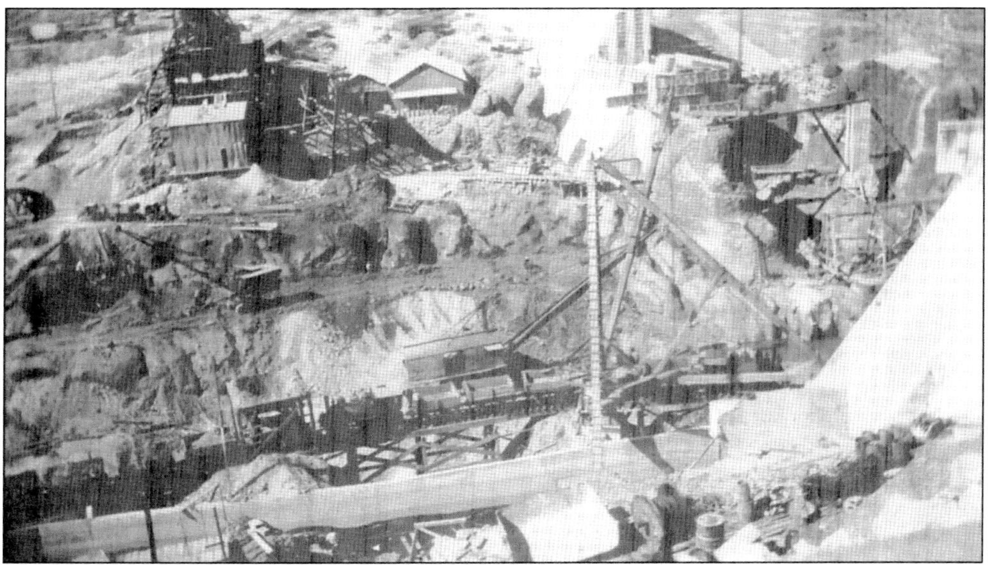

The dam reaches 183 feet from the center of the river channel, but only about 95 feet of the dam's height can be seen above the river level. The project involved 81,000 yards of concrete, 324,000 sacks of cement, 90,000 yards of gravel hauled, and 288,700 pounds of reinforced steel. The spillway has three drum gates, which are located at the top to regulate the height of the water in the reservoir.

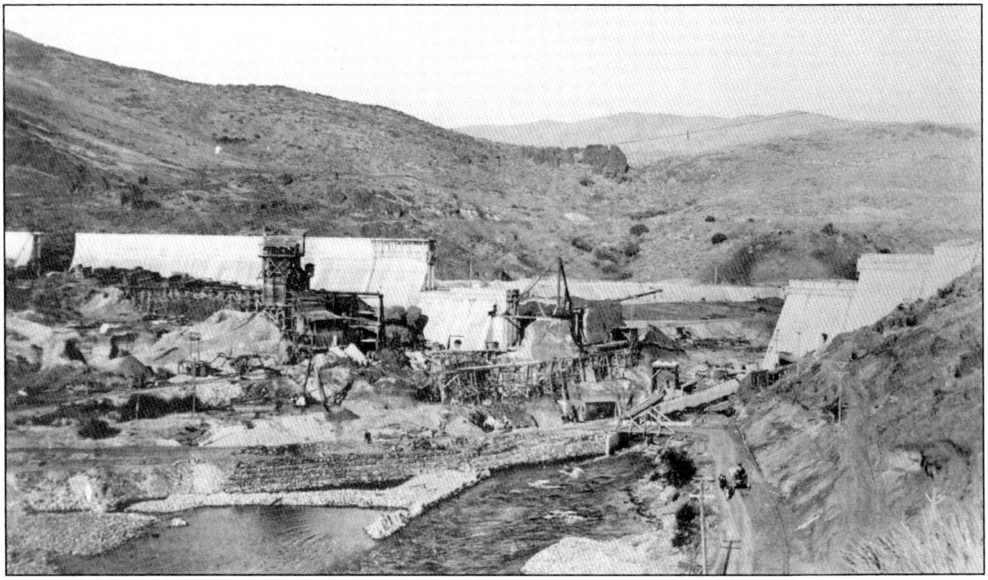

Black Canyon Dam is strictly a gravity-style diversion dam and provides no storage water for irrigation. The installation of the two generators and final construction of the powerhouse was completed in 1925. The dam, hydro pumps, generators, and powerhouse cost $1,771,435. Modernization of the power plant started in the early 1980s, and the facility has been brought up to date with today's technology. The supervisory control room remotely operates several facilities —including Black Canyon Dam and power plant, Anderson Ranch Dam and power plant, Deadwood Dam, Cascade Dam, Minidoka Dam and power plant, Palisades Dam, and Boise Diversion Dam and power plant—from one central point. An operator is on duty in the supervisory control room at all times. (Both, courtesy of US Bureau of Reclamation, Boise Payette Division.)

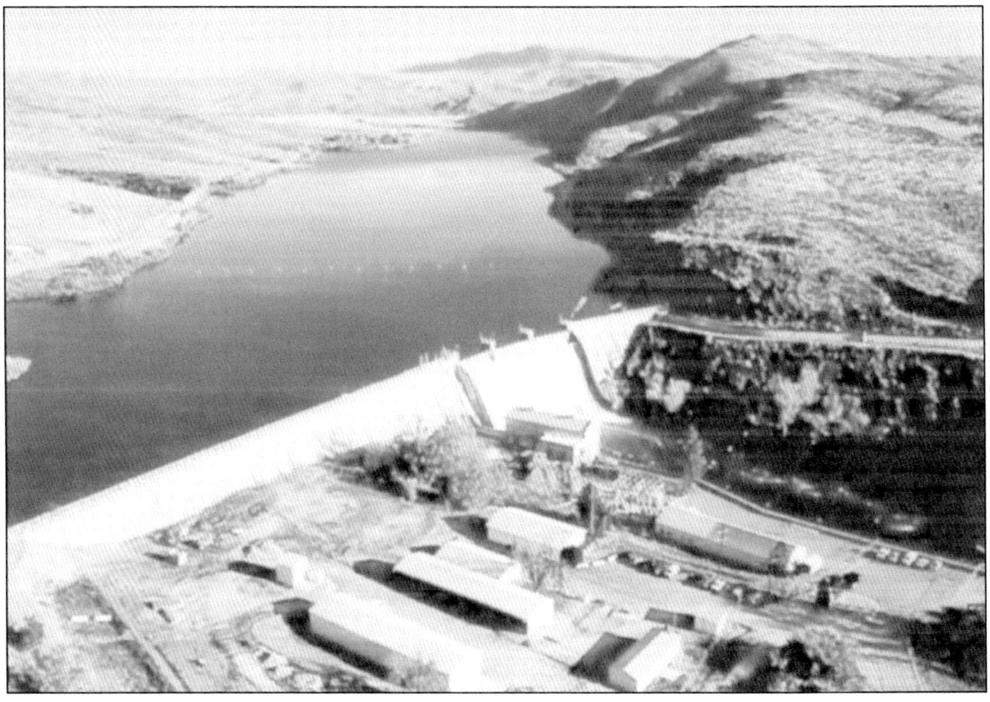

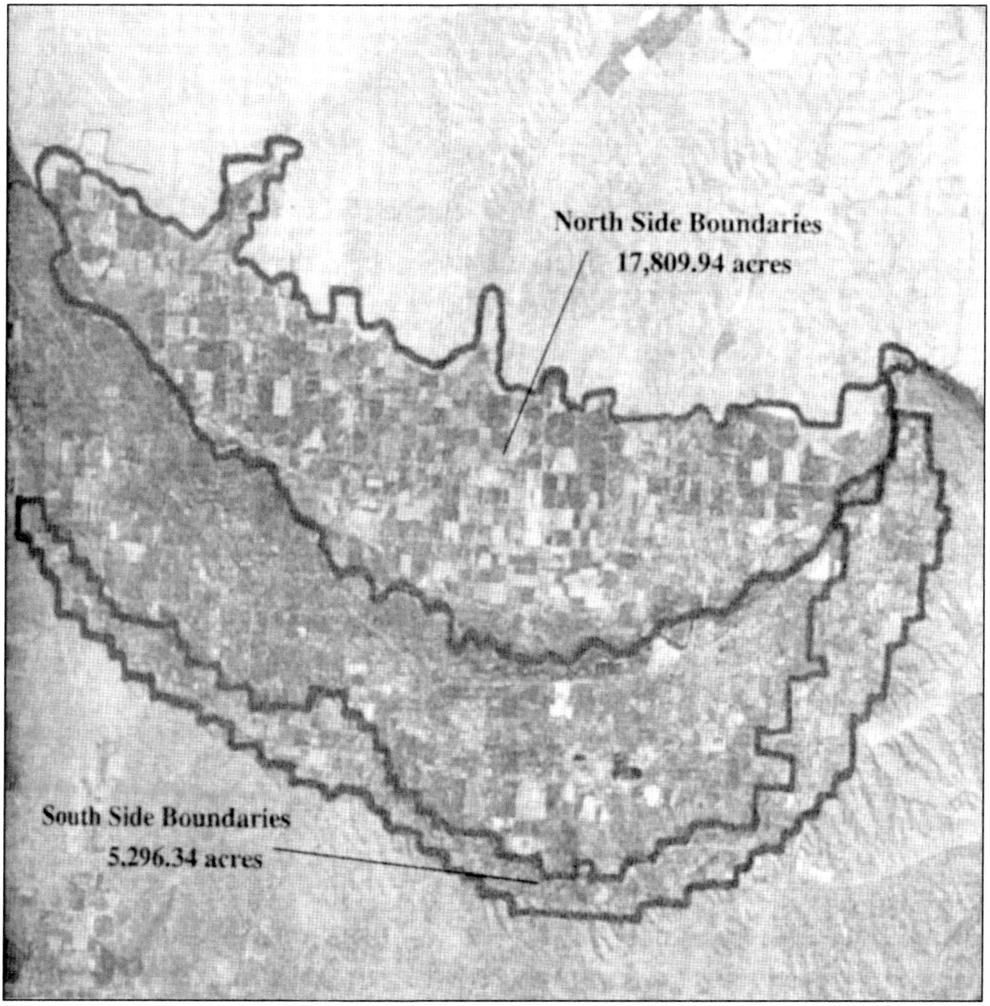

With 129 yes votes and only 6 no votes, the journey of the Emmett Irrigation District began on September 10, 1910. It was the strength, struggles, triumphs, and dreams of providing water to the Emmett Valley and the ventures of the early pioneers that built the foundation upon which the district was formed. The district is governed by seven people representing the patrons of seven divisions within its boundaries. Financial problems plagued the district at one time, and the Emmett Holding Company was formed to keep it from collapsing. As years passed and struggles have continued, the district has kept on improving. Its boundaries engulf a total of 23,106.28 acres, and the majority of the land is found on the north side and is known as the Bench area. Water is delivered to 17,809.94 acres via the North Side Canal. A total of 5,296.34 acres makes up the south-side boundary and water is delivered via the Black Canyon Canal. (Graph compiled by Carla R Standley.)

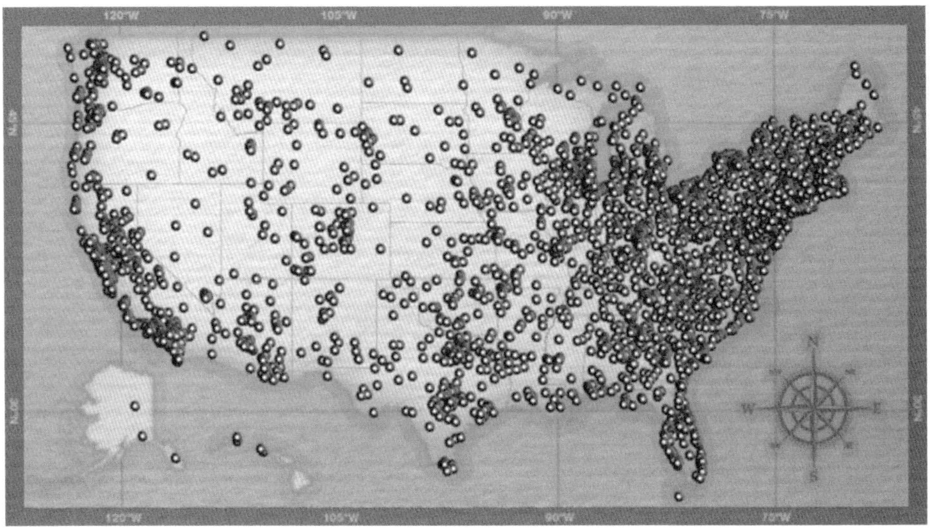